"In this valuable gathering of seven essays, one finds not only a fruitful remembrance of Marsha Dutton's distinguished career in Cistercian studies, but also the tracing of a soul's journey into God in the depths of memory. In that journey, Dutton has been a faithful companion of Augustine, Aelred, and Bernard; a trustworthy guide for their readers; and a friend to their friends."

— Ann W. Astell, John Cardinal O'Hara Professor of Theology, University of Notre Dame

"Marsha Dutton's close readings of Aelred's works bring a deeper understanding of a major unifying thread in Aelred's thought—the relationship between human beings and God. This collection of essays underscores the manner in which that relationship informs in unanticipated ways a diverse array of Aelred's texts. From iconographic imagery to theological philosophy, to ideological origins and contexts, the reader will find no shortage of illuminating insights in Dutton's work. Aelred scholars will not be disappointed."

— Christopher Coski, professor of French, Ohio University

CISTERCIAN STUDIES SERIES:
NUMBER THREE HUNDRED TWO

# Embracing God

## Essays on the Spiritual Treatises of Aelred of Rievaulx

Marsha L. Dutton

*Foreword by* Daniel J. Heisey, OSB

*Introduction by* J. Stephen Russell

Cistercian Publications
cistercianpublications.org

LITURGICAL PRESS
Collegeville, Minnesota
litpress.org

A Cistercian Publications title published by Liturgical Press

**Cistercian Publications**
Editorial Offices
161 Grosvenor Street
Athens, Ohio 45701
cistercianpublications.org

Cover art: *Jesus in the Temple.* Photo by Keith Barnes Photography Oxford. Used by permission of the photographer and the Provost and Fellows of Worcester College, Oxford.

Biblical quotations are generally taken from the New English Bible with Apocrypha, sometimes revised by Marsha L. Dutton.

Chapters 2, 5, 6, and 7 are reprinted here by permission from Cistercian Publications; chapters 3 and 4 are reprinted here by permission from *The American Benedictine Review.*



**Library of Congress Cataloging-in-Publication Data**

Names: Dutton, Marsha L., author.
Title: Embracing God : essays on the spiritual treatises of Aelred of Rievaulx / Marsha L. Dutton ; foreword by Daniel Heisey, OSB ; introduction by J. Stephen Russell.
Description: Athens, Ohio : Cistercian Publications ; Collegeville, Minnesota : Liturgical Press, [2025] | Series: Cistercian studies series ; three hundred two | Includes bibliographical references and index. | Summary: "In Embracing God Marsha L. Dutton surveys the interwoven structures and themes of five treatises of Aelred of Rievaulx. Individual chapters explore Aelred's meditations on Jesus's life, spiritual friendship, the eucharistic nature of Cistercian spirituality, and the nature of the soul"—Provided by publisher.
Identifiers: LCCN 2024044909 (print) | LCCN 2024044910 (ebook) | ISBN 9780879071950 (trade paperback) | ISBN 9780879075156 (epub) | ISBN 9780879074432 (pdf)
Subjects: LCSH: Aelred, of Rievaulx, Saint, 1110–1167.
Classification: LCC BR754.A325 D38 2025 (print) | LCC BR754.A325 (ebook) | DDC 230/.2--dc23/eng/20241206
LC record available at https://lccn.loc.gov/2024044909
LC ebook record available at https://lccn.loc.gov/2024044910

In thanksgiving for my children
David Stuckey, Emily Stuckey

And in loving memory of Gregory John Stuckey

# Contents

# Foreword

In *The Waters of Siloe,* Thomas Merton observed that the emergence of the Cistercian Order derived in part from a providential confluence of circumstances. Among other elements, there were the woods and hills and streams of northern Europe, the wisdom of the Benedictine Rule, the cultural developments of the twelfth-century renaissance, and "the ardent and poetic souls of a Bernard of Clairvaux, an Ailred of Rievaulx, a William of St. Thierry."[1] In this collection of seven papers, Marsha Dutton sheds light on those ardent, poetic Cistercians, especially Ailred, or Aelred, longtime twelfth-century abbot of Rievaulx, in Yorkshire.

Given Aelred's many facets, it is only right for a modern scholar to focus on some of them in a series of articles. After all, a book of seven essays or articles can cover more ground than a seven-hundred-page volume on one theme. Just as the seven times a day of monastic prayer can give glimpses into the seven-pillared house of Wisdom (Prov 9:1), so can seven vignettes open for readers Aelred's interior life and thus his devotion to the Trinity.

An essential insight offered by these seven studies underscores Aelred's spiritual and intellectual inheritance from Augustine of Hippo. Some seven hundred years separated those two Christian men, but Aelred saw in Augustine's writings truths that proved timeless. In particular, Aelred took within himself Augustine's understanding of the human soul's having three parts: intellect, will, and memory.

[1] Thomas Merton, *The Waters of Siloe* (New York: Harcourt, Brace, 1949), 289.

As Dutton shows us, notably in her "Clinging to God," memory serves as the key to appreciating Aelred's thought. In the Augustinian theological tradition, the three parts of the soul can align with the three Persons of the Trinity, "the image of God in man's soul."[2] Thus, the intellect can point to the Father; the will, being related to love, can refer to the Holy Spirit; and memory can indicate the Son. It is the incarnate Son, Jesus of Nazareth, who merits much of Aelred's meditations.

In "Intimacy and Imitation," Dutton points out that Aelred's fascination with the historical Jesus caused Aelred to dwell on the humanity of Jesus almost to the exclusion of Jesus' divinity. For example, Dutton notes, Aelred wrote about Jesus weeping at the death of his friend, Lazarus, but Aelred left out any mention of Jesus' raising Lazarus from the dead. While Aelred wrote on spiritual friendship, drawing upon Augustine, Ambrose, and Cicero, here he reminds us how sorrow over the loss of a dear friend really comes from memory.

As with all medieval monastic authors, Aelred of Rievaulx worked in continuity with the biblical and classical past. His intellectual curiosity, informed by his life of prayer, has left us a legacy of spiritual writings that still engage an attentive and patient reader. Such a student of Aelred and his contemporaries Bernard and William is Marsha Dutton. Her interconnected collection of seven studies of these profound, as well as ardent and poetic, writers stands as a worthy tribute to them and repays thoughtful rumination. As Merton wrote of the recurring round of contemplative life of those early Cistercians, "Yet it was never monotonous, any more than the seasons are monotonous."[3]

Daniel J. Heisey, OSB
Saint Vincent Archabbey, Latrobe, Pennsylvania

[2] Henry Chadwick, *Augustine of Hippo: A Life* (Oxford: Oxford University Press, 2009), 121.

[3] Merton, *Waters of Siloe*, 288.

# Preface

With the seven chapters in this book I seek to convey an understanding to which I have slowly come over many years of immersion in the sermons and treatises of Aelred of Rievaulx. I met Aelred in 1973, as a doctoral student at the University of Michigan. While a work of spiritual pedagogy by a twelfth-century monk was an unusual focus for a student of medieval English literature, I devoted my dissertation to editing the two Middle English translations of Aelred's *De institutione inclusarum*. Aelred's Latin original of that work has dominated my thought through the years since, guiding me to see as central to all of his work a determination to remind his readers of God as they have always known him, to recall them over and over to their knowledge of God and to confidence in God's readiness to reach out to them when they remember him. The image of himself that God placed within his human creatures in the three faculties of memory, reason, and will, Aelred says, allows each person to embrace him and to be embraced by him, for all eternity. In that truth is our beatitude.

I am grateful to Cistercian Publications for allowing me to collect and reprint these essays, most of them by now decades old, as embodiment of the lengthy process through which I have come to this understanding of the core of Aelred's thought. When I wrote them, of course, I was addressing different and apparently unrelated topics, but unsurprisingly, I now see, they were all pointing in the same direction.

For Aelred regularly offers his readers different paths to the same end. To an anchoress, for example, he offers either the quick flight of a dove to rest in the wounds of Jesus or a slow journey with Jesus through all the days of his earthly life. All of Aelred's works serve the same purpose, offering to those who read them a multiplicity of approaches: to follow the strict life of a Cistercian monastery, or to immerse oneself in Scripture, or to pray for a friend, or to read the works of the church fathers, or indeed to rule one's subjects in generosity and justice. So as the essays on the spiritual works that I have gathered here consider these diverse topics, they offer intersecting paths leading to the same end: to the God who invites us to his embrace.

In reprinting these chapters I have corrected minor orthographic and typographic errors in the original printings and occasionally replaced exclusive language with inclusive language. Otherwise they remain as originally published. The result of course is the presence of what now are some inaccuracies, as when I write "Only two scholars have noted" (p. 46 in "Christ Our Mother"), or internal inconsistencies, as when in different chapters I refer to the translations of Aelred's works under different titles, or, more significantly, as I changed my opinion from one year to another, often because of new learning. For some time I wrote incorrectly of three meditations in *The Formation of Recluses* rather than, correctly, of a single threefold meditation. Additionally, in my earlier articles I relied largely on published translations of the works, whereas as time passed I more regularly provided my own translations.

Because many of the Cistercian works I cite below have appeared in new critical editions and English translations since the articles were first published, I have added updated citations within brackets in footnotes while retaining the original ones, and I have altered footnotes to follow Cistercian Publications style. Unsurprisingly, there are a number of things that I would now do differently than I did forty years ago, changing some phrasing, emending some statements, clarifying thought. But as this volume is intentionally keeping what's good in the older articles rather than starting them fresh, I must consider the faults, as my Cistercian friend John-Baptist Porter once said, "part of the humility of the thing."

## Acknowledgments

My acknowledgments should include all those friends who helped me with these chapters in this book—all those who listened to me tell them much more than they had ever wanted to know about Aelred of Rievaulx, who read drafts of what I wrote, who heard and commented on my presentations at various conferences. That list, though, would be simply too long, so I offer merely a smattering. The presence of the original acknowledgments at the head of the individual chapters gives some insight into the number and names of those who have helped me.

Heading the list of those to whom I am grateful are my children, David Stuckey and Emily Stuckey, to whom I dedicate the book—it is a small enough recompense. And, in pure memory, I recall here my first son, Gregory John, who shared only a few hours of my life. I also thank my dear husband, R. T. Lenaghan. The too-few years we had together were full of joy and of constant conversation, often, as it happened, about Aelred (frequently ending with his hope that there wouldn't be a test).

I am particularly grateful to the Cistercian monks and nuns in the United States, the United Kingdom, the Republic of Ireland, and Norway who have become my dear friends over the years. They have been my most regular audiences, my best critics, my guides to what it means to lead the life. I dare not name most of them or their communities because I have such deep gratitude to so many. But I do want to acknowledge the guidance of Gethsemani Abbey's Br. William Leone, OCSO, who many years ago said to me, "You need to talk more about love."

I am so grateful for the longtime friendship of Dom Brendan Freeman, OCSO, at New Melleray Abbey, who has through so many decades welcomed me and made it possible for me to visit and speak repeatedly at New Melleray and at all the Irish Cistercian communities. Fr. Chrysogonus Waddell, OCSO, was the first Cistercian monk with whom I talked; I am so indebted to him, who knew so much and shared it so willingly. And to Fr. Luke Anderson, OCist, who bestowed understanding and laughter like jewels. And to Sr. Edith Scholl, OCSO, who allowed me to confide in her warmth and as she was dying encouraged me in editing Cistercian Publications and, for a term, CSQ. And—and I really dare not name all the others because of all those I would have to omit. I thank each of you for your friendship, and for your ready welcome, your warmth and conversation, and the model of your faith and lives. Everything I have done as a scholar of Cistercian thought and life is guided by time with you.

I also want to thank my many non-Cistercian friends, again a random sampling. Richard W. Bailey's now-stilled voice kept me from egregious errors of style until the too-early end of his life—and, to be honest, well beyond. Judith Avery's sharp wit and reliable insight informed much of what I wrote for many years; David N. Bell's erudition, academic rigor, and laughter advised and sustained me; Charles Flynn's friendship and confidence in me gave me opportunities I continue to value; Tyler Sergent's calm contributions to my need for information and evaluation and assistance kept me focused; John Stuckey's assumption that I could do anything let me do it; Elizabeth Thompson's readiness during sunny summers and chilly winters to listen and discuss over wine and snacks let me explore my ideas before imposing discipline on them; Niladri Mahato's quick perception provided meaning I had missed. I am also endlessly grateful to the librarians, and especially those in Interlibrary Loan, at the University of Michigan, Hanover College, and Ohio University.

Professionally, E. Rozanne Elder and John R. Sommerfeldt have pride of place in my gratitude, as editors of the earliest of the chapters below, as do Fr. Terrence Kardong, OSB, and Sr. Colleen Maura McGrane, OSB, who edited two of the last. In each case they taught me, shared ideas with me, and became my friends. I thank Cistercian Publications and *The American Benedictine Review* for permission to reprint the final six chapters in the book.

I am also particularly grateful to the Rev. Dr. Matthew Cheung Salisbury of Worcester College, Oxford, for the photograph on the cover of this book, which shows the boy Jesus in the temple as his parents walk unknowingly by, and to Worcester College and photographer Keith Barnes for permission to reprint it here. Dr. Salisbury's invitation to a concert at Worcester College let me see the chapel window with that image and at once to recognize its appropriateness for reproduction here. I also thank him for obtaining permission from Worcester College for its use.

Finally, I thank those who have helped to make this book possible: Hans Christoffersen at Liturgical Press, my friend and colleague for ten years now, who unhesitatingly accepted the book as appropriate for Cistercian Publications; Daniel Heisey, OSB, who willingly took on the challenge to read the chapters and write a welcoming foreword to the book; J. Stephen Russell, who brought his erudition, generosity, insight, and clear sharp prose to the introduction; and Emily Stuckey, who created the indices for the book with her reliable generosity and precision. I also thank all the staff members at Liturgical Press who turn word-processed manuscripts into books, make them beautiful, and sell them to the world: Stephanie Lancour, Colleen Stiller, Angela Steffens, Tara Durheim, Michelle Verkuilen, Deb Eisenschenk, Elizabeth Elin, Bernie Donlon, Christin Roskos, and Brian Woods. I am so very grateful to all of them.

The Feast of Saint Bernard, August 20, 2024

# Abbreviations

| | |
|---|---|
| ABR | *The American Benedictine Review* |
| ASOC | *Analecta Sacri Ordinis Cisterciensis/Analecta Cisterciensia* |
| CCCM | Corpus Christianorum, Continuatio Mediaevalis. Turnhout: Brepols. |
| CCCM 1 | *Aelredi Rievallensis Opera Omnia, 1 Opera Ascetica.* Ed. Anselm Hoste and C. H. Talbot. CCCM 1. Turnholt: Brepols, 1971. |
| CCSL | Corpus Christianorum Series Latina |
| CF | Cistercian Fathers series |
| *Cîteaux* | *Cîteaux: Commentarii Cisterciensis* |
| Coll | *Collectanea Cisterciensia* |
| CS | Cistercian Studies series |
| CSEL | Corpus Scriptorum Ecclesiasticorum Latinorum |
| CSQ | *Cistercian Studies Quarterly* |
| De am | Cicero, *De amicitia.* In Cicero, *De senectute, De amicitia, De divinatione.* Trans. William Armistead Falconer. Loeb. London: Heinemann, 1923. 108–211. |
| Ep | Epistle |
| H | Homily |
| Loeb | Loeb Classical Library |
| n.s. | new series |
| PL | Patrologia Latina. Ed. J.-P. Migne. |

SBOp Sancti Bernardi Opera. Ed. Jean Leclercq, H. M. Rochais, and C. H. Talbot. 9 vols. Rome: Editiones Cistercienses, 1957–1977.

SCh Sources Chrétiennes. Paris: Cerf.

{ } Dutton updating and corrections

## Works of Aelred of Rievaulx

The appendix of Aelred's Works (269–77) provides complete publication information.

Anima *De anima*

*On the Soul*

Iesu *De Iesu puero duodenni*

*On Jesus as a Boy of Twelve*

Inst incl *De institutione inclusarum*

*Formation of Recluses; A Rule of Life for a Recluse; On Reclusion*

Spec car *Speculum caritatis*

*Mirror of Charity*

Spir am *De amicitia spiritali*

*On Spiritual Friendship*

S(S) Sermon(s)

## Work of Ambrose

Duties *De officiis*

## Works of Augustine

Conf *Confessions*

De bono *De bono coniugali*

De Gen *De Genesi ad litteram libri duodecim*

## Works of Bernard of Clairvaux

Dil *Liber de diligendo Deo*

Hum *The Steps of Humility and Pride*

SC *Sermons on the Song of Songs*

## Works of Bonaventure

LV *Lignum Vitae*

TL *The Tree of Life*

## Works of William of Saint-Thierry

Cant *Expositio super Cantica canticorum*

Contemp *De contemplando Deo*

Ep frat *Epistola (aurea) ad fratres de Monte Dei*

Med *Meditativæ orationes*

Nat am *De natura et dignitate amoris*

Spec fid *Speculum fidei*

# Introduction

This is a book about the spirituality of Aelred of Rievaulx (1110–1167), the saintly abbot of the Cistercian abbey of Rievaulx in Yorkshire and the author of a large number of spiritual writings that are still read and treasured nine hundred years later.

In itself, a book about Aelred is not an unusual event: there are other books about Aelred's spirituality. This book is different, for it is not only about Aelred but it is also a record—a retrospective, perhaps—of the spiritual friendship between Aelred across the centuries with one of his most passionate and perceptive readers, Marsha Dutton. It consists of just some of Professor Dutton's essays on Aelred published over a period of almost forty years, essays that examine and respond to Aelred's own bold and luminous kerygma, his proclamation of the divinity and humanity of Jesus, of the mystical communion and real sustenance of the Eucharist, of *agape* and *philia*, of the love of God and friendship with the women and men around us. As we will see in the pages that follow, Professor Dutton's work has helped us—both as scholars and as believers—to meet Aelred for ourselves, to hear his voice and to encounter his profoundly human grasp of his faith.

Roughly half of the essays in this book originally appeared in two volumes produced in connection with the annual International Congress of Medieval Studies at Western Michigan University—or simply "Kalamazoo" to the initiated. These two books, *Goad and Nail* (1985) and *Erudition at God's Service* (1987) are particularly hard to come by these days, so these four essays' appearance here makes these earlier writings of Professor Dutton available to a new generation of readers. The other chapters, two expansive essays from *The American Benedictine Review* (2000 and 2010) and a new essay rooted in an unpublished conference address (2023), round out the volume as they round out Professor Dutton's deep and deepening understanding of Aelred's life of the spirit.

This little introduction will return now and again to these two areas—the spirituality of Aelred and Professor Dutton's unique grasp of Aelred's thought, but the principal focus here will be on this book as a casebook on *method,* on cognitive structures or templates that readers might bring to bear as they work to comprehend something wonderful and new. For this book is just that, a casebook: in the pages that follow one can watch Professor Dutton both grow as a scholar and also utilize and refine a particular group of analytical methods and then apply them to the study of Aelred.

To understand the roots of these methods we need to begin at the beginning. In 1981, Marsha Dutton Stuckey published her dissertation, "An Edition of Two Middle English Translations of Aelred's *De institutione inclusarum.*" This was a project completed in fulfillment of her doctoral degree from the University of Michigan *in English.* Like many other editions of medieval texts, both in and out of the Early English Text Society,[1] her work was the product of the meticulous and scrupulous examination of manuscripts, the extended examination of evolving definitions of antiquated words, and the constant alertness to the scribal fumble. In other words, it was the product of *historical philology,* that most demanding and least glamorous of specialties in English departments, often conducted in the lower levels of libraries, far from glittery metacriticism and poststructural *jouissance.*

[1] The EETS edition by John Ayto and Alexandra Talbot Barratt, *Aelred of Rievaulx's De Institutione Inclusarum: Two English Versions*, appeared in 1984 (Early English Text Society 87 [Oxford: Oxford University Press, 1984]).

For many aspiring medievalists, projects like these were means to an end, but not to (soon to be) Professor Dutton; the voice of Aelred—via a Middle English translator—spoke to her:

> For-asmuche as ydelnesse is a deedly enemy to mannys soule, whiche may be cleped moder of alle vices, wurcher of alle lustes, norsher of veyn thoughtes, former of vnclene affeccions, sturer of vnclene desires, greither of heuynesse, I wolde thou were not vnoccupyed, but with dyuerse honeste occupacions to voide this foule vice of ydelnesse.[2]

Along with its worthwhile warning to eschew idleness, a passage like this, early in *De Institutione Inclusarum* (On the Formation of Recluses), sits waiting to stir the mind of the student of language as well as the student of religion. Framing the pious message, the student of literary devices would see—like seeing both the knot and the rope, both the text and the textile—figures of speech, rhetorical periods, and the quiet, almost cardiac, rhythm that permeates the passage. Alongside the Latin in which he wrote his works Aelred probably thought in an English just a little earlier than this, and it was surely this voice that invited the student of literature to bring to it—with "dyuerse honeste occupacions"—the skills and methods of literary analysis.

It is these skills and methods, applied and refined by Professor Dutton, that are on view here. The essays may be seen broadly—and somewhat artificially—as either latitudinal or longitudinal. Latitudinal essays trace a topic or motif or theme across the width of an author's work. Its natural home, unsurprisingly, is literary study: think of studies like "race in Mark Twain" or "knighthood in Walter Scott." Longitudinal studies place an author's signature motifs or symbols along a line, either looking backwards and tracing influences *on an author* or looking forward *to an author's own influence*: imagine studies

[2] Ayto and Barratt, *Aelred of Rievaulx's*, 6.

of the influence of Dante on Spenser or of Spenser on Milton. Both of these approaches to authors and texts belong originally to literary study; applied here, to works of spirituality, these complementary approaches—the breadth of the *oeuvre* versus the line of influence—become powerfully illuminating, sharpening and contextualizing insights into the spirituality of these ancient writers.

An example of the latitudinal (or broad) template can be found in "Christ Our Mother: Aelred's Iconography for Contemplative Union," originally published in 1985.[3] The essay treats "the soul's consuming hunger for union with Christ" (45) through carefully tracing the motif of Christ as mother through Aelred's *On the Formation of Anchoresses*,[4] the only one of Aelred's works to be addressed to a single individual (his sister). Early on, the essay opens *Formation* up, arguing that—its title in the English translation notwithstanding—it is not simply a rule of life but a work of spirituality and spiritual direction, "a unified contemplative work; in it Aelred guides the contemplative toward union with God in this life, then depicts the beatitude she will enjoy in the next" (49).

What follows this is a treatment of maternal imagery associated with Christ, through both direct quotations and, more subtly, allusions to the writings of church fathers, forerunners of Aelred. In their footsteps, Aelred can tell his anchoress that she will

> be nourished by the gift of Christ's humanity, known in milk, but she is not yet able fully to know Christ in both flesh and spirit, in both humanity and divinity. That ability, possessed

[3] In *Goad and Nail: Studies in Medieval Cistercian History, X*, ed. E. Rozanne Elder, Cistercian Studies series [CS] 84 (Kalamazoo, MI: Cistercian Publications, 1985), 21–45; pp. 45–74 below.

[4] This work is often known by its inaccurate title in the English translation by Mary Paul Macpherson published by Cistercian Publications. In the course of her work Dutton uses different English versions of the title, finally settling on *The Formation of Recluses*.

> already by John, is represented by wine as well as milk, by inebriation as well as nourishment. John here lies upon Christ's bosom, receiving the wine and inebriated by it; his knowing of Christ is poured into him, not expressed by him. He knows God fully rather than in part. (58)

When motif criticism works well, as it does here, the occurrences of the motif in quotations will come to rest seamlessly in the text's own argumentation. The nest of images that comprise the motif, especially Jesus as nursing mother, are often stunning, perhaps even subversive, and they serve to introduce the reader to one of the central ideas of Aelred's spirituality, especially as documented by Professor Dutton: Aelred's thinking is deeply and unreservedly invested in the humanity of Jesus. For Aelred, Jesus is not simply pondered or imagined or worshiped from afar: in him God meets us person to person, as friend, as brother, and, in figure and spirit, even as mother. As Professor Dutton concludes, "Aelred embodies his profoundly incarnational understanding of mystical progress and union in the language of metaphor and image rather than in that of abstraction and speculation" (74).

The second of these latitudinal essays here is the dense and complex "Eat, Drink, and Be Merry: The Eucharistic Spirituality of the Cistercian Fathers."[5] Like its neighbor, "Intimacy and Imitation," this essay takes a broad look at Cistercian thought that stems from its core principles of incarnational and sacramental intimacy, flowing from the bedrock of Christianity as *Immanuel*, God with us, not simply in the promise of communion in heaven but also in the here and now.

[5] "Eat, Drink, and Be Merry: The Eucharistic Spirituality of the Cistercian Fathers," in *Erudition at God's Service: Studies in Medieval Cistercian History XI*, ed. John R. Sommerfeldt, CS 98 (Kalamazoo, MI: Cistercian Publications, 1987), 1–30; pp. 157–91 below.

The essay begins with a striking extended metaphor, this time from William of Saint-Thierry. William declares that the faithful see God through the eyes of charity, of love and reason, the coming together of two complementary "visions." William explains that reason

> cannot see God except in what he is not, but love cannot bring itself to rest except in what he is . . . . Reason . . . seems to advance through what God is not toward what God is . . . [whereas love], putting aside what God is not, rejoices to lose itself in what he is. (157)

However valuable as an heuristic, Professor Dutton observes that this distinction between reason and love is finally unsustainable, because we cannot love what we do not know, even as we cannot know what is transcendent to us. This spiritual impasse is the source of the Cistercians' bold new articulations of Jesus' humanity. This movement in Christology reached a plateau of sorts in the pietas to crèches of the thirteenth century, but its roots are, in large part, here in the twelfth century, with the Cistercians.

So this essay and its companion piece, "Intimacy and Imitation," approach William's two metaphorical eyes separately, dealing with the "eye of love" in "Intimacy and Imitation" and the "eye of reason" here. These three early Cistercian thinkers, Bernard, William, and Aelred, worked and thought and prayed over the foundational questions of the Eucharist and wrote, not from perfected confidence and assurance, but from need and yearning. Their

> unsatisfied longing to know and love God led the Cistercians of the twelfth century finally to a new way of understanding him and to intimate love shaped by that understanding. So they created a eucharistic and incarnational spirituality, one that was within a century to turn medieval Christianity toward the humanity of Christ and so to direct the attention of western Christianity from that time on to the incarnate God, Jesus of Nazareth. (158–59)

Specifically, the essay looks closely at three eucharistic questions:

1) Do we receive Jesus' earthly or glorified body—the Jesus who died, or the Jesus who was resurrected?
2) What does the Eucharist mean to believers in this life?
3) How does the Eucharist signify beyond this life; how does it participate in beatitude?

The body of the essay is devoted to looking at the thinking of Bernard, William and Aelred on these three questions. While the essay seems regularly to see Aelred's thinking on these issues as the culmination of the three Cistercians, "Eat, Drink" is still properly latitudinal, treating three evolving expressions of the same central ideas. On the first question, what it is that we consume when we receive the Eucharist, Aelred emerges as the clearest articulator of the importance of centering on Jesus' physical body as the natural point of contact with his followers on earth:

> [Aelred] identifies Christ's two natures with milk and wine in his meditation on the Last Supper and indicates the order in which they are known: "If you are not capable of greater things, leave John to inebriate himself with the wine of gladness in the knowledge of the Godhead while you run to feed on the milk which flows from Christ's humanity. (179)[6]

Aelred's language here, like his teaching, is carefully attenuated to balance the central doctrine of Jesus' divinity with the comforting intimacy of his humanity. Focusing on Aelred's metaphors, as she so often does in her work, Professor Dutton shows Aelred not so much obscuring or hiding dogma but clothing it in quotidian, even sensual experiences. Thus,

[6] Aelred, Inst incl 31 (CCCM 1:668, 1091–94; CF 2:87).

> Having emerged from the Eucharist, risen in the flesh from the manger, the cross, the tomb, and the altar, Jesus for Aelred is always fully human, fully flesh, but at the same time he is also always divine, his humanity always sacred. (170)

The Cistercians' and especially Aelred's response to the second and third questions grow directly from their approach to the first. For all three and especially Aelred, the Eucharist makes physical and tangible the intimacy to which Christians like Aelred's anchoress are called:

> Aelred argues not only that one may know Christ's divinity in this life, but that one may come into physical and spiritual unity with him here. He directs the contemplative to eat and drink of his body, then to enter into the wound in his side, "in which, like a dove, you may hide." (180)

The language here anticipated the affective spirituality of Teresa of Àvila and other *Brautmystik* figures. Hiding in the Lord's wounds perhaps silently evokes Jesus' dialogue with Thomas the apostle, including the sense that the human person's need for physical intimacy with Jesus is real and salutary.

On the third question, the place of the Eucharist in Christian thinking about the afterlife, Professor Dutton observes that

> as the Fathers emerged from their new and reasoned understanding of the humanity of Jesus they came to a new understanding of the Eucharist. No longer was receiving the species merely an act of faith, a blind tasting in unquestioning acceptance of what that tasting promised; now it meant feasting with both eyes open. (182)

The Eucharist is thus literally a foretaste of heavenly union with Jesus the Christ, both the literal feasting "with both eyes open"—both reason and love—and also the promise of communion that will not require sacramental intermediary.

The third latitudinal or broad study in this volume is "Intimacy and Imitation: The Humanity of Christ in Cistercian Spirituality," published, like the preceding essay, in the Kalamazoo-based *Studies in Medieval Cistercian History.*[7] It is a companion piece to "Eat, Drink, and Be Merry," turning from William's "eye of reason" to the "eye of love" and continuing Professor Dutton's program of fleshing out the radical incarnational spirituality of both Aelred and his brother Cistercians. It begins, almost seamlessly, where "Eat, Drink and Be Merry" ends:

> The incarnation represents the intimacy of the human state with God, says Gregory of Nyssa,[8] and the works of Cistercian spirituality echo that understanding. In his sermons on the Song of Songs, the great book of intimacy between the divine and the human, Bernard of Clairvaux lays a foundation for an incarnational and sacramental spirituality of just such intimacy, explaining the incarnation, the Holy Spirit, and the soul's reception of God's power and knowledge all in terms of a kiss. (193)

The essay thus begins with a master image—technically, a conceit, a metaphor embracing multiple logical bases and multiple, complementary interpretations, not wholly unlike the concept of the fourfold interpretations of Scripture. Here, Professor Dutton steps aside to allow Bernard the literary author to illuminate Bernard the spiritual master. Then come complementary passages from William of Saint-Thierry and Aelred, followed by a short passage that seems to me the inductive

[7] "Intimacy and Imitation: The Humanity of Christ in Cistercian Spirituality," in *Erudition at God's Service: Studies in Medieval Cistercian History XI*, ed. John R. Sommerfeldt, CS 98 (Kalamazoo, MI: Cistercian Publications, 1987), 33–69; pp. 193–236 below.

[8] Footnote in the original essay: *De virginitate* 2; PG 46:323; Gregory of Nyssa, *Dogmatic Treatises*, trans. William Moore and Henry Astin Wilson, Nicene and Post-Nicene Fathers, 2nd series, 5 (New York: Wipf and Stock, 1893), 344.

heart of the essay. Cistercian spirituality, writes Professor Dutton, is in its essence

> sacramental, grounded in the meeting of the worshiper with Christ on the altar and in Christ's revelation of himself there through the gift of the Holy Spirit. God channels his grace in the sacrament as in the incarnation, through the sensible, leading humankind through creatures of bread and wine to his son, begotten, not made, and so to himself. For *Cistercian spirituality, far from being rooted in a desire to escape the flesh and the world, begins and ends in God known in the flesh in this world.* (195, emphasis mine)

In some ways, this present book is an extended commentary on this passage and especially the italicized sentence. Because she is a Christian lay person whose career was in secular universities, Professor Dutton was and is perfectly situated to articulate Cistercian spirituality in language for the world beyond the cloister, a world that spends most of its waking moments surrounded by earthly, fleshly, *human* concerns. A bit later in the essay, Professor Dutton quotes William of Saint-Thierry making this very point, addressing Christ:

> It was not the least of the chief reasons for your incarnation that your babes in the Church, who still needed your milk rather than solid food, who are not strong enough spiritually to think of you in your own way, might find in you a form not unfamiliar to themselves. (202)

The reference here to breastfeeding and then to grown-up food looks back to both "Christ our Mother" and "Eat, Drink, and Be Merry," to Professor Dutton's continued exploration of the Cistercians' incarnational and sacramental spirituality and their multilayered catechesis on the Eucharist. Here, looking more specifically at the affective rather than the cognitive side of the Cistercians' eucharistic teachings, Professor Dutton comments,

> If Cistercian spirituality develops through the yearning that combines loneliness, anxiety, unwillingness to accept absolute exile in this life, and the desire to dwell in eternity within God's love, to "so pass through things temporal that we lose not the things eternal," that yearning is far from despair. It consists of love not hopeless but hopeful. (199)

This is a remarkable passage, one that would come to typify the scholarly dialogue that would develop from Professor Dutton's and her colleagues' writing, especially on Aelred. The nouns that dominate the first sentence—"yearning," "loneliness," and "anxiety"—might initially look peculiar in a theological or spiritual discourse, but it is precisely their messy, vulnerable human identity that earns them a place in this spirituality of intimacy and imitation. And the short included quotation, "so pass through things temporal . . .," is Professor Dutton's gentle nod to the warm incarnate relevance of these twelfth-century writers, for the quote is from the Book of Common Prayer.

The essay thus completes the circle begun in "Eat, Drink," as it fleshes out the human, affective reality of this evolving teaching on the humanity of Jesus and the sacrament of the altar—the last(ing) supper of intimacy with Jesus, both God and human Person.

Continuing—with quickly dissipating confidence in this introduction's cartological metaphor –we turn from *latitudinal* studies of motifs to *longitudinal* studies of influence. These essays, the alert reader may note, tend to have later publication dates than the ones already discussed. This development is due in no small part to what we might call the earnings of success: having worked to bring Aelred of Rievaulx to broader scholarly consciousness with her discussions of his thought, Professor Dutton (and others, to be sure) can move to his place in a continuum of Christian thinkers, both in the twelfth-century shorter term and the longer term from the early fathers to the Counter-Reformation and beyond.

The first of these longitudinal essays considered here is "The Cistercian Source: Aelred, Bonaventure, and Ignatius."[9] Though a study of influence, it was published in the 1980s along with the other studies of motifs. In some ways it is unique in this little collection, as it is the only study of influence that focusses on Aelred as the *influencer*. Building on "Intimacy and Imitation," the essay asserts Aelred as the "Cistercian source" or influence on or inspiration for the thinking of Bonaventure and Ignatius of Loyola on what could come to be known as affective spirituality. This thinking on spirituality stems from the twelfth-century emphasis on the humanity of Jesus to urge pious, imaginative imitation of the life of Jesus as the entryway to spiritual communion with the Lord. Like the other "earlier" writings, this essay draws particularly on *Formation of Recluses*, paying particular attention to the work's insistence on meditation on Jesus' earthly life as the source of entry into spiritual intimacy with the divine. As she noted in "Intimacy and Imitation," Professor Dutton here emphasizes that *Rule* alone among Aelred's

> works was written for a woman, it alone exalted the life of Mary over that of Martha. Further, it guided the contemplative toward union not, like *On Jesus*, through imitation of Jesus, but through intimacy with him. This approach to contemplative union depended on the imaginative involvement of the contemplative in the human life of Jesus. (239)

There is much to unpack here. First, of course, is Professor Dutton's emphasis on Aelred's crafting this work for a woman in consecrated life. Beyond the remarkable fact of its being addressed to a woman. *Formation* is striking for the contemplative *demands* it makes on its audience: far from "talking down"

[9] In *Goad and Nail: Studies in Medieval Cistercian History, X*, ed. E. Rozanne Elder, CS 84 (Kalamazoo, MI: Cistercian Publications, 1985), 151–78; pp. 237–67 below.

to the anchoress, *Rule* asks of her a sophisticated level of contemplative energy and skill, to aspire to an intimacy with the Lord that "depended on the imaginative involvement of the contemplative in the human life of Jesus."

The essay then looks forward to the way in which the great Franciscan and Jesuit understood (or misunderstood) this Aelredan goal of "imaginative involvement." The essay itself treats this much more fully and powerfully than any synopsis or appreciation could, but in the end the essay records a large—and largely unacknowledged—debt to Aelred's writing and thinking. This sort of criticism cannot be done casually or gently: when source and influence criticism is at its best, it is relentless, specific and even insistent. Thus, Professor Dutton takes great care in detailing Bonaventure's extensive reliance on Aelred's *Formation:*

> The passages in [Bonaventure's] *The Tree of Life* revealing influence from Aelred fall into four rough categories: (1) near-identity with slight variation in phrasing, (2) extensive verbal parallels with embellishment or rearrangement, (3) some verbal similarity and likeness in technique and purpose but with considerable independence in phrasing, and (4) stylistic imitation of Aelred with little overlap of content or phrasing. (251)

True to form, the essay goes on to detail multiple examples of each level of borrowing.

"The Cistercian Source" does not spend time speculating on the reasons that Aelred's place in the development of affective spirituality has been so widely unacknowledged. Some of this slight comes, certainly, from misattribution of the work, but just as much stems from the later writers' incomplete understanding of Aelred's thinking and milieu, especially by Bonaventure. The essay concludes,

> Bonaventure and Ludolph were able to use Aelred's words and, in the case of Bonaventure, imitate his method, but in the absence of Aelred's particular purpose and understanding—and with

> their own understanding of Christ as exemplar and of contemplative union as emerging from imitation of Christ—they were never able really to understand what Aelred had in mind. (266)

There is a real boldness and assurance in such a sentence by a young scholar, along with a healthy partisanship towards a figure whose place in a line of influence has yet to be established. And we read Professor Dutton today and will continue to do so in the future in large part because we no longer have to make arguments like this one, arguments that assert that Aelred is unique and uniquely valuable.

We turn now to two more recent essays by Professor Dutton, published in the early 2000s in *The American Benedictine Review.* Both of these essays, "Friendship and the Love of God: Augustine's Teaching in the *Confessions* and Aelred of Rievaulx's Response in *Spiritual Friendship*" and "A Model for Friendship: Ambrose's Contribution to Aelred of Rievaulx's *Spiritual Friendship*," are rich, classic examples of the longitudinal (or influence) essay, mature studies that begin by establishing a line of influence and then move on towards a supple, nuanced understanding of the relationship, especially how the recipient of the influence—here, Aelred—worked with Augustine's and Ambrose's thinking as he crafted his own unique understanding of *philia*.

"Friendship and the Love of God" is the first of these two influence essays that deal with Aelred's signature teaching on friendship; it is an essay that focuses on the influence of Augustine's *Confessions* on Aelred's *Spiritual Friendship.* The essay begins with an unexpected caveat, a distinction at home in the rhetoric-sensitive analyses of literary study as distinct from historical or biographical writing:

> Comprehension of Augustine's and Aelred's teaching requires analysis of what they wrote rather than what they may have experienced, a recognition of their use of personal narrative as a vehicle through which to explore the relationship of human beings with one another and with God. (83–84)

This is, again, a distinction and an approach rooted in the study of literature and its mechanisms and tropes—of the weave of the tapestry as constituent of and yet as distinct from the image the tapestry depicts. Here, for Augustine and Aelred, the avenues of analysis that open with this subtle distinction—between narrative artifact and biographical reminiscence—are wide and rich, taking readers beyond questions of biography or remembrance to deeper insights into what the writers were expressing through these rhetorical strategies, real or embellished. When seen as expressive strategies Augustine's and Aelred's remembrances of friendships become brightly illuminated windows into the two writers' thoughts on *philia* as a spiritual, even a theological experience. Specifically, the *Confessions* and *Spiritual Friendship* both

> contain within their narratives of apparently candid autobiographical reminiscence narrative *personae*—the first-person narrator in Augustine and the abbot-teacher in Aelred—who articulate their authors' teaching while remaining distinct from those creators. Both *personae* have many friends, but these friendships serve as dramatized explications of the authors' views on friendship. (84)

Far from minimizing or disrespecting the two writers' life experiences, Professor Dutton's method, as the passage suggests, frees the reader to reach the *intentionality* that sits beneath the narrative vignettes, an intentionality that gives them their outsized rhetorical power. When Augustine, for example, relates the death of his unnamed boyhood friend in *Confessions* IV, he moves resolutely from narrative to meditation and to prayer, remembering the event to allow himself to draw from it and learn from it. And in the end, readers often find themselves uncomfortable with Augustine's conclusions, feeling that he rejects what is healthy and innocent in this life as he yearns for the next.

Professor Dutton's signal insight here—and one of the most important insights that she has contributed to Aelred studies—

is that Aelred very consciously steps away from his "influences" and declines to make these sorts of rejections. Here, for example, while in the end Augustine feels he must reject earthly friendship as incompatible with beatitude, Aelred steadfastly refuses to do this and celebrates spiritual friendship as essentially Godly:

> Aelred, however, consistently expresses confidence in God's gift of friendship as good in itself. He treats it as part of the order of Creation and as God's image in his creatures. Furthermore, he says, God sanctified friendship through his incarnation and will perfect it in eternity, when God himself will be the friend of all. (87)

For Aelred this is not an exaggeration, not a figure of speech, though time and again his expression of this divine gift of human friendship seems to be at odds with institutional Christian teaching. It is not, as Aelred well knew, and as he would have whispered as he celebrated Mass,

> O God, Who wonderfully formed the dignity of human nature, and more wonderfully restored it, grant us through the mystery of this water and wine, to be made participants of His divinity, Who condescended to become a partaker of our humanity, Jesus Christ, Thy Son, our Lord . . . .[10]

This mystical fusion of the human and the divine, repeated and celebrated every time the Mass is offered, led to Aelred's most radical expression of the divine nature, from the lips of Ivo in *Spiritual Friendship*:

[10] "*Deus, qui humána substántia dignitátem mirabiliter condidísti et mirabilius reformásti: da nobis per hujus aqua et vini mystérium, ejus divinitatis esse consórtes, qui humanitátis nostræ fieri dignátus est párticeps, Jesus Christus Filius tuus Dóminus Noster . . . .*" Extraordinary form of the Latin Mass of the Roman Rite, https://extraordinaryform.org/ExtraordinaryFormTextLandscape.pdf, accessed 8 May 2024. This prayer, the secret, survives in shortened form in the revised vernacular prayers of the Offertory.

> Should I say of friendship what John, the friend of Jesus, said of charity, "God is friendship"?[11]

As Aelred, his translators, and Professor Dutton well know, the various Latin words that end up getting translated into English as *love* run the gamut from the sensual to the transcendent, and *amicitia* or *philia* are among the most rarified of these words. Ivo is wrong about John and his Gospel, of course—and his abbot Aelredus duly corrects him—but the point has most elegantly been made: for Aelred, true friendship, far from being something to be pushed aside as Augustine counsels, is to be embraced, as it is from God.

This emphasis on the value of friendship for Aelred has been one of the central themes of Professor Dutton's writings, and, more broadly, a prime focus of the explosion of scholarly (and general) interest in Aelred, especially in the new century. Some of this interest has moved into speculation about Aelred's sexual orientation, but Professor Dutton and most mainstream Aelred scholars treat the issue as only speculation, an example of the dangers of imposing contemporary social constructs and clues on cultures and people of long ago and far away. Like many men and women in consecrated and cloistered life today, Aelred speaks of his friendships and relationships with his brothers with an openness and tenderness that sound, somehow, more than friendly, too fervent to us, but this disconnect probably stems more from our own diluted notion of friendship than from what we perceive to be Aelred's unusual fervor. And, as accomplished as Aelred was in English and medieval Latin, he would have recoiled at the use of "friend" as a verb.

So this topic—of powerful, spiritual but earthly friendship—would rightly come to dominate Aelred studies and would inspire essays like "Friendship and the Love of God," and the next longitudinal essay, "A Model for Friendship: Ambrose's

[11] Spir am 1.69; CF 5:69.

Contribution to Aelred of Rievaulx's *Spiritual Friendship*."[12] Published ten years after "Friendship and the Love of God," "Model for Friendship" is a significant and expansive reconsideration of the relationship between Ambrose's "On Duties" and Aelred's *Spiritual Friendship.*

At the outset this essay resembles Professor Dutton's earlier essay on Augustine's *Confessions* and *Spiritual Friendship*, opening here with a measured and carefully constructed overview of Ambrose's thinking on human friendship:

> Two Ambrosian threads are of particular importance in shaping the theological argument of *Spiritual Friendship*. From beginning to end, Aelred interweaves God's role in creating, modeling, and participating in human friendship with the human experience of friendship, as friends share their every thought and emotion with one another. (122)

Unlike Ambrose, however, Aelred does not treat these two strands as separable but integrates them,

> so enunciating unified and sacramental understanding of friendship as both a reminiscence of Paradise and anticipation of beatitude, with the friend the other half of oneself, known and loved always in Christ. (123)

This move closely mirrors Aelred's reimagining of Augustine's thinking on friendship, blotting out the boundary between earthly and heavenly friendship.

The essay then proceeds into a detailed treatment of Ambrose's thinking on friendship in *On Duties*. This work, written as a master guide for the proper ethical and ecclesial behavior of the clergy, is not, clearly, a philosophical work, let alone a work about *philia* or *amicitia*: the topics come up, logically enough, in Ambrose's discussion of the proper limits of earthly attachments among the clergy. Though solidly basing his work on Cicero, Ambrose carefully articulates a place for *amicitia*

[12] ABR 64 (2010): 39–66; pp. 121–56 below.

within and subordinate to righteous and ethical Christian behavior, again especially for clergy. His approach and focus to the issue thus clearly moves Ambrose to a positive but limited celebration of Christian *amicitia* as a worldly value instituted and blessed by God but ultimately a value subordinate to *caritas*.

As with his encounter with Augustine and the *Confessions*, it is precisely here—in his response to *On Duties*—that Aelred finds where to reach beyond his source to articulate a stronger more integrative understanding of spiritual friendship. In general, the essay finds Ambrose's thinking closer to Aelred's than Augustine's was—a surprising observation given that Augustine is so eloquent about his own friendships in the *Confessions*. Here, with Ambrose, Professor Dutton shows Aelred working much more closely with the bishop of Milan, responding and adapting almost point by point to the thinking of *On Duties*. This relationship gives "Model for Friendship" a unique, almost musical quality, playing Aelred's agreements against his innovations like a toccata and fugue; for example,

> both Ambrose and Aelred locate the origins of human friendship in God's intention in creation. Ambrose's passage on the subject comes at some distance from his discussion of the social instincts of animals, and . . . credits God not with creating friendship itself but with placing good will in the man and the woman . . . . Aelred, however, connects the social behavior of animals and angels directly to the natural social attachment of humans, attributing that attachment to God's eternal purpose.Further, he translates Ambrose's good will into friendship itself as God's gift. (140)

And again, a little later:

> [B]oth Ambrose and Aelred explain that the friendship begun in Paradise expanded into human communities. For Ambrose, that development is directly tied to God's action in Paradise and indeed articulated within the passage where he says that from its beginnings in Paradise "it has filled the world." Aelred, however,

> ties his discussion of the expansion of individual friendship not to Paradise but to Christ's call to his followers, and he does so not within or after but well before his passage on the divine origins of friendship. (142)

In each of these instances and others in the essay, we can watch Professor Dutton lead the reader to see the very atoms and molecules of Aelred's thought and to watch him sit beside the great mind of Ambrose and thoughtfully, fraternally take the thoughts of *On Duties* and make them, subtly but unmistakably, his own.

This is the gold standard of the longitudinal essay. When essays like this one really work—and this is rare—the reader is allowed to watch the evolution of image or theme or thought or *topos* at the most granular level. Especially in the sphere of spiritual writing, work like this is immensely valuable both to scholars and to every motivated reader, since it celebrates the balance between continuity and change, between tradition and innovation, continuities that can only be truly seen in the patient, deliberate long (-itudinal) view.

The book's table of contents notwithstanding, we come at last to the first essay of the collection, "Clinging to God: The Pedagogy of Memory in Aelred's Spiritual Treatises." This is the most recent essay in the book, originating in an address to the international online conference "Our Aelred," sponsored by the British Archaeological Association in January 2021. This was a remarkable event, and its sessions can still be viewed online;[13] as the title might suggest, the event centered on a broad appreciation of Aelred and included both scholarly and nonacademic perspectives.

"Clinging to God: The Pedagogy of Memory" is an expansive and challenging essay, not quite the longest of the collection but broad and subtle in scope and managing both latitude and longitude, that is, focusing both on a discrete nest of ideas

[13] https://thebaa.org/event/our-aelred-man-monk-and-saint/. Accessed 10 May 2024.

in Aelred's works and also examining their most relevant source, in the writings of Augustine. This relationship, between Augustine's thinking on memory and learning (drawing especially on the *Confessions* and *On the Trinity*) and Aelred's, is what we might call the longitudinal axis of this essay. This dense and subtle discussion takes up roughly the first third of the discussion, returning again and again to the centrality of *memoria* in Augustine's pedagogy, that is, how the process of membering, dismembering, and re-membering for Augustine is the way humans learn as they walk through life.

With these insights in hand, the essay turns to Aelred:

> [B]eginning with *Mirror*, while still a novice director and then a new abbot, [Aelred] shaped his spiritual treatises to guide readers to cling to God without forgetfulness, using Augustine's explanation of the power of memory as the theological core of his pedagogical praxis. (18)

It might be possible to miss the boldness of this assertion: of the ascent to communion with God in this life *through memory*, "without forgetfulness," as Professor Dutton puts it. This movement to *fides* through *memoria*, says Professor Dutton, can be seen to happen in all five of Aelred's relevant treatises, written to dramatize conferences or dialogues between a mature abbot and one or two other people, who come to him not only requesting aid but often phrasing their requests to define the terms of his answer, requests that often provide a prologue to and an outline of what follows. But rather than imposing his own authority by then giving a lecture, in the treatises he provides reminders of their experience of God "to help them remember God as they already know him" (19).

In the balance of this very rewarding essay Professor Dutton illustrates this gentle, communal pedagogical (or evangelical) process at work in the treatises. In *On Jesus at the Age of Twelve*, for example, Aelred can begin with Mary's sudden *memory* of her missing son and move effortlessly from this to Brother Ivo's own truant memories of events in Jesus' life that can and ought to shape him. And the treatise ends, says Professor Dutton, with another truant memory gently recovered by the abbot, that Jesus' own behavior must be our model in this world, for the work ends

> with the audience's continuing participation in Jesus' life, as both he and they must return to minister in obedience to Joseph and Mary [and] . . . fulfill the never-ending demands of human life. Just as Jesus was able to spend only three days in Jerusalem contemplating his Father before returning to Nazareth and his human obligations, so Ivo and Aelred's readers must put aside the joys of anticipated beatitude to care for those who depend on them. (29)

This little hint about what can be found in this essay and the others needs to serve as the last foretaste of what awaits the reader in this collection of Professor Dutton's essays. As I suggested at the beginning of the introduction, Professor Dutton's career has enriched the spiritual thinking—and the spiritual lives—of thousands of people, from scholars listening to her papers at Kalamazoo (with varying degrees of professional envy), to Cistercian monks and nuns whose communities she has visited, to readers in monastic and medieval and spiritual studies, and to readers who come to her after wondering what that Aelred fellow was actually all about.

Professor Dutton's works do many things: they explain, they introduce, they illuminate. But I would like to think they do more: I would like, in fact, to believe that what Professor Dutton says in these pages of Aelred's writings might justly be applied to her own. For it seems to me, at their best, Professor Dutton's works provide her readers with reminders of their experience of God to help them remember God as they already know him (19).

J. Stephen Russell
Department of English
Hofstra University, retired

# Embracing God

*Let your voice sound in my ears, good Jesus, that my heart may learn how to love you, my mind how to love you, the intimate parts of my soul how to love you. Let the inner essence of my heart embrace you, my one and only true good, my dear and delightful joy.*

Aelred of Rievaulx, *Mirror of Charity* 1.2

*Chapter 1*

# Clinging to God: The Pedagogy of Memory in Aelred's Spiritual Treatises[1]

Aelred begins *Mirror of Charity*, his first known work, by celebrating God's creation of the world and the excellence of his creatures. The characteristics shared by all creatures, he explains, are given by God and therefore mirror God: "Because he from whom they come is utterly and unalterably beautiful, all things are beautiful; because they come from him who is utterly and unalterably good, all things are good; because they come from him who is utterly and unalterably wise, all things are well ordered."[2] This praise of creation reaches its climax two chapters later when Aelred narrows his focus from those traits common to all creatures to those reserved to rational creatures: humankind:

> Created in the image of its creator, the rational creature may therefore cling to the one whose image it is: that is its only good . . . . This clinging is clearly not that of the flesh, but of the mind,

[1] I presented an early version of this article at *Our Aelred*, a conference sponsored by English Heritage on January 11–12, 2021. I am grateful to Michael Carter for his organization of the conference, and to Dr. Niladri Mahato, Fr. Lawrence Morey, Fr. Placid Morris, and Sr. Judith Sutera for bibliographical assistance.

[2] Aelred, Spec car 1.2.4 (CCCM 1:14; CF 17:89). All translations in this chapter are mine.

> in which the author of all natures inserted three things by which his divine eternity might be shared, his wisdom participated in, and his sweetness tasted. These three, I say, are memory, knowledge, and love or will. Memory is indeed capable of eternity, knowledge of wisdom, and love of sweetness. In these three humankind was created in the image of the Trinity. Memory held God without forgetfulness, understanding knew God without error, and love embraced God without a selfish desire for anything else. So we were blessed [*Hinc beatus*].[3]

As humankind is created in God's image, Aelred says, in these uniquely human attributes God is always present, always able to be known. With this passage and its emphatic chain of reiteration and restatement he establishes the theme that governs *Mirror* and another four of his six spiritual works, guiding his readers to look into their memory to find and hold fast to God—to cling to God into eternity.

## The Format of the Spiritual Works

*Mirror* begins with a letter to Aelred from Bernard, abbot of Clairvaux, requiring Aelred to write, "among other things, to resist the complaints of some who have difficulty with stricter ways," and telling him "not to delay in recording by pen the excellence of charity, of its fruit, and of its order."[4] The work that follows fulfills Bernard's request. This letter and Aelred's

[3] Aelred, Spec car 1.3.9 (CCCM 1:16; CF 17:91–92). By beginning *Mirror* with praise of creation Aelred echoes Genesis 1 as well as the beginning of Augustine's *Confessions*, but where Augustine at once defines humankind as "bearing around him his mortality, bearing around him the witness of his sin," Aelred speaks instead of humans' search for God, then defines the presence of God's image in the human soul and God's desire that humans be blessed. John R. Sommerfeldt, translating *beatus* as *happy*, emphasizes Aelred's insistence on God's intention for human happiness (*Aelred of Rievaulx: On Love and Order in the World and the Church* [New York and Mahwah, NJ: Newman Press, 2006], esp. xvii–xviii, 3–7).

[4] Aelred, Spec car Prol. 1, 6 (CCCM 1.3, 4; CF 17:69, 71).

response, both included in all manuscripts of *Mirror*, thus identify the work's immediate audience and serve as its prologue.

With this structure Aelred anticipates the form of four other treatises: *Jesus as a Boy of Twelve, The Formation of Recluses, Spiritual Friendship*, and *On the Soul*. Each of these begins as Aelred responds to someone requesting guidance, which he provides in the treatise that follows.[5] These requests establish the topics of the treatises and define Aelred's purpose in writing, while also providing personal audiences to serve as surrogates and models for readers.

The ostensible instigators of these works pose specific questions, such as "Where did friendship originate?" and "What does Augustine mean?" In answering them, Aelred also addresses a larger, unspoken, concern: "How can I know and love God?" It was a timely issue. As Elizabeth Connor has written, "twelfth-century people . . . were preoccupied with questions such as: who is man?—who am I? How can I reach God?"[6] Philippe Nouzille comments, "for a monk like Aelred, one of the great questions is that of the possibility of salvation and thus of closeness [*proximité*] to the Christ who came to bring that salvation."[7]

Aelred's response in these works relies on the doctrine he enunciates in the third chapter of *Mirror*, the patristic definition of the human soul as comprising the three inseparable faculties of memory, reason, and will. After explaining the doctrine early in *Mirror*, Aelred returns to it again and again in sermons written throughout his abbatial career, and he articulates it one last

[5] Aelred's sixth spiritual work, *The Pastoral Prayer*, begins as Aelred addresses Jesus, the Good Shepherd.

[6] Elizabeth Connor, "Saint Bernard's Three Steps of Truth and Saint Aelred of Rievaulx's Three Loves," in *Bernardus Magister*, ed. John R. Sommerfeldt, CS 135 (Kalamazoo, MI: Cistercian Publications, 1991), *Cîteaux* 42, nos. 1–4 (1991): 226.

[7] Philippe Nouzille, "Temps et liturgie: présence et representation," in *Intentio Cordis: Temps, histoire, mémoire chez Aelred de Rievaulx*, Coll 73, no. 1 (2011): 174.

time in one of his last works, *On the Soul*. In each case he emphasizes the role of the memory in receiving God, retaining God, and clinging to God, and in all five treatises, even the three in which he does not explain the nature of the soul, he guides readers through their own memory of things past, present, and future, always offering a vision of the beatitude awaiting them. Repeatedly he guides his readers to remember what they may not know they have forgotten: the presence of God with and within them.

## Augustine on the Soul

Aelred's discussion of the soul echoes that of Augustine, who in his work repeatedly explains the way that the tripartite human *mens* or soul bears the image of the trinitarian God. Although he uses a variety of terms for what David N. Bell calls "this psychological trinity,"[8] he consistently explains it as composed of three inseparable faculties,[9] writing in book fourteen of *De Trinitate*, "We think that the trinity of the mind should be put forward under these three names: memory, understanding, and will."[10] This mirroring of the Trinity, he says, enables a person to know and love God, to participate in God, and to embrace God forever.

Augustine also explains that what enters one's memory remains there always, even when silent and unrecognized: "As with a person expert in many disciplines, the things such a person knows are contained in his memory, while nothing is in his mind's sight except what he is thinking of. The other things are stored in a certain secret knowledge that is known

[8] David N. Bell, *The Image and Likeness: The Augustinian Spirituality of William of Saint Thierry*, CS 78 (Kalamazoo, MI: Cistercian Publications, 1984), 40. Bell's book explains the doctrine within the context of Cistercian thought.

[9] Bell, *Image and Likeness*, chap. 1, esp. 27–29, 37–45.

[10] Augustine, *De Trinitate* 14.6.8 (PL 42:1041); Saint Augustine, *The Trinity*, trans. Edmund Hill (Brooklyn, NY: New City Press, 1990), 376.

as memory. . . . we say someone knows letters even when he is thinking about something else, not letters."[11]

Whereas in *On the Trinity* Augustine works to explain the doctrine in general terms, in the *Confessions* he focuses on its significance for the individual. He puts particular emphasis on the role of memory in preserving knowledge of God, presented through his own experience: "Behold how far I have walked about in my memory seeking you, Lord, and I have not found you outside it. For I have found nothing of you that I did not remember from what I was taught of you. For from the time I was taught of you, I have not forgotten you. . . . and so from what I have been taught of you you remain in my memory, and there I find you when I remember you and delight in you."[12] He goes on to explain that this memory of God is not only for the moment, but eternal, linking past, present, and future: "Perhaps it might appropriately be said that there are three times: a present of past things, a present of present things, and a present of future things, for indeed there are three of these in the soul, and I do not see them anywhere else. The present of past things is memory, the present of present things is sight, the present of future things is expectation."[13]

While the doctrine of the tripartite soul precedes Augustine,[14] and Aelred's knowledge of it was probably not limited to Augustine's works, Aelred's frequent citations of Augustine and his extensive discussion in *On the Soul* show that he identified

[11] Augustine, *De Trinitate* 14.6.8 (PL 42:1042).

[12] Augustine, Conf 10.24; *St Augustine's Confessions*, trans. William Watts, 2 vols., Loeb (Cambridge, MA: Harvard University Press, 1912), 2:140–43.

[13] Augustine, Conf 11.20; Watts, trans., *St Augustine's Confessions*, 250–53.

[14] Bell says, "Augustine took over this idea from Neo-Platonic thought, adapted it to his own purpose, and never found it necessary to prove the principle" (Bell, *Image and Likeness*, 22). On Augustine's notion of memory and its influence on later writers, see Patrick J. Geary, *Phantoms of Remembrance: Memory and Oblivion at the End of the First Millennium* (Princeton, NJ: Princeton University Press, 1994), 16–19.

it with Augustine.[15] Augustine's conceptualization provided the core of the doctrinal understanding incorporated into the pedagogy of Aelred's spiritual treatises.

## Aelred on the Tripartite Soul

Aelred found Augustine's explanation of the tripartite soul, and of memory as the means through which men and women know God, so compelling that he included it near the beginning of *Mirror of Charity*. After repeatedly in the first two chapters of the work emphasizing his own desire for God—"Lord, I shall seek you, and by loving you I shall seek"[16]—and declaring that God granted blessedness to humans,[17] he moves to the practical issue of how they may find God. His answer is essentially Augustine's: "Memory held God without forgetfulness, understanding knew God without error, and love embraced God without a selfish desire for anything else. So we were blessed."[18]

Over twenty years later, in *On the Soul,* Aelred returned to Augustine's teaching on the soul, now exploring it at length in a dialogue between himself and John, a young monk. Although in *Mirror* Aelred had presented the doctrine without mentioning Augustine, in *On the Soul* he repeatedly cites Augustine. In book one Aelred answers John's questions about the nature and capacity of the soul, identifies its three inseparable faculties, and begins to explain the role of memory in knowing God: "What surpasses all else, the memory has the capacity for God. For from the moment that a person begins to know God, from that moment God begins to live in his

[15] C. H. Talbot tacitly makes the point by citing twenty-four of Augustine's works in his translation of Aelred's *De Anima*, CF 22 (Kalamazoo, MI: Cistercian Publications, 1981).

[16] *Domine, quaeram te, et amando quaeram te.* Aelred, Spec car 1.1.3 (CCCM 1:14; CF 17:89).

[17] Aelred, Spec car 1.3.8 (CCCM 1:16; CF 17:91).

[18] Aelred, Spec car 1.3.9 (CCCM 1:16; CF 17:91–92).

memory, and there he finds God as often as he remembers him."[19] In book two he continues the discussion of memory, so indicating its importance to him, then considers reason and will.

Like Augustine, Aelred recognizes that what enters memory is not always immediately retrievable. He explains humans' predictably unpredictable experience of trying to remember:

> the memory receives all these things, with the mind seeking now this, now that. Some are so readily available that they appear at once and offer themselves to the one thinking, while some, as others are being sought, rush to the center and can hardly be driven away. Some, in truth, are stored in such a deep pit that they can hardly be retrieved even with great effort of mind, as if concealed in a cave. Other unperturbed thoughts, however, appear in order as they are requested.[20]

In the years between defining the tripartite nature of the soul in his first and possibly his last treatise, Aelred repeatedly spoke of the doctrine in his sermons as he explained the faculties of the soul and their role in human experience. In Sermon 49, on Christ's nativity, he writes of the soul as God created it, saying of the first humans, "their happiness was in the presence of God, the knowledge of God, the love of God: the presence of God in memory, knowledge in reason, love in will. Memory was like a certain embrace of the soul by which it kept God without forgetfulness; reason was like a certain eye by which it knew God without error; love was like the palate of the heart by which it tasted God without selfish desire for anything else."[21] In Sermon 9 on the annunciation, he approaches the topic by noting the ways in which humans have fallen away from the knowledge of God given in creation while

[19] Aelred, Anima 2.12 (CCCM 1:710; CF 22:77).

[20] Aelred, Anima 2.3 (CCCM 1:708; CF 22:72).

[21] Aelred, S 49.5 (CCCM 2B:23; CF 80:29–30).

also emphasizing the compensating power of memory restored by Christ:

> While receding from us physically, our Lord and Savior Jesus promised us the presence of his divinity, the presence of his grace and loving-kindness, saying, "Behold, I am with you always until the end of the world" [Matt 28:20]. But because it was expedient for the memory of his benefits to be always present to us—those he had showed us through his physical presence—and because he knew that our memory is corrupted by forgetfulness, our intellect by error, and our attentiveness by selfish desire, he lovingly provided for us that his benefits would be not only recounted to us by the Scriptures but also re-presented to us by certain spiritual actions. Thus when he gave his disciples the sacrament of his body and blood he said to them, "This do in my memory."[22]

Aelred frequently explains this doctrine in sermons showing the Virgin Mary as the embodiment of human nature, particularly because of her faculty of memory, recalling Luke's words at Christ's birth: "Mary kept these words and pondered them in her heart" (Luke 2:19). In a sermon on the annunciation he writes, "Truly she is full of grace . . . whose memory considered nothing except God, whose reason looked on nothing else, whose love tasted nothing other than him."[23] A sermon on the assumption portrays Mary as the Bride recalling having looked upon the Bridegroom in her memory: "that vision had impressed on her soul the image of his sweetest face, whose memory aroused her soul with spiritual arrows for seeking him whom she loved."[24]

[22] Aelred, S 9.1–2 (CCCM 2A:70; CF 58:155–56).

[23] Aelred, S 57.5 (CCCM 2B:99; CF 80:128).

[24] Aelred, S 73.9 (CCCM 2B:243; CF 80:305). Bell also calls attention to Aelred's explanation in S 75 of "how the rational soul in general, and the rational soul of Mary in particular, experiences God," noting Aelred's summary in this sermon of Augustine's explanation of the trinitarian soul (David N. Bell, *Handmaid of the Lord: Mary, the Cistercians, and Armand-Jean de Rancé*, CS 293 [Collegeville, MN: Cistercian Publications, 2021], 161–62).

In *Homilies on the Prophetic Burdens of Isaiah*, concerning Isaiah's prophecies against the foreign nations (Isa 13–16), Aelred identifies the faculties of the soul in a darker way, explaining that having fallen, those faculties tend to lead away from God: "all of Philistia is brought low when reason falls into error, memory falls into forgetfulness of God, and the will falls into wantonness."[25] Later he makes the same point: "the tripartite power of the soul through which all sin comes [is] memory, will, and reason . . . . Those who yield to threefold concupiscence, who transgress in thought, word, and deed, [are those] in whom thought corrupts memory, delight soils will, and agreement in sin weakens reason."[26]

Oddly, the importance of the Augustinian depiction of the soul in Aelred's works has largely escaped attention over the years, with readers focusing on the defined subjects of the individual works while overlooking Aelred's consistent concern with the way the memory allows one to know God. Many have been so attracted to Aelred's writing about the love and friendship manifested in humans' affection for one another that they have allowed that theme to dominate their evaluation of all his spiritual writing. Distinguished Cistercian scholars C. H. Talbot and Aelred Squire, for example, seem unaware of the centrality of memory in Aelred's works. Talbot concludes in his introduction to his translation of *On the Soul* that Aelred "made no claim to originality and contented himself with providing a synthesis of the ideas culled from" Augustine's works, though he also refers to the work's "clarity and searching analysis."[27] Of Aelred's anthropology in *Mirror* Squire states, "Substantially it is common Augustinian doctrine. Thus, it is fitting that man who is made to the image of God should cleave

[25] Aelred, *Homiliae de oneribus propheticis Isaiae*, H 22.10 (CCCM 2D:200; CF 83:215).

[26] Aelred, *Homiliae de oneribus propheticis Isaiae*, H 24.27 (CCCM 2D:222–23; CF 83:242).

[27] Talbot, Introduction, 23.

to his creator."[28] Ignoring the role of memory in such cleaving, he goes on to declare that "the crucial conversion is that of the will," suggesting that it is "the affection of the soul" and "the delights of loving and being loved" that dominate Aelred's understanding of Augustine's teaching. Devoting just over three pages to *On the Soul*, Squire dismisses it as a failure: "The *Dialogue on the Soul* must be regarded as no more than a brave attempt at a task which might well have proved beyond Aelred's powers even had they not been failing as he wrote."[29]

Both Talbot and Squire dismissed Aelred's treatment of the soul partly because of their judgment that Cistercians, and specifically Aelred, were less interested in theology than in spiritual direction. Talbot wrote, "it is doubtful whether the Cistercians were concerned with the purely theoretical aspects of the question . . . . It seems more likely that these treatises were intended to promote an interest in spiritual and mystical matters."[30] And Squire wrote of Aelred, "His gifts lay in another direction, not in the world of speculations and abstractions, but in the world where men move and act, led on perhaps by an ultimate vision, but passing through conflicts and obscurities and alternations of darkness and light."[31] Neither apparently noticed Aelred's concern throughout his works to integrate theological clarity and understanding into all of his teaching.

More recent scholars, however, have corrected such earlier neglect of Aelred's effort to recall his readers to the presence of God, sometimes connecting that effort to his concern with memory. Historian Elizabeth Freeman notes the importance

[28] Aelred Squire, *Aelred of Rievaulx: A Study*, CS 50 (1950; Kalamazoo, MI: Cistercian Publications, 2020), 44.

[29] Squire, *Aelred of Rievaulx*, 134–35. Of Augustine's *Confessions*, however, Squire notes that "The large perspectives of its closing books are indeed . . . vital for the theoretical groundwork Aelred has to lay in the first part of his *Mirror of Charity*" (138).

[30] Talbot, Introduction, 8.

[31] Squire, *Aelred of Rievaulx*, 134–35.

Cistercians placed on the patristic doctrine of the soul, and especially on memory, noting its particular significance to Aelred:

> references to memory carried particular significance in the Cistercian theological context. . . . more so than other orders, Cistercians were committed to writing about the soul; indeed, almost every Cistercian of note wrote a treatise on this topic. In these texts Cistercians frequently stressed the three vestiges of God that could be found in the soul: *memoria, intelligentia,* and *voluntas*. Along with the will and knowledge, memory had a locus in the soul and thus by definition of relation with the divine. Although damaged by the fall, it had the potential to lead one to God. This is standard in Cistercian theology overall and, especially, in Aelred's personal theology.[32]

Philosopher Janet Coleman is similarly clear about Aelred's use of the Augustinian trinitarian model of the soul, though crediting Aelred's concern with memory most directly with the Rule of Benedict rather than with the Augustinian doctrine: "For Aelred, such perfection consists in remembering without forgetfulness (inspired by the *semper memor* of the Rule), knowing without error, and loving without satiety."[33] She notes Aelred's explanation of the memory's capacity to receive God and then to find him there,[34] and she is particularly insightful concerning Aelred's authorship of historical treatises and his role in "the historical revival in twelfth-century monasteries." She is thus more explicit than Freeman in linking his historical treatises to his concern with memory:

[32] Elizabeth Freeman, *Narratives of a New Order: Cistercian Historical Writing in England, 1150–1220*, Medieval Church Studies 2 (Turnholt: Brepols, 2002), 36–37. In a footnote Freeman calls attention to Aelred's explanation of the patristic doctrine of the soul in *Mirror* (36 n. 14).

[33] Janet Coleman, *Ancient and Medieval Memories: Studies in the Reconstruction of the Past* (Cambridge, UK: Cambridge University Press, 1992), 208–15, here 209.

[34] Coleman, *Ancient and Medieval Memories*, 212.

> His understanding of the memory as a faculty that recalls sequences of events and with the help of reason links these together truly or falsely, tells us what he self-consciously took his own historical enterprise to be as it depended on the operations of higher mind. . . . The primary function of memory was to recall rational souls to a divine similitude through contemplation of scriptural reminiscences or historical events endowed with higher universal meaning.[35]

Other scholars have written of Aelred's emphasis on re-presentation (*re-presentatio*) of Christ in Scripture and liturgy, especially in *Formation of Recluses*. Charles Dumont succinctly noted that "the *memoria-praesentia* theme occurs frequently in Aelred's writings, especially when he speaks of the mystery of the liturgy,"[36] and Nouzille expands this idea by comparing Aelred's treatment of the liturgical re-presentation of Christ in his eleventh sermon as paralleled in *Formation*:

> Scripture addresses itself to the memory and to a vision that cannot be other than interior. Liturgy equally places the mystery celebrated under our corporal eyes, as does the crucifix of the recluse elsewhere, and when it is a question of the Eucharist, it places it also on the tongue. . . . It is necessary finally to note that the *re-presentatio* not only bears on the past but also allows sight of the present and the future.[37]

[35] Coleman, *Ancient and Medieval Memories*, 214. M.-D. Chenu wrote, "it was not the least splendid achievement of Latin Christendom in the twelfth century to awaken in men's minds an active awareness of human history," identifying sequences of events shaped by the realities of human experience, and past events leading to events in the present and future as essential characteristics of that awareness (M.-D. Chenu, "Theology and the New Awareness of History," in *Nature, Man, and Society in the Twelfth Century*, trans. Jerome Taylor and Lester K. Little [Chicago: University of Chicago Press, 1968], 162).

[36] Charles Dumont, "Aelred of Rievaulx: His Life and Works," in Aelred of Rievaulx, *Mirror of Charity*, trans. Elizabeth Connor, CF 17 (Kalamazoo, MI: Cistercian Publications, 1990), 43.

[37] Philippe Nouzille, *Expérience de Dieu et Théologie Monastique au XII^e^ Siècle* (Paris: Cerf, 1999), 148.

Elsewhere Nouzille again points out that for Aelred *re-presentatio* also appears outside the liturgy: "he employs the term and especially illustrates what he understands by it even more in the treatises than the liturgical sermons."[38]

Pierre-André Burton also notes the presence of liturgical re-presentation in both *Formation* and Aelred's ninth sermon:

> The role of these [liturgical] celebrations . . . is to "re-present now" (*re-praesentatio*) the mysteries of [Christ's] birth, passion, resurrection, and ascension. One anthropological result of this re-presentation is that "that wondrous loving-kindness, that wondrous gentleness, that wondrous charity that he showed for us in all these, will always be fresh in our memory." On a theological level, the result of this re-presentation is that, as in the threefold meditation of *Formation*, our faith might be fortified "whenever we hear with our ears and almost see beneath our eyes what Christ suffered for us [memory of the past], and what he gives us in this life [memory of the present], and what he promises us after this life [memory of the future]."[39]

Like Squire, however, several of these scholars minimize Aelred's concern with memory in their focus on what they find more compelling: *affectus*—"attachment, affection." While acknowledging the Augustinian inspiration of Aelred's anthropology as seen in books 1 and 3 of *Mirror*, Burton emphasizes not Aelred's attention to the memory, which allows one to cling to God, but to affectivity: "To these three faculties [of the soul] Aelred added another, insisting more than any of his contemporaries on the primordial importance of humans' affective dimension—in other words, the natural dynamism of desire

[38] Nouzille, "Temps et liturgie," 177.

[39] Pierre-André Burton, *Aelred of Rievaulx (1110–1167): An Existential and Spiritual Biography*, trans. Christopher Coski, CS 276 (Collegeville, MN: Cistercian Publications, 2021), 223–24 (bracketed notes in the first sentence are mine; those in the last sentence are Burton's), quoting Aelred, S 9.2 (CCCM 2A:70–71; CF 58:155–56). The same passage from S 9 appears nearly identically in Aelred's S 26.3 (CCCM 2A:210; CF 58:354–55).

that runs through their being. . . . Such dynamism presides over all the inner forces that drive men and women to act, even before the discernment of reason and the consent of the will come into play."[40]

Damien Boquet also calls attention to the way in *Formation* Aelred prompts his reader to remember God: "Notably in the *Formation of Anchoresses*, Aelred leads the contemplative in an affective meditation that rests on a *recordatio* of the Gospels, a memorial voyage whose fruit is an affective participation in the life of Christ." Boquet goes further than Burton, however, in eliding the role of memory in Aelred's teaching by explicitly suggesting that Aelred allows *affectus* to subsume memory: "Without ignoring [the Augustinian] schema, Aelred slides incidentally toward a new proposition, full of consequences, imposing a new three-way division into affect, will, and reason." Qualifying this statement, however, Boquet is careful not to eliminate memory: "That division does not however mean diminution of the role of memory. More than ever the religious function of memory, linked to *recordatio Dei*, is shaped by affect."[41]

## Memory in the Spiritual Treatises

Aelred seems early on to have seen the value of the Augustinian doctrine of the soul for teaching, especially in the memory's ability to know and remember God. So beginning with *Mirror* while still a novice director, he shaped his spiritual treatises to guide readers to cling to God without forgetfulness, using Augustine's explanation of the power of memory as the theological core of his pedagogical praxis.

Although frequently explaining the doctrine of the soul's three faculties in his sermons, Aelred includes it explicitly only

[40] Burton, *Aelred of Rievaulx*, 184.

[41] Damien Boquet, "Affectivity in the Spiritual Writings of Aelred of Rievaulx," in *A Companion to Aelred of Rievaulx (1110–1167)*, ed. Marsha L. Dutton, Brill's Companions to the Christian Tradition 76 (Leiden: Brill Academic, 2017), 173.

twice in the treatises, in *Mirror of Charity* and *On the Soul*. But in those and three others, he relies on the concept to help readers find God in their memory. He usually refers to Jesus in his humanity but regularly reminds his readers that Jesus is God indeed. So in *Formation* he writes of Jesus as "the lord who fills heaven and earth," and he notes that on the cross "the mediator of God and humankind, hanging in the middle between heaven and earth, unites the heights with the depths and joins earthly things to heavenly."[42] In *Friendship*, promising the beatitude to come, he segues from Christ to God: "So from that holy love by which one embraces a friend we ascend to that by which one embraces Christ, we will take the fruit of spiritual friendship joyfully and fully into the mouth while awaiting the fullness of all things in the future, when that friendship to which we here admit but few will be poured out into all and from all will be poured again into God, when *God* will be *all in all*."[43]

The ease with which humans forget is not a theme on which Aelred dwells, but it is always implicit in these works, underlying his audience's need for assistance in remembering what has slipped their mind.[44] Regularly for example he recounts experiences of his own and of his readers to help them remember God as they already know him. The works are rich in such reminders, grounded in four aspects of memory through which God may be found and brought back to mind. Two of these aspects concern past and present experience: (1) the memory

[42] Aelred, Inst incl 29, 31 (CCCM 1:663, 670; CF 2:80, 89).

[43] 1 Cor 15:28; Aelred, Spir am 3.134 (CCCM 1:349–50; CF 5:126).

[44] Geary calls the tenth and eleventh centuries "an age of forgetting," noting that the period has been neglected by historians of memory, who "have tended to dichotomize memory and written record, as though the two were mutually exclusive . . . . historians are normally interested primarily in what is remembered, while this period was more concerned with the other vital component of memory—the ability to forget" (Geary, *Phantoms*, 28). Although Aelred is writing in the better-studied twelfth century, his consciousness of the ease of forgetting underlies his efforts to remind his readers, with particular emphasis in *On Jesus*, as is reflected in the cover image of this book.

has the capacity to receive God, and (2) one can reliably find God whenever one brings him to mind.[45] The other two move from present experience of God into the future: (3) memory allows one to cling to God without forgetfulness and so to share God's eternity,[46] and (4) memory connects past to present to future: "by it what follows is remembered and connected to things before, and future things to those past."[47] This emphasis on the linked memory of the past, present, and future is essentially eucharistic, familiar from Jesus' words: "this do in memory of me."

Mary Carruthers explains the concept of "remembering the future" as central to the lives of medieval monks, grounded in their profound familiarity with the Psalms, "the one book that every monk in the Middle Ages learned by heart."[48] As the Psalmist's longing for Jerusalem became allegorically associated with Christian anticipation for the New Jerusalem, she says, it became "a fundamental model of the monk's life. . . . 'Remember Jerusalem,' . . . is a call not to preserve but to act—in the present, for the future. The matters memory presents are used to persuade and motivate, to create emotion and stir the will. Though it is certainly a form of knowing, recollecting is also a matter of will, of being *moved*."[49] She quotes the explanation of the thirteenth-century Italian rhetorician Boncompagno da Signa: "*memoria*, the means by which humans comprehend time, enables us to recall past things,

[45] Aelred, Anima 2.12 (CCCM 1:710; CF 22:77); Augustine, Conf 10.24.35 (*St Augustine's Confessions*, trans. Watts, 140–43).

[46] Aelred, Spec car 1.3.9 (CCCM 1:16; CF 17:91–92).

[47] Aelred, Anima 2.15 (CCCM 1:711; CF 22:78).

[48] On memory of the future, see Mary Carruthers, *The Craft of Thought: Meditation, Rhetoric, and the Making of Images, 400–1200*, Cambridge Studies in Medieval Literature 34 (Cambridge: Cambridge University Press, 2000), 66–69, here 67. On historical considerations of memory and specifically its significance in medieval society, see Mary Carruthers, *The Book of Memory: A Study of Memory in Medieval Culture*, 2nd ed., Cambridge Studies in Medieval Literature 10 (Cambridge, UK: Cambridge University Press, 2008).

[49] Carruthers, *Craft of Thought*, 67.

embrace present things, and contemplate future things *through their likeness to past things*."[50] So Aelred writes his spiritual treatises to recall God to his readers in their remembered knowledge of him.

### *Mirror of Charity*

In *Mirror of Charity* Aelred writes for monks about the way Cistercian discipline strengthens charity. Early in the first book he explains the Augustinian description of the soul, which allows one to cling to God. He then appears personally within the work in three first-person passages whose common thread is the memory of God's bringing someone to monastic life, passages presented as Aelred's reminiscences. In the first case, Aelred recalls his own conversion, when God rescued him from his unhappy approximation of well-being, held in "the chain of my worst habits, the love of my kin, the bonds of gracious society." It was God, he says, who led him to accept Christ's easy yoke at Rievaulx: "You who *hear the groans of prisoners and loose the children of the slain* shattered my bonds . . . . I breathe again under your yoke, and I rest again under your burden, because *your yoke is pleasant and your burden light*."[51]

In the second such passage, at the end of book one, Aelred remembers the life of his friend Simon. His lament begins with his own grief at Simon's death but quickly moves to awareness that Simon now dwells in the bliss of heaven, the first of the visions of beatitude in the spiritual treatises: "introduced *into the joy of your Lord*, at the table of that great father of our family you delightedly feast, and with *that new fruit of the wine* in the

[50] Carruthers, *Craft of Memory*, 69; citing Boncompagno da Signa, *Rhetorica novissima*, 8, ed. A. Guadenzi, in *Scripta anecdota glossatorum*, Bibliotheca Iuridica Medii Aevi (Bologna, 1892), 2:275. Emphasis hers.

[51] Ps 102:20; Matt 11:30; Aelred, Spec car 1.28.79–82, here 79, 82 (CCCM 1:46–58, here 47, 48; CF 17:133–36, here 134, 136).

kingdom of the father with your Jesus you become happily inebriated."[52] Having linked his consuming grief directly to Simon's consummate joy, Aelred proceeds by remembering Simon's life—his following Jesus into the monastery, devotedly serving Jesus there, and then, in dying, following the scent of Jesus' ointments into heaven: "All things are yours, Lord, who dedicated the beginning of his conversion by these marvels, who later received the welcome sacrifice of his loving life, who have now mercifully translated that most acceptable offering into your temple on high."[53] So, implicitly contrasting his own recently recalled hard conversion with Simon's easy one, Aelred integrates past, present, and future not only through the events of those times but through the syntactic complexity with which he interweaves them.

Finally, midway through the second book, Aelred shows himself as a novice master to whom a young monk comes full of anxiety, recalling his repeated tears for the love of God before entering the monastery but complaining that now, living under monastic discipline, he rarely tastes that sweetness. His current failure to feel moved as he formerly did causes him to fear that he no longer loves God as much as before. In this first of Aelred's three dialogues, Aelred leads the novice through recollection of his experiences before and since his monastic conversion to an understanding that God had led him with the gift of tears to his current life of discipline and charity. So for the

[52] Spec car 1.34.99 (CCCM 1:57; CF 17:148).

[53] Spec car 1.34.103 (CCCM 1:59; CF 17:150–51). Aelred may have included the death of Simon, and of Ivo in *Friendship*, in allusion to the recollected deaths of the authors' friends in Cicero's *De amicitia* and Augustine's *Confessions*, illustrating his emphasis on friendship as lasting even after death (e.g., Spir am 1.24 [CCCM 1:293; CF 5:59]). James McEvoy also notes Aelred's use in *Friendship* of the "literary device of separating the first book from the second and third by a period of many years" (James McEvoy, "Notes on the Prologue of St Aelred of Rievaulx's 'De Spirituali Amicitia,' with a Translation," *Traditio* 37 [1981]: 402). See Marsha L. Dutton, "Friendship and the Love of God: Augustine's Teaching in the *Confessions* and Aelred of Rievaulx's Response in *Spiritual Friendship*," chap. 3 below, 113–14.

second time in *Mirror* Aelred defines conversion as the acceptance of Christ's easy yoke: "the clemency of our most loving savior by a taste of a certain inner sweetness draws toward salvation those who are immersed in the enticements of the flesh. . . . He places on them the yoke of his service."[54]

With these three instances drawn from among his own memories of knowing, loving, and embracing God in monastic life, Aelred reminds his audience of God's loving care. He does not articulate the link among the passages or between them and his earlier Augustinian explanation of the soul, but he instructs his readers by drawing on his own memory of God's leading men and women to monastic life and then into beatitude. It is no wonder that these three episodes recalling God's love and deeds are among the best-known passages from *Mirror*, as Aelred has incorporated them precisely to show his readers the ease of finding God in the memory, and to tell them of God's quick response to such recollection.

### *On Jesus as a Boy of Twelve* and *The Formation of Recluses*

Throughout *On Jesus as a Boy of Twelve* and *The Formation of Recluses*, Aelred insistently reminds his readers of God, recalling God as they already know him through Scripture and through their own experience. Aelred also again incorporates some of his own memories of God. Finally both works invite the questioner to stand contemplatively before God, looking into the loving face of Jesus in beatitude, remembering the

[54] Aelred, Spec car 2.19.57 (CCCM 1:93; CF 17:203). Gabriel Ghislain rejects the view that Aelred prioritizes *affectus*, arguing that he shows *affectus* as assisting conversion rather than being its goal, that the sweet yoke that one takes on in conversion is charity, which "joins labor (*jugum*) and sweetness (*suave*); the labor is not thus done away with, but it has paradoxically become easy to bear: . . . what is more important than all is obedience to the commandments, even without tears, rather than tears or even miracles, but without the commandments" ("À la recherche de la réponse juste: un novice interroge son père maître," *Intentio cordis*, Coll 73, no. 1 [2011]: 103–4).

future, when they will cling to him forever without forgetting. Nouzille has emphasized Aelred's use of *re-presentatio* in these two works: "Aelred proposes the meditations from Scripture on the life of Christ, which render us contemporaneous with him, because the one praying is invited to participate fully in the scene meditated upon . . . . Aelred's aim is not to call from that meditation some moral or doctrinal teaching, but simply to engage the one praying in abandoning oneself to that closeness and that intimacy with Christ that is before us."[55]

*On Jesus* follows the Lukan pericope of Jesus' remaining behind in Jerusalem as his parents travel homeward (Luke 2:41-52).[56] Aelred begins with the request he has received from the monk Ivo for an explanation of the story: "you ask me, my dearest son Ivo, to draw from the gospel reading . . . seeds of loving meditation and holy love. Entrusting them to little baskets of letters, I am sending what I have collected to you."[57] After replying with his own long-ago memories of the story, Aelred then focuses on Mary and Joseph's loss of Jesus and search for him. So the work begins not with Luke's explanation of the family's annual Passover visit to Jerusalem, but with their discovery of Jesus' absence, their search for Jesus, and finally their finding him and taking them home with him.

Aelred is explicit in this work about the role of memory, his and Ivo's, noting that after both have for a while forgotten the story and its meaning, they are now recovering it. His response resonates with the words of memory: *remember, recall, come to*

[55] Nouzille, "Temps et Liturgie," 177.

[56] Someone has referred to Homer's *Odyssey* as beginning with a man-sized hole as Telemachus searches to find his long-absent father; Aelred's *On Jesus as a Boy of Twelve* has a similar structure, beginning not with the presence of Jesus but with his loss.

[57] Aelred, Iesu 1.1 (CCCM 1:249; CF 2:3). Aelred returns to this image in his final words to Ivo at the end of the work: "And you should know that we have taken care not so much to expound the Gospel reading as to draw from it some seeds for meditation for you, as you asked" (Iesu 3.32 [CCCM 1:278; CF 139]).

*mind*, and *looking back* (*uenit in mentem, respexi, recordatus sum*).[58] He writes not an exegesis but a personal narrative, intertwining his and Ivo's forgetfulness of Jesus with Mary's loss of her son.

Recounting his receipt of Ivo's request, Aelred recalls his own long-ago familiarity with the story and his subsequent loss of the devotion that it then inspired in him: "suddenly there came into my mind where I was once, what I felt, what effect these same words of the Gospel brought out in me sometimes when they were read or sung. I looked back, I looked back—a wretch, I looked back—and I saw how far behind me I had left those sweet and pleasant things, how far from those delights the bonds of occupation and obligation had removed me."[59] Then he demonstrates God's readiness to respond, again recalling from his own experience that remembering God results not in nostalgia, but in God's presence, past and present: "I remembered these things, and I was pouring out my soul within myself when the hand of the Lord, stretched out to me, touched my heart and anointed it with the unction of his mercy."[60]

At once, though, Aelred turns from his experience of God to Ivo's, emphasizing Ivo's tears of regret and prayers, linking them also to Mary's search for Jesus: "You demanded that I tell you where the boy Jesus was during that three-day period when his mother was looking for him: how he found lodging, by what food he was fed, in what company he was made happy, with what business he was occupied."[61] Soon, though, he asks Jesus the reason for his lack of compassion on his mother during that time of loss, then reminds Mary of her apparently having forgotten just who her son was: "My sweetest Lady, why were you looking for the boy who—as you well knew—was God? . . . Is it not he who feeds all, who nourishes

[58] Aelred, Iesu 1.1 (CCCM 1:249; CF 2:3).
[59] Aelred, Iesu 1.1 (CCCM 1:249; CF 2:3).
[60] Aelred, Iesu 1.1 (CCCM 1:249; CF 2:4).
[61] Aelred, Iesu 1.1 (CCCM 1:249–50; CF 2:5).

all?" And finally these gentle reminders turn to chastisement, of Mary and implicitly of himself, Ivo, and his larger audience, for the lack of attention that caused them all to forget her son: "If I may say, my Lady, respectfully—why did you so easily lose your most dear Son, why did you watch him so carelessly, why did you notice so late that he was gone?"[62] The work has thus begun with three absences, as three people—Aelred, Ivo, and Mary—remember the one they have lost. In this way Aelred writes to assist all who need guidance in recovering lost understanding and lost devotion, to arouse in them a renewed love for Jesus.

After having chastised Mary for having forgotten Jesus, Aelred continues by commending her subsequent care to keep Jesus in mind. As is common in Cistercian writing, Mary appears here as a representative of and model for all humans, and specifically for all Christians, but in this case she so serves not through humility and obedience but by remembering Jesus' explanation to her when she found him in the temple: "But with others not understanding what Jesus had said, Mary, as knowing and understanding, 'preserved all these words, comparing them in her heart.' She preserved in memory, she pondered in meditation, and she compared them with other things that she had seen and heard about him."[63]

With this echo of Luke's words from Jesus' nativity, Aelred identifies Mary with the power of memory, despite her temporary forgetfulness.[64] He portrays Mary as doing what he wants his readers to do, pointing out the long-term value of her exercise of memory for those who will follow her through the centuries ahead:

[62] Aelred, Iesu 1.2 (CCCM 1:250; CF 2:5).

[63] Aelred, Iesu 1.9 (CCCM 1:257; CF 2:5).

[64] Domenico Pezzini says that Mary "is also the one who becomes the living memory of the story of Jesus, charged as such with transmitting it to the apostles so that they in turn preach it" (Aelredo di Rievaulx, *Gesù Dodicenne[;] Preghiera Pastorale*, trans. and intro. by Domenico Pezzini, Letture Cristiane del Secondo Millennio 29 [Milan: Paoline Editoriale Libri, 2001], 47).

> So the most blessed Virgin even then was mercifully providing for us, lest things so sweet, so healthful, so necessary, slip away through neglect and therefore not be written down or preached, with followers cheated of the delights of this spiritual manna. All these things therefore this most prudent virgin faithfully preserved, modestly kept in silence, opportunely provided, and committed to the holy apostles and disciples to be preached.[65]

By focusing on Mary's having for a while overlooked her son's absence, he expands the meaning of the episode for his larger audience, extending the reach of Luke's familiar words by explaining that Mary ultimately served not only herself but also the others who would recall and pass on the story.

This first book of *On Jesus* thus begins and ends with a demonstration of memory's ability to receive God, to find God when bringing him to mind, even after long forgetfulness, and to be assured of his presence. Mary, Aelred, and Ivo have in different ways all known Jesus but lost him, moving onward in the business of their lives while failing to keep him in mind. Now, however, all have recovered him, Mary by returning to the place where she last saw him, and Aelred and Ivo by looking into their memory and finding him there. Mary's loss, search, and recovery take place in her present but the readers' past; having found him, she clings to him with her memory for the benefit of those in her future. Aelred and Ivo imitate her in their present, bringing Jesus to mind and so knowing him not only now but in time to come.[66]

[65] Aelred, Iesu 1.9 (CCCM 1:257; CF 2:12). After *through neglect*, Theodore Berkeley's CF 2 English translation here appropriately adds *lost to memory*, despite the absence of the phrase from the Latin.

[66] Pezzini's introduction to his Italian translation of *On Jesus* concludes with the insight that Mary's question to Jesus—"Son, why have you done this to us?"—is that of all readers of the treatise, her question recognizable as "that of someone who questions herself and continues to question herself about Jesus, . . . like all those who for centuries have not stopped losing, seeking, and finding Jesus" (Aelredo di Rievaulx, *Gesù Dodicenne*, 64–65).

The second book of *On Jesus* moves to the third and fourth aspects of the soul's knowledge of God: its ability to share God's eternity and the way it links past to present to future. While still addressing Ivo, Aelred moves from a literal reading of the Gospel pericope to a moral one, repeatedly asking his audience to combine scriptural understanding with personal experience: "my dearest son, whose desire [*animus*] is to be conformed to Christ and to cleave closely to Jesus' footsteps, perhaps I will be able to explain to you your progress in the Gospel passage, so that you may read on these pages [*schedulis*] what you experience in yourself with interior sweetness."[67] In books two and three Aelred guides his hearers to follow Jesus along his life's journey to Jerusalem, "so that you will be able to read hidden things [*mystica*] not so much in books as in your own experience [*moribus*]."[68]

Whereas in the first book Aelred focuses on Jesus as a vulnerable human boy and explores what it means to have loved and then forgotten him, in the second book he is clear that that boy known and lost in his humanity is in fact the Lord God: "this our eternal, non-temporal, unchangeable God was in our nature made changeable and temporal, so that he might make our changeableness and temporality—which he took on for us—the way to his eternity and stability, so that in our one single savior should be the way through which we might ascend, and the life to which we might come, and the truth that we might enjoy."[69] He then explains that following in Jesus' footsteps will allow one not only to participate in Jesus' life but also to share in his eternity: "So his bodily progress is our spiritual progress, and those acts described to us as done by him in all the ages of his life are felt to be done in us through each step of our spiritual progress."[70]

[67] Aelred, Iesu 3.19 (CCCM 1:265–66; CF 2:25).
[68] Aelred, Iesu 3.19 (CCCM 1:266; CF 2:25).
[69] Aelred, Iesu 2.11 (CCCM 1:258; CF 2:15).
[70] Aelred, Iesu 2.11 (CCCM 1:258; CF 2:15).

Having followed Jesus to "the contemplation of celestial secrets,"[71] Aelred's readers are now led to beatitude (imaged as another monastery) to join Jesus where he waits to welcome them: "the light of contemplation . . . raises the fervent soul to the celestial Jerusalem, unlocks heaven, opens the gates of paradise, and exhibits to the eyes of the pure mind the Bridegroom himself—the most beautiful of the sons of the men—as if *looking out through the enclosure*."[72] Later, Aelred returns to the original story, now leading his audience to join Mary and Joseph in finding Jesus in the temple and so to gaze upon God: "The person who can see eternal things in those of time, celestial in earthly, divine in human—that is, the Creator in created things—may exult as if admitted into the forecourts of Jerusalem. . . . One who with veil removed can contemplate God's glory with face revealed in Sacred Scripture may glory at having entered the portals of Jerusalem."[73]

The work does not end with that vision of beatitude, though, but with the audience's continuing participation in Jesus' life, as both he and they must return to minister in obedience to Joseph and Mary, identified here as the Holy Spirit and Charity, to fulfill the never-ending demands of human life. Just as Jesus was able to spend only three days in Jerusalem about his Father's business before returning to Nazareth and his human obligations, so Aelred, Ivo, and Aelred's readers must put aside the joys of anticipated beatitude to care for those who depend on them.[74]

Scholars have dated *On Jesus* and *Formation* only speculatively, usually to the early 1160s, but it is appealing to suggest

[71] Aelred, Iesu 2.19 (CCCM 1:266; CF 2:25).

[72] Aelred, Iesu 2.20 (CCCM 1:267; CF 2:27); Song 2:9. The Latin word I have translated as *enclosure* is *cancellos*, often translated as *lattice*, as in Song 2:9: "My beloved . . . . Look! There he stands behind our wall, . . . peering through the lattice." I am grateful to Kitty Turley for reminding me of this passage.

[73] Aelred, Iesu 3.29 (CCCM 1:275–76; CF 2:36).

[74] Aelred, Iesu 3.30–31 (CCCM 1:276–78; CF 2:37–39).

that after having focused in that first work on a single biblical pericope, Aelred decided to expand the approach in *Formation*, now inviting his audience to engage imaginatively in Jesus' whole human life from conception through resurrection. Whereas in *On Jesus* Aelred shows himself and Ivo as sharing in Mary's loss of and search for Jesus, in *Formation* he assigns that role to the anchoress who he says asked him to write, encouraging her to join with those who knew and loved Jesus in his manhood. Thus this first of what was to become the popular medieval genre of Lives of Christ uses fundamentally the same pedagogical method as *On Jesus*,[75] and scholars such as Burton and Nouzille are quite right in recognizing the work's echoes of the liturgical *re-presentatio* of the passion in the Eucharist.

After beginning *Formation* with a practical guide for anchoritic life,[76] Aelred turns to the anchoress's spiritual development, guiding her to grow in love for Jesus. He offers her a constant visual reminder of Jesus through the crucifix on her altar, showing him to her as her lord, bridegroom, and mother and emphasizing the role of her memory in loving him: "On your altar let an image of the Savior hanging on the cross suffice you; it may represent to you his passion, which you may imitate; with outstretched arms he invites you to his embraces, in which you may delight; from his naked breasts will flow to you the milk of sweetness, by which you may be consoled."[77]

[75] Popular examples of the genre include *Meditations on the Life of Christ* by the Pseudo-Bonaventure, *Life of Jesus Christ* by Ludolph of Saxony, Bonaventure's *Tree of Life*, and Ignatius of Loyola's *Spiritual Exercises*. See Marsha L. Dutton, "The Cistercian Source: Aelred, Bonaventure, and Ignatius," chap. 7 below, 237–67.

[76] Jean Leclercq has suggested that Aelred, like other Cistercians of his time, "was a reformer," but that others had already taken on "every state of life in the church" except reclusion, and so Aelred took that task upon himself (Jean Leclercq, "Solitude and Solidarity: Medieval Women Recluses," in *Peace Weavers*, ed. John A. Nichols and Lillian Thomas Shank, Medieval Religious Women, vol. 2, CS 72 [Kalamazoo, MI: Cistercian Publications, 1987], 70).

[77] Aelred, Inst incl 26 (CCCM 1:658; CF 2:73).

Having brought Jesus to her mind visually and imaginatively, Aelred guides the anchoress to understand her role as a follower of Mary of Bethany, sitting at Jesus' feet and learning from him by listening to his words, and then invites her to engage in the memory of Jesus' birth, life, passion, and resurrection, not following behind him, as in *On Jesus*, but imaginatively engaging actively and intimately with him as his contemporary, first in his human life and then in beatitude: "And so that that sweet love of Jesus may grow in your affection [*affectu*], you need a triple meditation, on things past, present, and future, that is, remembrance of things past, experience of things present, and contemplation of things future."[78]

The long meditation that follows begins with Jesus' conception, asking the contemplative to identify with the Virgin Mary while remembering God's action in her. Aelred points out what the contemplative is about to see as the first of the promised memories of the past, then explains what she is to do in that moment: "Turn your now purified eyes to the past; first enter the cell with Blessed Mary and read the books in which the Virgin's giving birth and the coming of Christ are foretold. . . . Contemplate and marvel at the Lord who fills earth and heaven being enclosed within the womb of one girl, whom the Father sanctified, the Son fecundated, the Holy Spirit overshadowed."[79]

After asking Mary to recall her experience, he directs the anchoress to understand its meaning for her: "O sweet Lady, how greatly you were inebriated with sweetness, by what a fire of love you were set on fire, when you felt in your mind and in your womb the presence of majesty. . . . All this was on account of you, O virgin, so that you might diligently attend to the Virgin whom you have proposed to imitate and to the Virgin's son, to whom you are married [*nupsisti*]."[80]

[78] Aelred, Inst incl 29 (CCCM 1:662; CF 2:79).

[79] Aelred, Inst incl 29 (CCCM 1:662; CF 2:80).

[80] Aelred, Inst incl 29 (CCCM 1:663; CF 2:80).

Aelred develops the long first part of this meditation around Jesus' life as recounted in Scripture, guiding the anchoress to join those who knew and loved Jesus. He urges her to go with the holy family to Egypt, to watch Jesus forgive the woman taken in adultery, to visit Mary and Martha with him, and to be present at the Last Supper, giving Jesus her feet to wash and joining John at Jesus' breast. She is to embrace Jesus' body on the cross, receive blood and water from the wound in his side, enter into the wound itself, and help to carry his body to the tomb. Finally she is to join Mary Magdalene at the resurrection, with her to clasp the feet of their resurrected Lord.

In the next portion of the meditation Aelred directs attention to the present, to his reader's current experience of Jesus. Echoing the personal reminiscences in *Mirror* and *On Jesus*, Aelred begins with his own memories of falling away from God but being rescued by God's mercy, recalling the language of God's effecting his conversion in *Mirror*: "he broke the unbreakable bonds of bad habits, and when I was removed from the world, he kindly received me."[81] He then asks the anchoress to recall her own experiences of Christ, no longer through events in the scriptural past but now through those of her own life, finding him in her memory of his repeated visits to her. Reminding her to see what is to come, he lifts her from daily devotion to future joy:

> Now see the gifts of divine goodness of which only you know. . . . How often he stood beside you . . . in loving consolation, how often when you were singing songs or reading he illuminated you with the light of spiritual understanding, how often when you were praying he seized you with a certain unspeakable longing for himself, how often he lifted your mind from earthly things and carried it into celestial delights and paradisal pleasures.[82]

[81] Aelred, Inst incl 32 (CCCM 1:675; CF 2:95).

[82] Aelred, Inst incl 32 (CCCM 1:676; CF 2:97).

So *Formation*, like *On Jesus*, begins with the first two aspects of memory—the certainty of God's continual presence in one's memory, and God's reliable response when called to mind. Guiding the anchoress to identify with the Virgin Mary, with Mary and Martha of Bethany, with Saint Peter and Saint John and Mary Magdalene, he gives his larger audience models and companions for their own remembering and loving God. Then calling upon the anchoress to remember her experience of God as including foretastes of heaven, Aelred pulls her forward to time to come, introducing the last two key aspects of memory: linking past and present to future, and clinging to God in eternity.

Such past and present experience culminates in the third section of the meditation as he guides the anchoress to anticipate standing before Christ the Judge, recognizing his face, "not terrible but lovable, not bitter but sweet, not frightening but comforting."[83] After anxiously awaiting Christ's judgment, fearing and expecting eternal punishment, she finds herself by Christ's mercy placed among the blessed: "Now stand as though in the middle, not knowing to which ones the judge's sentence will send you. Oh, how hard the wait! . . . Truly, Lord, life is in your will. You see then how your soul ought to be spent in the love of him who could have justly also given to you the sentence of the wicked, but he chose rather to put you among those who are to be saved."[84]

The meditation thus concludes with the promise of what awaits the anchoress and all who have joined her in loving Christ: "He will be seen in himself, he will be seen in all his creatures. . . . That lovable and desired face on which the angels desire to look will be seen. . . . The Father will be seen in the Son, the Son in the Father, the Holy Spirit in both. He

[83] Aelred, Inst incl 33 (CCCM 1:679; CF 2:99).

[84] Aelred, Inst incl 33 (CCCM 1:679; CF 2:99–100).

will be seen *not as a riddle in a mirror, but face to face*. For he will be seen as he is."[85]

### *Spiritual Friendship* and *On the Soul*

In these two works from the late 1160s Aelred guides his audience to find God in memory not through scriptural recollections but with the help of classical and patristic sources. These two also differ from the earlier treatises in the kinds of questions the interlocutors raise, and most noticeably by Aelred's expanding the discursive approach of the earlier works into full-length dialogues.

Three monks appear as questioners in *Friendship*: Ivo in book one, and Walter and Gratian in books two and three. Ivo is an anxious young man whose initial inquiry appears only peripherally related to his monastic life and his relationship with God. Approaching Aelred hesitantly, he raises some apparently long-considered questions about friendship: "Would you teach me something about spiritual friendship? What is it? What values does it offer? What is its beginning and its end? Can friendship exist among all persons? If not among all, then among whom? How can it remain unbroken and so without any troubling disagreement reach a blessed end?"[86] He has already made a start in thinking about the topic by reading Cicero, he explains, but he regrets the absence of Christ from that work and wants to hear Aelred's explanation of spiritual friendship, one that begins, continues, and ends in Christ, for Christ, he says, "is the beginning and end [of friendship]."[87]

In books two and three, Ivo having died some time before,[88] Walter and Gratian express their desire to hear further about

[85] Aelred, Inst incl 33 (CCCM 1:681; CF 2:101).

[86] Aelred, Spir am 1.5 (CCCM 1:290; CF 5:56).

[87] Aelred, Spir am 1.8 (CCCM 1:290; CF 5:57). In this speech Ivo echoes some of what Aelred writes in the Prologue to the work about his own experience.

[88] See n. 53 above.

the nature of friendship, similarly making clear their familiarity with Cicero and Augustine. Aelred also insists on the relevance of Cicero's thoughts about friendship with his reiterated dependence on Cicero's definition, which, with variations, appears four times in the dialogue: "Friendship is agreement in things human and divine, with good will and charity."[89]

The work begins, though, before Ivo speaks, as Aelred greets him by defining the friendly context of their encounter, with Christ at its center: "See, you and I, and I hope that between us Christ is third. Now there is no obstreperous person, no one disrupting friendly conversation [*amica colloquia*]. No voice or storm invades this our pleasant solitude. So now, beloved, open your heart and distill whatever you please into friendly ears [*amicis auribus*]."[90] A little later, Aelred identifies the relationship between himself and Ivo as the friendship defined by Saint Ambrose, shaped by mutual confidence and responsibility: "Speak therefore safely, and share with a friend [*amico*] all your cares and thoughts, so that you may either learn something or teach, may give and receive, pour out and drink in."[91]

Aelred then explains to Ivo that friendship originated in creation, as part of God's plan for his creatures and indeed as sharing in God's own nature: "So from him who is supremely and purely one, all should be given a certain vestige of his unity. . . . So nature impressed on human minds from the very beginning the attachment of friendship and charity."[92] In

[89] Aelred, Spir am 1.11, 29, 46; 3.8 (CCCM 1.291, 294, 297, 319; CF 5:57, 61, 64, 90). J. M. Ziolkowski notes the "interaction between an intense orality and an equally intense textuality" in this work ("Translation and Commentary on Aelred of Rievaulx: *De spiritali amicitia* 2.27–29," in *Corpus Christianorum 1953–2003: Xenium Natalicum: Fifty Years of Scholarly Editing*, ed. John Leemans [Turnhout: Brepols, 2003], 314–18).

[90] Aelred, Spir am 1.1 (CCCM 1:289; CF 5:55); see Ambrose, *De officiis* 3.132, 136, and 139.

[91] Aelred, Spir am 1.4 (CCCM 1:289–90; CF 5:56).

[92] Aelred, Spir am 1.53, 58 (CCCM 1:298; CF 5:65, 67). Here Aelred echoes the first chapters of *Mirror*, where he tells of God's creatures embodying God's characteristics (see pp. 5–6 above).

a few steps Aelred has thus fulfilled Ivo's desire to hear about spiritual friendship, introduced the idea of humankind's creation in God's image, and explained in what way that fact allows participation in God, insisting on God's eternal presence in human relationships. The dialogue as it develops does not provide new information but simply confirms what both men already know: that friendship is grounded in God's nature and imbued with God's love and purpose for his creatures, beginning with God's intention for humankind and continuing with Christ present within it. Toward the end of this book Aelred emphasizes to Ivo that "*the one who remains in* friendship *remains in God, and God in him*."[93] So Aelred reminds a larger audience, one that has perhaps assumed friendship to be purely secular and unrelated to God, that God created it and is present within it.

Book two begins as a new questioner, the monk Walter, reminds Aelred of his earlier conversation with Ivo. In seeking to resume that conversation, though, Walter, later joined by Gratian, asks questions different from Ivo's. He says nothing about spiritual friendship; he is concerned not with friendship's origins or continuation in Christ but with its present-day value and practicality, and he is hesitant to accept Aelred's praise of true friendship—*vera amicitia*—as being worth the trouble.[94] For the rest of the treatise, then, Aelred leads Walter and Gratian to see spiritual friendship as desirable not merely for lighthearted companionship, as Walter prefers, but as a

[93] Aelred, Spir am 1.70 (CCCM 1:301; CF 5:69). Aelred's words here respond to Ivo's question about whether perhaps one might say that God is friendship, gently rejecting the suggestion. This passage is regularly misrepresented by readers who fail to note Aelred's courteous but firm opposition to Ivo's error.

[94] J. Stephen Russell, considering the four speakers in *Friendship*, writes of Walter that "for him, *amicitia* is a logical problem, a concept that might or might not be made consonant with Scripture but whose rewards are beyond his understanding . . . . he has no patience for concepts and ideas, so he dryly presses for *certam metam*, something he can define or measure" ("The Dialogic of Aelred's *Spiritual Friendship*," CSQ 47, no. 1 [2012]: 61).

way to God: "Was that not like the portion of beatitude, so *to love and* so *to be loved*,[95] so to help and to be helped, and so from the sweetness of brotherly love to fly away toward that higher place in the splendor of divine love, and on the ladder of charity now to climb to the embrace of Christ himself, now to descend to the love of the neighbor, there sweetly to rest?"[96]

Throughout this dialogue Aelred calls his interlocutors to consider their own memories of friendship and the friendships of holy men and women, and he emphasizes Jesus' words identifying himself as a friend of God.[97] As in the other spiritual works, Aelred also contributes his own experiences, in this case, of friendship with individuals and with members of his community.[98] Through these models and the young monks' memories, he shows them how to find God, as friendship guides them to oneness with one another, with their fellow monks, and with God. That movement concludes the dialogue, with an anticipation of beatitude, now shown as eternal friendship:

> Thus praying to Christ on behalf of a friend and wishing to be heard by Christ on behalf of a friend, we reach out to Christ with love and desire, when sometimes suddenly and imperceptibly, affection crossing into affection [*affectus affectum transiens*], as if touching the neighboring sweetness of Christ, one begins to see *how pleasant he is* and to feel *how sweet* he is.[99]

[95] Augustine, Conf 2.2.2, 3.1.1; cf. Aelred, Spir am Prol.1 (CCCM 1:287; CF 5:53); Aelred, Spec car 1.25.71 (CCCM 1:42; CF 17:128).

[96] Aelred, Spir am 3.127 (CCCM 1:348; CF 5:124). This passage recalls the end of *On Jesus* as Jesus returns from the joys of Paradise to his responsibilities in Nazareth (Iesu 30–31).

[97] Aelred, Spir am 3.8 (CCCM 1:334–35; CF 5:108).

[98] See e.g., Aelred, Spir am 3.82, 119–27 (CCCM 1:334, 345–48; CF 5:108, 121–24). Russell writes, "Both the recovered text of the earlier dialogue with Ivo and Aelredus himself together serve as *memoria* in these last two books, the written and memorial recollections of a time long ago" (59).

[99] *quasi e uicino ipsius Christi dulcedinem tangens, incipit gustare quam dulcis est, et sentire quam suauis est*. Aelred does not specify the subject of *est*.

> So from that holy love by which one embraces a friend we ascend to that by which one embraces Christ; we will take the fruit of spiritual friendship joyfully and fully [*pleno*] into the mouth while awaiting all plenitude in the life to come, when that friendship to which we here admit few will be poured out into all and from all will be poured again into God, when *God* will be *all in all*.[100]

In this treatise Aelred presents friendship not as a distraction from the love of God, as does Augustine in *Confessions*,[101] but as a way to know God, fulfilling God's intention for all his creatures and participating in his nature, coming finally to his eternal embrace. True friendship, Aelred explains, leads to Paradise—the second Eden, where one may eat fully of all the fruit God has provided. So he directs the audience to find God through their memories of their friendships, recognizing the presence of Christ within them. There are many ways to know God, Aelred shows—remembering what Scripture has shown is one way, but another way is friendship, created by God, participating in God's own nature, and enjoyed in God's continuing presence.

Although the voices of Augustine and Ambrose are clear throughout *Friendship*, Aelred's second dialogue, *On the Soul*, is almost entirely Augustinian. It begins without prologue or narrative episode, as a monk named John asks Aelred to explain an Augustinian passage that he doesn't understand: "I would like to have your help and to ask what you think about certain problems. . . . I should like to know what you hold about the soul. For Augustine does not think the same about it as I have been accustomed to think."[102] Both here and in *Friendship*, then, the questioners come not requesting spiri-

[100] See Ps 34:8 [33:9]; 1 Cor 15:28; Aelred, Spir am 3.133–34 (CCCM 1:349–50; CF 5:125–26).

[101] See Augustine, Conf 4.4. 8; Dutton, "Friendship and the Love of God," 87, 92 below.

[102] Aelred, Anima 1.1 (CCCM 1:685; CF 22:35).

tual assistance, but instead to ask Aelred's opinion on something that they have had on their mind, having already developed thoughtful questions and their own opinions, which allow them sometimes to dispute Aelred's answers. Taking his cue from the questions put to him, Aelred for the most part offers not scriptural models but insight into what older authorities have written. So in both works he shows that topics explored outside Scripture may also lead to memories of God.

*On the Soul*, perhaps Aelred's last treatise, is concerned from beginning to end with Augustine's teaching on the soul, with Aelred at the end of his career giving clear evidence of his broad knowledge of Augustine's works and his indebtedness to Augustine's thought. After exploring what John understands on the subject, Aelred briefly defines the nature of the soul as tripartite, created by God in his own image and likeness in order that humankind might participate in him: "These three, then, the memory, reason, and will, are themselves the soul or are certainly in the soul."[103] Then, before going on to explain each of the three separately, he demonstrates the inseparability of the three faculties:

> For they can be separated from one another in thought. But on consideration it seems clear to me that these three—memory, reason, and will—are one substance. For even if they seem to have single properties, they can never work separately, nor can they be separated from each other. Memory can indeed do nothing without reason and will, reason nothing without will and memory, and will nothing without memory and reason. And so although memory is not reason or will and vice versa, these three are one substance and one soul.[104]

This least read of Aelred's treatises departs from the mostly untheorized teaching of the other spiritual treatises. It is still

[103] Aelred, Anima 1.32 (CCCM 1:694; CF 22:50).

[104] Aelred, Anima 1.36 (CCCM 1:695; CF 22:52); cf. Anima 2.1 (CCCM 1:707; CF 22:70).

pedagogically intentional, but it also now carefully articulates the theory found in Augustine's works, all explained within a dialogue that advances painstakingly through explanations of each of the soul's three faculties and discussions of other concerns regarding the soul. But despite the work's careful presentation of its theological essence, while responding thoughtfully to John's questions and concerns Aelred insists on the way one finds God in memory.

After explaining the tripartite structure of the soul to John, Aelred focuses on memory, from time to time linking his explanation to John's own experience and implicitly to his own. So when John objects to the idea that the soul can hold images of all the objects it has perceived, Aelred explains in terms of what John already knows, reminding him first of the size of his own reflection in a mirror, then of his memory of London, centered on its cathedral: "Do you remember London, how great it is? How the river Thames flows under it, how the monastery of blessed Peter decorates its western side, how the eastern side is guarded by the huge tower, and how the middle is adorned by the church of the teacher of the Gentiles?"[105] Having reminded John of how much can be clearly present in the memory and recalled by thinking of it, and by tacitly suggesting to him the structures of faith that shape the great city, Aelred builds on that understanding to introduce the crucial topic: the presence of God in the soul: "For what surpasses all, the memory has the capacity for God."[106]

This work is the most explicit of Aelred's treatises in uniting psychological theory with pedagogical practice. While unconcerned to retheorize the doctrine he has inherited, Aelred guides his audience—John and other readers—step by step through what that doctrine means and why it matters to them. He first explains the concept and then brings God into the memory of his audience, reminding them of God's continuing

[105] Aelred, Anima 2.5 (CCCM 1:708; CF 22:73).

[106] Aelred, Anima 2.12 (CCCM 1:710; CF 22:77).

presence in the soul. While the work is clearly not fully successful, with most readers unwilling to persevere through the long theological tutorial, it is a reminder that despite scholars' tendency to dismiss Aelred's theological expertise, Aelred had not only immersed himself in the theological anthropology of his age but was also eager to explain it to others and to rely on it in teaching his monks. And, as in his other spiritual treatises, he uses this one again to lead his audience to a vision of beatitude, here drawn from an episode from the life of Saint Benedict, as being "suffused with so great a light of celestial secrets that all the world seems narrow, perceived as though gathered under a single ray, the saints enjoying that immensity of divine light in their sight of God."[107] The work is theologically and intellectually centered rather than affective, a matter of instruction rather than lyrical contemplation. But like the other spiritual treatises, it insists throughout on God's creation and shaping of the soul, and ultimately it leads its audience to know itself as, with all the saints, illuminated by God's light now and in time to come, when in that light they may look upon God forever.

## Conclusion

Aelred's five spiritual works are carefully linked formally, thematically, and theologically. Though only the first and last of the five present the Augustinian doctrine of the soul, all of them begin with a familiar figure requesting that Aelred explain something, all of them proceed with Aelred's prompts to his audience to remember the God they already know, all of them link past, present, and future, and all of them call on personal experiences of Aelred and his interlocutors as well

[107] Anima 3.50 (CCCM 1:754; CF 22:148). See Terrence G. Kardong, trans., *The Life of Saint Benedict by Gregory the Great: Translation and Commentary* (Collegeville, MN: Liturgical Press, 2009), 130–37.

as on Scripture, the Augustinian doctrine of the soul, and the ability of the memory to hold God.

Readers have generally treated these five treatises as discrete entities, a little here and a little there, exploring mostly unrelated ideas ranging from the benefits of Cistercian monasticism through meditation on the sacred humanity of Christ through the meaning of human friendship through Augustinian psychology. Aelred's practice of attributing each topic to a request from someone requiring instruction has tended to be regarded as autobiographical, with more scholarly speculation devoted to the possible identity of the questioners and their relationship with Aelred than to Aelred's intellectual and pedagogical reasons for beginning and often ending these works with their requests.

And while scholars often credit Aelred with originality and influence as a writer, by and large his intellectual and authorial skills in the spiritual treatises have been undervalued, as though he were something of a spiritual dilettante rather than, like Bernard, a serious and committed teacher and writer, with a range of works revealing the depth and breadth of his reading and understanding, the vitality and energy of his mind, and the variety of his concerns and insights. The great David Knowles has written, "Ailred was not a deep speculative or mystical theologian; . . . he lacked Bernard's gift of grasping and expounding in magisterial manner a question of moral or spiritual importance. . . Ailred was not of the schools and did not probe deeply into the mysteries of the faith." Instead he praises Aelred's "limpid sincerity" and "wish to help others."[108]

But it is not, clearly, that Aelred lacked the ability to probe deeply or to speak magisterially (as his *De oneribus* homilies make clear), but rather that he chose to reap where systematic theologians had sowed, to use their work to nourish and guide

[108] David Knowles, "Ailred of Rievaulx," in *Saints and Scholars: Twenty-Five Medieval Portraits* (Cambridge, UK: Cambridge University Press, 1962), 48.

his monks, his readers, and to deliver seeds for meditation in baskets of carefully chosen words. Incorporating into his teaching the patristic understanding of the soul as God's creation and God's resting place, in work after work he thoughtfully reminded his readers of God as they already knew him and assured them that God was not only already present in their memory but that he would immediately—*subito*—respond whenever they remembered him. His careful work to shape a theological core of instruction for those who would follow him, designing a reliable and natural format through which he could write as though responding to personal requests for guidance and relying on personal memories of himself and his readers, provides an enduring way to remember and so to cling to God forever. Like Mary, Aelred received and pondered on all that he had received and then bequeathed it to the use of those who would follow.

*Chapter 2*

# Christ Our Mother: Aelred's Iconography for Contemplative Union[1]

The soul's consuming hunger for union with Christ governs Aelred of Rievaulx's single treatise on the contemplative life, *A Rule of Life for a Recluse*, addressed to an anchoress and directing her toward a life of purity and devotion.[2] Unlike other works of the genre, however, *A Rule* contains more than guidance for her quotidian life and devotional practice; it promises

[1] {I first presented this chapter at the Cistercian Studies Conference as part of the International Medieval Studies Congress at Western Michigan University, May 1983. It was first published in *Goad and Nail: Studies in Medieval Cistercian History, X*, ed. E. Rozanne Elder, CS 84 [Kalamazoo, MI: Cistercian Publications, 1985], 21–45. I have enclosed corrections and citations added to update the original version of these chapters in braces, as in this note.} It is with real gratitude that I acknowledge my indebtedness in this paper to several friends and students. Many have discussed the ideas and position here developed with me, but I owe special thanks to four in particular, Macklin Smith, Michael P. O'Connor, Judith Avery, and Stephen Rawson. In a variety of important ways they have contributed to my understanding of *A Rule*, to the shaping of my argument here contained, and even to the language in which I present that argument.

[2] {Aelred of Rievaulx, *De institutione inclusarum* (hereafter Inst incl), ed. C. H. Talbot, in *Aelredi Rievallensis Opera Omnia, 1 Opera Ascetica*, ed. Anselm Hoste and C. H. Talbot, CCCM 1 (Turnhout: Brepols, 1971), 636–82; *A Rule of Life for a Recluse*, trans. M. P. Macpherson, in Aelred of Rievaulx, *Treatises; The Pastoral Prayer*, CF 2 (Spencer, MA: Cistercian Publications, 1971), 43–102.}

her the direct, unmediated knowledge of God in this life, not just in the next. While Aelred, like the fathers who preceded him, always presents such mystical knowledge as available only at God's initiative and through his gift, he repeatedly encourages the contemplative to play an active role in obtaining that gift, to hasten to Christ's embrace, to entice him "to love and bestow gifts."[3] In the course of the work Aelred invites her to her bridegroom's chamber and brings her, like Mary of Bethany, to drink "from the fountain of divine love."[4] Through meditation on the humanity of Christ she comes finally to full spiritual union with him as her spouse, her mother, and her Lord.

The received text of *A Rule* contains two largely discrete portions linked by a common audience and subject matter. The first is a short manual for the daily life of the anchoress, 454 lines in C. H. Talbot's edition; the second is a treatise of spiritual direction in 1100 lines.[5] The disjunction between the two parts is largely responsible for readers' failure to recognize the strong contemplative concern of the larger portion; because the two-part work is not itself unified or centrally contemplative, the contemplative core of the second portion has not been generally identified.[6]

Only two scholars have discussed the contemplative content of the work, and both have failed to note just how many contemplative elements it contains and how they combine to de-

[3] Inst incl 14 (CCCM 1:650, CF 2:63). {CF page numbers refer to the Macpherson translation, but I have regularly adjusted the translation to fit it more closely to the Latin.}

[4] Inst incl 29 (CCCM 1:662; CF 2:79).

[5] Aelred of Rievaulx, "The 'De Institutis Inclusarum' of Aelred of Rievaulx," ed. C. H. Talbot, ASOC 7 (1951): 12–217; repr. CCCM 1:636–82.

[6] See my discussion of the questions surrounding the structure of the received text of *A Rule* in Marsha Dutton-Stuckey, "Getting Things the Wrong Way Round: Composition and Transposition in Aelred of Rievaulx's *De institutione inclusarum*," in *Heaven on Earth: Studies in Medieval Cistercian History*, ed. E. Rozanne Elder, CS 68 (Kalamazoo, MI: Cistercian Publications, 1983), 90–101.

fine the journey toward mystical union. C. H. Talbot's most pointed statement of the work's mystical qualities appears in the introduction to his edition:

> The Rule is . . . a warm and enthusiastic exhortation to the practice of the highest form of religious asceticism and contemplation. The recluse should [be] . . . a contemplative like Mary, sitting at the feet of Christ, listening to his words and gazing upon his blessed countenance . . . . She must rest like Saint John on the bosom of Christ and become a partaker of his secrets . . . . In this way, the renuntiation of all human company and consolation will not condemn her to absolute solitude but will ensure her the enjoyment of God's ineffable presence.[7]

Teresa Ann Doyle speaks of the work primarily as a conventional quasi-monastic rule: "The first section treats of outward observance which should regulate the life of a recluse; the second portion is devoted more exclusively to the development of the interior spirit of prayer and mortification."[8] Only once does she note mystical significance within the work, this in reference to the Last Supper passage also cited by Talbot: "Ailred comes to the last supper and dwells devoutly on the scene where St John rests his head on the breast of Christ. The incident represents the fulfillment of the mystic's quest, the meeting of human and divine love in sweet embrace." Like Talbot, Doyle notes but fails to develop this perception of the contemplative center of the work; she continues immediately: "Ailred encourages his sister to meditate in the manner he has illustrated and by this means to grow in the love of Christ."[9] The statement is accurate but incomplete; both the meditation and the love of Christ are intended by Aelred to culminate in "the meeting . . . in sweet embrace," in mystical union.

[7] Talbot, "The 'De Institutis Inclusarum,'" 173–74.

[8] Teresa Ann Doyle, "Aelred of Rievaulx's Rule for a Recluse," *The Benedictine Review* 6 (1951): 33.

[9] Doyle, "Aelred of Rievaulx's Rule," 36–37.

Other writers too have treated *A Rule* as an introduction to the devotional life, or even perhaps as a first step toward true contemplation, but no more than that. In his important study of Aelred's writings Aelred Squire summarizes the work: "Fundamentally, Aelred's work too is an ascetic letter on the preservation of virginity, which incorporates a Benedictine timetable and dietary, together with some glowing advice on how to meditate." Elsewhere he notes that "there can be little doubt that the unsophisticated would find Aelred the easiest and plainest guide to the practical question of how to begin to pray." Squire does acknowledge Christ's appearance in the work as the bridegroom to the soul, the defining element of *Brautmystik* in contemplative literature, but he perceives it here rather as a spur to asceticism than a mystical promise: "The recluse's purpose is to please God in body and soul in the perfect Christian life. Her virginity is to be preserved in view of a true espousal with Christ."[10] Mary Felicitas Madigan also comments that "Aelred regarded meditation on the humanity of Christ as preparatory purification for higher contemplation."[11] The same conclusion has been expressed most deliberately and forcefully by John Sommerfeldt. In his recent study of *A Rule* he states, "Aelred, I am forced to conclude, simply does not mention the possibility of the contemplative experience to his sister, the recluse. The route laid out in the *Rule* passes from meditation to Beatific Vision, with no foretaste of that Vision in contemplation."[12]

[10] Aelred Squire, *Aelred of Rievaulx: A Study*, CS 50 (London: SPCK, 1969; Kalamazoo, MI: Cistercian Publications, 1981), 120, 124, 127–28.

[11] Mary Felicitas Madigan, *The Passio Domini Theme in the Works of Richard Rolle* (Salzburg: Institut für Englische Sprache und Literatur, The University of Salzburg, 1978), 40.

[12] John R. Sommerfeldt, "The Vocabulary of Contemplation in Aelred of Rievaulx' *On Jesus at the Age of Twelve, A Rule of Life for a Recluse*, and *On Spiritual Friendship*," in *Heaven on Earth: Studies in Medieval Cistercian History*, ed. E. Rozanne Elder, CS 68 (Kalamazoo, MI: Cistercian Publications, 1983), 75.

In fact, however, the second part of *A Rule* is a unified contemplative work; in it Aelred guides the contemplative toward union with God in this life, then depicts the beatitude she will enjoy in the next. While his concern is primarily with the mystical joys available now, he indicates that these anticipate those to come. The pathway toward temporal union is centrally defined in three passages where Jesus is visually portrayed as mother; a number of associated images and propositional passages reinforce the promise to the contemplative that she may come to full knowledge of God in her life.

Aelred's direction for contemplation, the second portion of *A Rule*, has itself been generally understood as divided into two parts, each of which contains three smaller sections. The first part, according to this view, presents Aelred's teaching on the virtues of chastity, humility, and charity, while the second contains three meditations in the past, the present, and the future. The first of these meditations invites imaginative participation with Christ in his humanity, the second contains Aelred's confessional recollection of his own sinful youth and of God's insistent grace, and the third depicts a conventional Last Judgment.

This two-part understanding of the structure, however, is not in fact correct; for Aelred explicitly incorporates the three meditations into his discussion of charity, "the end and border of the spiritual garment."[13] The three speak separately and together of the contemplative's experience of God's love in this life and the next:

> There are two elements in the love of God, interior dispositions and the performance of works. The latter consists in the practice of the virtues, the former in the sweetness tasted by the spirit . . . . So, if that sweet love of Jesus is to grow in your affections,

[13] Aelred, Inst incl 26 (CCCM 1:659; CF 2:74).

> you need a threefold meditation, on the past, the present, and the future.[14]

Thus the three meditations emerge naturally from within the section on charity rather than standing apart from it.

Aelred's teaching on the three virtues presents the ascetic stage of the contemplative life, the preliminary step of purification and purgation on the mystical journey. Subsequently the first two meditations, those concerning the temporal life, present both meditation and contemplation, and the third presents beatitude in life to come, the eternal experience of what in this life is only temporary.

The structure of the treatise does not, then, exactly mirror the contemplative's spiritual progress. Although the maternal scenes themselves depict the journey from purification to union simply and schematically, the structural units of the treatise exemplify Aelred's understanding that the contemplative life is neither so simple nor so straightforward. Precisely because "in this wretched life nothing is stable, nothing eternal, and one never remains in the same state,"[15] the contemplative never lingers long in union with her Lord in Aelred's work. Hence within the two meditations on this life's experience Aelred insists on a movement from the active search for union to its achievement, then once again to its loss and a renewal of the search. The language in which he speaks of contemplative experience in this life recurs in the third meditation, however, showing both that true contemplative experience, however transitory, is available in this life and that it is a foretaste of that to come in and last through all eternity.

[14] Aelred, Inst incl 29 (CCCM 1:662; CF 2:79). The division into three parts of the CF translation of *A Rule* has probably contributed to the conventional misunderstanding of the relationship between the three virtues (titled "The Inner Life" in the translation) and the three meditations. {My discussion in this chapter inaccurately refers to three meditations rather than to a single threefold meditation.}

[15] Aelred, Inst incl 31 (CCCM 1:673; CF 2:92).

Jesus appears as spouse and as mother in passages throughout the teaching on the virtues and the first meditation. Of the three maternal passages the first stands at the center of preparation for the contemplative journey, within the discussion of humility, and the other two come in the meditation on the past. Aelred supplements the metaphorical promise of mystical union contained in the maternal passages and disallows any denial of literal significance to that promise when he twice speaks plainly of the purpose of the contemplative life, first stating the anchoress's goal, then recording her experience of it. The first of these statements comes immediately after the first of the three maternal passages, as a transition between the discussions of humility and charity, moving the anchoress from preparation for the life of true charity into the living of it. The second comes toward the end of the second meditation, summing up the contemplative experience in this life. During the stage of preparation, then, Aelred first metaphorically invites the anchoress to travel forward toward the love and knowledge of Christ and then plainly states that the goal of that journey is contemplative union. Within the meditation on the past he guides her careful steps to that union, schematically displaying her gradual progress on the way, and in the meditation on the present he records her experience as part of her personal history and as a token of what she may expect in life to come.

The theme of Christ's motherhood is introduced subtly when Aelred speaks of Christ the bridegroom in the words of Ecclesiasticus 24:27: "His spirit is sweeter than honey and his inheritance above the honeycomb."[16] The biblical passage itself, however, defines a mother, not a spouse. Wisdom there introduces herself: "I am the mother of fair love and of fear and of knowledge and of holy hope" (24:24-25).[17] Aelred uses

[16] Aelred, Inst incl 14 (CCCM 1:650; CF 2:63).

[17] The introduction of Christ through the words of Wisdom should not be taken to mean that she is to be understood as equivalent to him; she is only

this passage to delight the anchoress with the charms of her lover and bridegroom but depends at the same time on its biblical context within the words of a maternal child of God. This merging of the spouse and the mother prefigures a thematic interweaving throughout the treatise of the two kinds of mystical knowledge and union available to the contemplative, the familiar *Brautmystik* and what may be termed *Muttermystik*.

The first of the three central passages of maternal imagery appears within the exhortation to humility. Aelred says to the anchoress,

> It should suffice you to have on your altar a figure of the Savior hanging on the cross. That should represent to you his Passion which you are to imitate, invite you to the clasp of his embracing arms in which you should take delight, and pour out for you from his naked breasts the milk of sweetness by which you may be comforted.[18]

While Christ has already been identified implicitly as both bridegroom and mother, this passage is far more explicit. The anchoress is asked now to ready herself for the spiritual journey, no longer merely in virtuous cleanliness but now in active pursuit of the goal. She is invited to imitate Christ her Lord's passion, to delight in Christ her Bridegroom's embrace, and to take comfort in Christ her Mother's milk.

The milk here receives its definition from the sweetness that throughout the text epitomizes both the purity of the anchoress and the unity of Christ's nature. The chastity of the contempla-

---

a portion of his total definition. Finally all partial perceptions of Christ's nature find completion and fulfillment in the crucified Lord, and this Old Testament type is only a type. The eucharistic language unifying the various understandings of Christ in the treatise is at work here. Wisdom's words in Ecclesiasticus continue: "My memory is unto everlasting generations. They that eat me shall yet hunger, and they that drink me shall yet thirst" (Sir 24:28-29). Cf. Christ's own words in John 4:13-14.

[18] Aelred, Inst incl 26 (CCCM 1:658; CF 2:73).

tive draws her bridegroom to her; it "breathes out its fragrance even in heaven and leads the king to desire your beauty, him who is the Lord your God."[19] At the same time sweetness is Christ's nature. At his conception Mary was "inebriated with sweetness . . . when [she] felt in mind and womb the presence of majesty,"[20] in anticipation of his marriage with the contemplative his spirit is said to be "sweeter than honey and his inheritance above the honeycomb," and at his death the contemplative is exhorted to "eat the honeycomb with your honey."[21] He is throughout the work associated with sweetness and with honey; in this scene the sweetness is intrinsic to his definition in oneness, his identity as God and man, as infant, spouse, mother, and Lord.[22] The anchoress and Christ are fitting mates, and the sign of that fact is the sweetness of the milk here offered to her.

That sweetness, especially in its resonance with the earlier definitions of Christ through sweetness and honey, also introduces the eucharistic theme that underlies the maternal imagery of the treatise. Aelred suggests throughout that there are many paths to God, that the mystical one by no means winds alone, even for the contemplative. All Christians may come to union with Christ through the Eucharist, and indeed the union of the contemplative with him through his motherhood and spousehood is itself presented by Aelred as essentially eucharistic. The vocabulary of contemplation in *A Rule* centers in words of eating and drinking: its characteristic verbs are *bibo, comedo, inebrio*, and *nutrio*, its nouns *mel, favus, dulcedo, vinum, lac*, and *fons*. Aelred explicitly establishes this vocabulary as intrinsic to the contemplative's search for God when he says

[19] Aelred, Inst incl 14 (CCCM 1:650; CF 2:63).

[20] Aelred, Inst incl 29 (CCCM 1:663; CF 2:80).

[21] Aelred, Inst incl 31 (CCCM 1:671; CF 2:90).

[22] This idea also appears in Iesu: "his words sweet as honey" (Iesu 5 [CCCM 1:253; CF 2:6]). In *A Rule* the contemplative participates in this sweetness when her words become sweet as she kisses Christ's wounds.

that the first of "the two elements in the love of God" is "the sweetness tasted by the spirit."

Moreover, the three central passages through which the contemplative advances to union with God are all eucharistic in language and in imagery. In this first of the three she is still a beginner, young in contemplation; the sweetness of the milk may be understood to allude to the first communion of the young in faith, the newly baptized, and especially to the early church's practice of offering mingled milk and honey to new communicants before they first received the chalice. Hippolytus in his third-century *Apostolic Tradition* explains this rite:

> And then the offering is immediately brought by the deacons to the bishop, and by thanksgiving he shall make the bread into an image of the body of Christ, and the cup of wine mixed with water according to the likeness of the blood, which is shed for all who believe in him. And milk and honey mixed together for the fulfilment of the promise to the fathers, which spoke of a land flowing with milk and honey; namely, Christ's flesh which he gave, by which they who believe are nourished like babes, he making sweet the bitter things of the heart by the gentleness of his word. And the water into an offering in a token of the laver, in order that the inner part of man, which is a living soul, may receive the same as the body. The bishop shall explain the reason of all these things to those who partake . . . . And the recipients shall taste of each three times.[23]

The crucifix is only a representation, an object, in the first scene of maternal invitation, and while it invites the anchoress to consider its significance for her, she is not yet expected to respond imaginatively. It is static, frozen in time, a memorial of past events. Further, Aelred does not at this point encourage her to linger in thought or prayer at the crucifix; he adds instruction on adorning the altar instead:

[23] *Apostolic Tradition* 21; trans. Burton Scott Easton, *The Apostolic Tradition of Hippolytus* (Cambridge, UK: Cambridge University Press, 1934; repr. ed. 1962), 48–49. See also Tertullian, *De corona militis* 3 (PL 2:99).

> If you like, in order to bring home to you the excellence of virginity, a picture of the Virgin Mother and one of the Virgin Disciple may stand on either side of the Cross, so that you may consider how pleasing to Christ is the virginity of both sexes.[24]

These figures are to commend chastity to her and to lead her to think about it; their purpose is entirely deliberative. She is now to recognize those who stand at Christ's side as representatives of the defining virtue of her life; they demand nothing of her in return.

Immediately after this passage, however, Aelred plainly expounds the goal of her asceticism and purification:

> Let these things serve to increase your charity, not to provide empty show. From all of them you must ascend to unity, for only one thing is necessary. That is the one thing, the unity which is found only in the One, by the One, with the One with whom there is no variation, no shadow of change. The one who unites oneself with him becomes one spirit with him, passing into that unity that is always the same and whose years do not come to an end. This union is charity, as it were the edge and the border of the spiritual vesture.[25]

Her purification is not self-sufficient, her virtue not its own reward; rather are they necessary stages on the way to spiritual unity.

The other two passages in which Christ appears as mother are both within the meditation on the past, that extended life of Christ in which the contemplative is repeatedly urged to participate imaginatively in each event. Now she has moved beyond purification and preparation—packing her bags for the journey, as it were—and is on the road.

Some five years before writing *A Rule*, Aelred had expressed in *On Jesus as a Boy of Twelve* his understanding of the significance of Christ's human life for the spiritual traveler: "Thus

[24] Aelred, Inst incl 26 (CCCM 1:658–59; CF 2:73).

[25] Aelred, Inst incl 26 (CCCM 1:659; CF 2:74).

his bodily progress is our spiritual progress, and what we are told he did at each stage of his life is reproduced in us spiritually according to the various degrees of progress."[26] In *A Rule*, however, Aelred asks not that the anchoress imitate Christ, but that she meet him within his human life. She is asked not to walk in his footsteps, but to embrace his crib, wash his feet, pray beside him, bear up his bloody limbs. She is to be his friend and his disciple, and she imitates those who in his human life were mother, friend, and disciple to him. Her place in Paradise is earned not by imitating him but by ministering to him, and so she too may in this life experience a foretaste of that eternal joy.

The contemplative's changed status in this meditation is marked in the second maternal scene, at the Last Supper:

> Why do you hasten to leave? Delay a little. Do you not see? Who is that, I ask, who is reclining on his breast and bends back his head to lay it in his bosom? Happy is he, whoever he may be. O, I see: his name is John. O John, tell us what sweetness, what grace and tenderness, what light and devotion you are imbibing from that fountain. There indeed all the treasures of wisdom and knowledge, the fountain of mercy, the abode of loving kindness, the honeycomb of eternal sweetness . . . . Exult now, virgin, draw near and do not delay to claim for yourself some portion of this sweetness. If you are not capable of greater things, leave John to inebriate himself with the wine of joy in the knowledge of the divinity, {while you, running to the breasts of the humanity, press out the milk by which you may be nourished}.[27]

In this passage the anchoress, by Aelred's guidance now advanced to the stage of meditation on Christ in his humanity,

[26] Aelred, Iesu 11 (CCCM 1:258; CF 2:15).

[27] Aelred, Inst incl 31 (CCCM 1:668; CF 2:87). {The original version of this chapter followed the Macpherson translation in CF 2, which omitted the final clause of this passage. In this reprinting I have added my translation of the Latin: *tu currens ad ubera humanitatis, lac exprime quo nutriaris.*}

has become an active, assertive participant in the Last Supper itself. She is to go forward, to claim for herself the sweetness of Christ's embrace, to run to the breasts and press out their milk. In the Latin all the verbs of which she is subject are active except *nutriaris*; the nourishment of the milk remains in the gift of God. In the previous maternal passage the crucifix was chief actor, the subject of all active verbs, while the anchoress was the subject of only passive constructions.[28] Even the first verb of that passage, a verb of direction, was not an active imperative, but an impersonal construction with a dative, *sufficiat tibi*.

The milk in this second maternal passage has taken on different significance as it flows from the breasts of Christ's humanity, and it receives additional definition as it is complemented by Christ's divinity. Aelred here supports his iconographic contemplative theology with an orthodox speculative theology, a Pauline insistence that one comes to God, even on contemplative paths, only through the Son, the Incarnate Lord, who in his humanity manifests the Godhead, but that knowledge of Jesus only in that humanity is insufficient: one must pass beyond it.

The sweetness is still present here, but no longer only through the milk, and it is now explicitly available to the one who knows the living Christ while before it was only offered by the naked breasts of the crucified one. In the first maternal passage milk represents the sweetness of spirit, but now that the milk is to be redefined as representing only one portion of that spirit, Christ's human nature, the sweetness must be understood as no longer that of the milk alone. The no-longer-beginning contemplative is still not ready to know Christ in his divinity, but she has become able at least to recognize the

[28] The verbs of which she is subject in the first passage are *imiteris*, *delecteris*, and *consoleris*, only the second of which is truly passive, as both *imitor* and *consolor* are deponents.

presence of that divinity, which completes his humanity while remaining separate from it. Sweetness characterizes Christ in both his human and his divine natures, but when she knew him only in his humanity she could associate the sweetness only with that humanity. The sweetness, his intrinsic oneness, remains undivided, the indivisible issue of the fountain of his nature and his love. Meanwhile the contemplative can as yet receive only "some portion" of "this honeycomb of eternal sweetness," as she can receive only the milk, a partial emanation of his spirit, while John, who receives the divinity with the humanity, imbibes sweetness "from that fountain." Aelred insists again on the oneness and indivisibility of Christ at the same moment that he first speaks of Christ's dual nature, just as he earlier defined Christ in his sweetness as one when enunciating his triple way of being known by the anchoress.

The contemplative has taken an important step forward on her path to union, but she is still only halfway there. She is nourished by the gift of Christ's humanity, known in milk, but she is not yet able fully to know Christ in both flesh and spirit, in both humanity and divinity. That ability, possessed already by John, is represented by wine as well as milk, by inebriation as well as nourishment. John here lies upon Christ's bosom, receiving the wine and inebriated by it; his knowing of Christ is poured into him, not expressed by him. He knows God fully rather than in part.

In fact Aelred qualifies his direction to the contemplative at this point, not altogether sure how quickly she has traveled or how far progressed. He begins his exhortation to her in this passage with "if you are not capable of greater things"; presumably if she has taken the journey at a single bound she may already join John at the breast, to drink not only milk but wine with him. The rapidity with which a contemplative may come to full knowledge of Christ is, as Aelred shows elsewhere, variable and unpredictable.

Surprisingly, Aelred does not here mention the feast, the other disciples, or the words in which on this occasion in the

Gospel narrative Jesus instituted the Eucharist. The bread and wine are not explicitly present; the disciples and their Lord do not eat and drink together. Contemplative metaphor replaces sacramental and liturgical narrative; John at the table of the Last Supper partakes of Christ's body and blood as he reclines against him and receives the "wine of joy in the knowledge of the divinity." The spiritual transformation of Christ's flesh takes place in the receiving of it by him who loves and experiences Christ in his humanity and through it approaches his divinity. No physical symbol for the body is necessary for one who can reach the body itself, and the anchoress, new traveler that she is, is like John in her ability to drink from that body. The Eucharist needs no words of institution here; its true celebration appears in John's inebriation through the wine of joy.

The third maternal passage accomplishes the journey to union, through the same vocabulary and a crucifix already familiar in its implications from the first such passage. Now that crucifix upon the altar has become the cross with the dying Christ upon it; now the small figures of John and Mary are come to life, weeping together at the foot of the cross:

> But you, virgin, who can feel more confidence with the Virgin's Son than the women who stand at a distance, draw near to the Cross with the Virgin Mother and the virgin disciple, and look at close quarters upon that face in all its pallor . . . . Then one of the soldiers opened his side with a lance, and there came forth blood and water. Hasten, linger not, eat the honeycomb with your honey, drink your wine with your milk. The blood is changed into wine to inebriate you, the water into milk to nourish you. From the rock streams have flowed for you, wounds have been made in his limbs, holes in the walls of his body, in which, like a dove, you may hide while you kiss them one by one. Your lips, stained with his blood, will become like a scarlet ribbon and your word sweet.[29]

[29] Aelred, Inst incl 31 (CCCM 1:671; CF 2:90–91).

Here the anchoress has come to full knowledge of God through Christ. She knows him still through the milk of his humanity, but now the wine of his divinity is also available to her. She can now go beyond Mary and John, after first briefly standing and weeping with them, to receive the sweetness of Christ's body—the honeycomb with the honey—and the mingled milk and wine, humanity and divinity, no longer distinguished or distinguishable for her. The milk no longer flows from his two breasts, but as a fountain from his opened side, just as in the previous passage John received the wine while "imbibing from that fountain." The sweetness is now fully present for the anchoress at last, no longer associated merely with Christ's humanity or reserved for John.

At the culmination of this scene the contemplative actually enters Christ, becomes one with him by entering the hole in the wall of his body. There she dwells. In the perfection of contemplation the anchoress has moved beyond the partial knowledge of Christ as the God who nourishes as a mother nurses her child to full knowledge of the God who bears his lover within him as a mother bears her unborn child. Here union occurs at last, total knowing imaged forth in physical terms. The contemplative at rest within the womb of her mother Christ is enfolded in an embrace even closer than the sexual union with her bridegroom for which she has so long prepared.

At the same time, this is a sexual union as well: the contemplative in entering the body of the crucified Christ becomes indeed flesh of his flesh. The bridal union so long anticipated here takes place; the marriage has begun. While the anchoress has all along been understood as a fitting bride for Christ through their mutual sweetness, at the moment of union she has come to resemble him even more closely: as she kisses his wounds her lips take on the color of his blood and her word becomes newly sweet.

The biblical texture of the passage reinforces the blended maternal and spousal themes defining the contemplative's union with Christ. As the verse from Ecclesiasticus earlier introduced Christ explicitly as bridegroom and implicitly as mother, so here the text's narrative level, especially through its resonance with earlier maternal passages, presents Christ as a mother, while the language of the Song of Songs, of which this passage is a pastiche, language inherently erotic rather than maternal, recalls his identity as bridegroom. In both cases Aelred transforms a biblical metaphor so as to allow the passage to show Christ both as mother and as lover-spouse.[30] At the same time he alerts readers familiar with the mystical uses and interpretation of the Song of Songs in medieval contemplative writing to his central idea throughout the work, the love of and longing for union with God.

One version of *A Rule*, a late-fourteenth-century English translation found in the Bodleian Vernon manuscript, concludes its scene of maternal and spousal union at the passion

[30] Caroline Walker Bynum (*Jesus as Mother: Studies in the Spirituality of the High Middle Ages* [Berkeley: University of California Press, 1982]) suggests that this combined presence of two kinds of feminine imagery for mystical union is unusual, saying: "*Brautmystik* . . ., the use of maternal names for God, and devotion to the Virgin did not occur together in medieval texts; the presence of some kinds of feminine imagery seems to have inhibited the presence of other kinds" (141). While this perception may be simply an error on her part, it is equally possible that this treatise is in fact unique, that Aelred's curious and almost inadvertent shifts from an explicitly female audience to an undefined male audience and back again may explain the presence of both *Brautmystik* and *Muttermystik* in the text. Bynum argues that the latter form is typically male in origin and significance: "Given the twelfth-century partiality for metaphors drawn from human relationships, religious males had a problem. For if the God with whom they wished to unite was spoken of in male language, it was hard to use the metaphor of a sexual union with a male God . . . . We . . . have many examples of monks describing themselves or their souls as brides of Christ—that is, as female. But another solution . . . was of course to see God as female parent, with whom union could be quite physical (in the womb or at the breast). We should not ignore the possibility that in such writings males could express as males certain sexual desires: play at the breasts and entry into a female body" (161–62). Certainly in *A Rule* the union involves the contemplative's entering Christ rather than he her; he is physiologically female in the passion scene.

with birth of living offspring, so binding the two metaphors even more explicitly together than do any of the extant Latin manuscripts: "And just as in a dovecote holes are made in the walls to wash the doves in, so in the wall of Christ's flesh are made nests all hot with blood that you should hide in and bring forth spiritual birds."[31] Here the wound in the side becomes a physiologically recognizable womb, and the sexual union produces living issue.[32]

In defiance of normal physiology, the final maternal passage presents Christ, who appeared earlier as a nursing mother, now as a gestating one, though milk is normally produced only upon the birth of a child.[33] The inversion of the expected temporal and physiological sequence here is part of Aelred's treatment of time throughout the three meditations and, more specifically, in the three maternal scenes. The first of the scenes remembers past events; the second and third move forward in the narrative context, but the anchoress has had to move imaginatively backward in real time to participate in the

[31] Marsha L. Dutton Stuckey, ed., "An Edition of Two Middle English Translations of Aelred's *De institutione inclusarum*," PhD dissertation, University of Michigan, 1981, 160.

[32] Bynum says of Cistercian use of maternal imagery: ". . . where birth and the womb are dominant metaphors, the mother is described as one who conceives and carries the child in her womb, not as one who ejects the child into the world, suffering pain and possibly death in order to give life. Conceiving and giving birth, like suckling, are thus images primarily of return to, union with, or dependence upon God . . . . Moreover, other physiological images, such as . . . Aelred's reference to hiding inside Christ, express not merely the compassion or love that God offers man but also the closest possible binding of self to God . . . . Thus the most frequent meaning of mother-Jesus to twelfth-century Cistercians is compassion, nurturing, and union" (150).

[33] For Bernard the relationship between childbearing and milk is equally obscure, apparently; in Sermon 9 of the Sermons on the Song of Songs the bridal kiss results immediately in conception, and the sign of that fact is the production of milk: "For so great is the potency of that holy kiss, that no sooner has the bride received it than she conceives and her breasts grow rounded with the fruitfulness of conception, bearing witness, as it were, with this milky abundance" (SC 9.7; [SBOp 1:46; CF 4:58]).

present reality of the event represented in the first scene and recalled there as long past. Aelred insists on the beginning and the end as identical rather than distinguishable in language and imagery and in the confusing presentation of time. Time past and time present merge in the scene of unity, the return from alienation and separation.[34]

The two central metaphors through which Aelred has guided the contemplative to union with Christ also cease to be distinct; they achieve unity in this passage. Just as physically the water and blood, symbolically the milk and wine, theologically the humanity and divinity, and temporally the past and present merge in the passion, so do the two humanly conceived relationships through which the contemplative has been aided to love and to know her Lord. As the early definition of Christ presented him as both mother and spouse, and as the anchoress's altar invited her to come to him as both mother and spouse, so here finally this union must be understood as that of the contemplative with Christ in all the ways she has come to know and love him. In his passion he is no longer merely mother or merely spouse, but Lord, and his motherhood and spousehood are partial but essential understandings of that lordship. Just as Aelred insists that one cannot know God in his divinity except by knowing him first in his humanity, knowledge that is itself incomplete, so too he insists that while a contemplative may approach union with God envisaged as mother or spouse, finally the mother and the spouse must be subsumed in the crucified Lord. No partial understanding is sufficient. With

[34] Aelred treats time similarly in the three-part meditation. The meditation on the past describes "what happened long ago" but relies on present tense verbs, both imperative and indicative, and demands that the present-day contemplative involve herself in those past events; the meditation on the present discusses the life of the author himself, but it emphasizes his past and God's mercy toward him in that past and in the future through the use of past and future verbs. The meditation on the future resolves the temporal paradox, for in it the past and the future become one in God's eternal present. See Dutton Stuckey, "An Edition," 56–58.

Paul, Aelred brings the contemplative finally "to know nothing . . . but Jesus Christ and him crucified" (1 Cor 2:2).

Still another instance of unity from diversity occurs in the scene at the culmination of the passion, when the contemplative is for the second time in the treatise portrayed as a dove. In the discussion of chastity the anchoress was directed to look into Scripture, which flows "from the clear fountain of wisdom," Christ, for warning of the devil's approach.[35] Having previously found Christ's protection and her safety in the written word, now in the meditation on the past, while meditating on his humanity, she is able to find protection in his incarnation and his passion, by taking refuge in his wounded side. Here animal and maternal images merge, as do spousal and maternal ones.

In both animal and maternal images for union the contemplative first knows Christ from a distance, through a memorial of past events, and then comes to him in his living flesh. At the same time in both cases the first, static image is presented in the lively language of liquid flowing from its fount, Christ: to the dove-anchoress streams of water promise safety, and to the anchoress at the altar naked breasts offer milk of sweetness. In the passion scene, however, the two figures become one—the dove merges with the enclosed worshiper, and the promised safety and sweet milk are both attained and surpassed in present union with Christ.

For Aelred the preparation for the contemplative journey is essentially passive, demanding that the traveler consider God's saving action in history, the giving of the Law and of his Son. The would-be contemplative must begin the journey by looking on, thinking about, understanding. Once she has begun the search, however, she becomes more like God, her passivity turns into action. The journey may be swift—taken in one beat of the wings—or slower, achieved in daily footsteps among Jesus' followers. Finally the speed is unimportant and unpredictable; the goal is available and equally attainable to all, and

[35] Aelred, Inst incl 20 (CCCM 1:654; CF 2:68).

the means of travel or the time it takes does not matter. One may begin by reading Scripture or by praying before the crucifix; one may come suddenly to union, without struggle, without meditation, soaring above the plodders, or one may walk with them laboriously toward the dwelling place.

Aelred links his three maternal scenes through common language and imagery. The first and third are essentially the same, the first comes to life in the third, and the shared eucharistic language of the second and third creates a narrative continuity between them. What has changed in the course of the three scenes is the anchoress's relationship with her Lord. She has moved from invitation through active participation to total union, from ascetic preparation through active pursuit to infused contemplation, the stages of the contemplative journey in this life. Where at first she was invited by his breasts, then was able herself to press the milk from them, finally she enters his very flesh. She has ceased to be a passive observer and become active in union.

The contemplative's progress is described and enabled through incarnational and eucharistic language, so that finally she receives union with Christ precisely through the elements of the Eucharist, through eating his body—the honeycomb—and drinking his blood, the wine. The transformation undergone by the blood and water that issue from Christ's side is an inversion of the transformation in the Mass, a necessary and perhaps heuristic inversion for the anchoress's benefit. It is clear, in any case, that in the scenes of the Last Supper and crucifixion the contemplative comes to know Christ through his body and blood. Caroline Walker Bynum says in *Jesus as Mother*, "Maternal imagery is part of a new sense of God, which stresses his creative power, his love, and his presence in the physical body of Christ and in the flesh and blood of the eucharist."[36]

[36] Bynum, *Jesus as Mother*, 135. Bynum also comments at some length on the intersection of the Eucharist and the desire for mystical union in the lives of women mystics of the thirteenth century, for whom the union was not so

The three incrementally developed maternal passages conclude with the scene of mystical union presented as the physical interpenetration of Christ and a woman. Aelred's iconography for the contemplative journey is complete. But this last step has in fact taken place once before in the work, at the conception of Jesus himself, early in the first meditation and so between the first two passages in which Christ appears as mother. That passage, however, is non-visual.[37] Aelred speaks first to his anchoress, then to Mary herself, and finally again to the anchoress:

> Wonder at the Lord who fills earth and heaven being enclosed within the womb of a maiden, whom the Father sanctified, the Son fecundated, and the Holy Spirit overshadowed. O sweet Lady, with what sweetness you were inebriated, with what a fire of love you were enflamed, when you felt in your mind and in your womb the presence of majesty, when he took flesh to himself from your flesh and fashioned for himself from your members members in which all the fullness of the Godhead might dwell in bodily form. All this was on your account, virgin, in order that you might diligently contemplate the Virgin whom you have resolved to imitate and the Virgin's Son to whom you are betrothed.[38]

This union is mental and physical, and Mary, in this case the one whose womb is being entered, is inebriated by the sweetness of the union while herself being, like the contemplative whom Aelred addresses, defined in terms of chastity and sweetness. Immediately the contemplative is reminded both that she is to imitate Mary and that she is betrothed to Mary's

---

much understood in the language of the Eucharist, but achieved through its celebration (257–58).

[37] Perhaps the scale implied in the first quoted sentence makes any visualization impossible. It is worth noting that in the course of the three maternal passages the anchoress grows small in relationship to Christ, an inversion of that physical phenomenon at which Aelred marvels here.

[38] Inst incl 29 (CCCM 1:663; CF 2:80).

son. The maternal and the spousal could hardly be more explicitly linked. In fact, Mary apparently not only conceives Christ within her as a son but knows him also in some sense as lover; Aelred insists on both relationships in his language of conception: "the womb of a maiden, whom . . . the Son fecundated."[39]

Christ is conceived in wholeness, in humanity and divinity, and Mary, though no contemplative, receives infused grace and union. Where Aelred's contemplative audience receives different tastes at different times—now milk of sweetness, later milk of humanity, then wine of divinity mixed with milk of humanity and honey with the honeycomb—and is nourished by the milk and inebriated by the wine, Mary is inebriated by the sweetness, all at once, non-incrementally, with no stages to traverse. She knows God in his own unity at the moment of her union with him. The annunciation scene is then in some sense a lyric, ecstatic prefiguring of the highly visual scene at the cross; in both cases Christ and a virgin woman come together in spousal and maternal union.

The theological basis for Aelred's combination of the spousal and the maternal union of a woman with Christ appears in chapter 6 of Augustine's *On Holy Virginity*: Mary "is mother, indeed, in the spirit, not of our Head, who is our Savior himself, of whom she was rather born spiritually, since all who believe in him (among whom she, too, is included) are rightly called children of the bridegroom."[40]

[39] In Iesu Aelred briefly raises the idea of imitating Mary as the mother of Christ, but without a corresponding spousal significance, and the central idea there is essentially that mentioned above, that of growing spiritually in intimacy with Christ: "For just as the Lord Jesus Christ is born and conceived in us, so he grows and is nourished in us, until we all come to perfect manhood, that maturity which is proportioned to the complete growth of Christ" (Iesu 4 [CCCM 1:252; CF 2:8]).

[40] PL 40:399; trans. John McQuade, "Holy Virginity," in St. Augustine, *Treatises on Marriage and Other Subjects*, The Fathers of the Church: A New Translation 27 (Washington, DC: The Catholic University of America Press, 1955), 149.

Aelred's passage containing the conception of Jesus not only adds theological definition to the union at the crucifixion, but, occurring at an early stage of the contemplative's meditative movement toward union, it clarifies her goal. It gives her in Mary a model to imitate and to follow, and it promises a specific reward. Aelred provides two such models and two such rewards for the anchoress; both appear at each of the three essential stages of her life: preparation, meditation, and union. On her altar the images of John and Mary draw her to consider the excellence of chastity; in her meditation she considers first the annunciation—and is told to "contemplate the Virgin whom you have resolved to imitate"—and then the Last Supper, where she observes John's joy in the knowledge of Christ's divinity. Finally, when she is ready for contemplative union, John and Mary are together again, at the foot of the cross, showing her the way.

Having followed, observed, and learned from these two models, having imitated both in virginity, assisted Mary in caring for the infant, drunk beside John at Christ's breast, and finally watched and wept in their company, she is now able herself to go forward to union with Christ. She has not advanced beyond them—chronologically they have preceded her in union—but she is no longer in need of their showing her the way, guiding her steps. She has become one with them, a contemplative bride and child of Christ in her own right. Not only does Aelred guide the anchoress toward her goal through these two models, but he indicates to non-contemplative readers her position on the pathway through comparison with the two who knew Jesus most intimately.

Two passages that stand on either side of the passion in the first meditation, passages verbally though not visually almost identical, insist on a theologically correct understanding of the Christ elsewhere known as mother. These two passages echo the imagery and language of the three maternal passages, but the echoes are inversions; Jesus is twice known again in his humanity, but for the moment only in his humanity. In these passages Aelred insists that contemplative progress is not possible unless Christ's humanity is properly understood, that his carefully shaped maternal images can only serve as steps on the contemplative way if they are de-allegorized and understood to be only metaphors for the Christ who is man *and* God.

In the first of these two scenes Jesus prays in the garden of Gethsemane, and Aelred addresses him, saying, "Your compassion for me makes you show yourself human to the extent that you seem almost to be no longer aware that you are God. You pray prostrate on your face, and your sweat has become like drops of blood running down onto the ground." At once Aelred turns his direction to the watching anchoress, saying, "Why are you standing there? Run up, consume those sweet drops and lick the dust from his feet."[41] Once again liquid comes from Christ, but it is not now life-giving, like the Scriptural streams of water or the flowing milk and wine. As will be true so soon at the passion, blood and water are mingled, or rather in fact confused, but they are only blood and water, and they neither nourish nor inebriate. The drops of sweat, naturally salt, are become sweet as they come from the body of Jesus, but the dust insists that he is mortal.

The second of the scenes comes after the crucifixion, as Christ is being carried to the tomb, now defeated, broken, and dead. Aelred again implores the contemplative to assist the human Christ, to bear up the feet or arms, "or at least gather up the drops of precious blood as they fall one by one and lick the dust from his feet."[42]

In these two scenes the anchoress is led not to milk and wine but to dust and blood and sweat. Dust here replaces milk as a

[41] Aelred, Inst incl 31 (CCCM 1:669; CF 2:88). The verb translated as *consume* in the first of these passages is *adlambe*, a verb commonly used in reference to the action of flame or water in licking against and so washing or eating away at its object. The sense of *consume*, then, is accurate here, but it should not be understood as equivalent to taking into oneself for nourishment.

[42] Aelred, Inst incl 31 (CCCM 1:672; CF 2:91).

symbol of Christ's humanity, even to the point that it is the dust that the anchoress is twice instructed to lick up rather than the transformed blood and water of the maternal scenes. The dust is not transformed into anything, nor is the blood, precious for its own sake; the sweat may be misunderstood or misidentified—and in its identification with blood, it of course becomes blood for the reader—but it is not in itself changed into something life-giving.

The echoing and inversion of maternal imagery in these scenes serves primarily to draw a theological contrast between these and the truly maternal ones. Christ here does not represent God's motherhood; he is in neither of these scenes active, offering himself to the contemplative and nourishing her. Rather, she must support him, wiping the sweat from his face, watching while he prays, bearing up his limbs. Here the inviting, embracing, nourishing Christ is turned away from the contemplative, and in the withdrawal of her now-expected food she must seize whatever she can from him. The very absence of the mother God calls attention to her earlier presence, and the impotent humanity of Jesus in these scenes emphasizes his Majesty, his wholeness as God and man in the other three.

The near identity of these scenes allows Aelred through them to make not two separate statements, but rather one emphatic one, and their position on either side of the passion scene allows him more fully to articulate his incarnational understanding of the Christ whom the contemplative knows as mother. The two passages insist on the ineluctable humanity of Christ, but they stand on either side of that moment of unity in which the contemplative finally knows Christ fully, in humanity and divinity, as spouse, mother, and Lord. At last she has come to know the God who bears and nourishes her children in a full human nature. But if her children do not understand that her nature is divine as well as human, they cannot know her. Only when the water and blood become milk and wine, only when grace transforms the physical outflowing of

Jesus into the sacramental elements of the Eucharist, does the union between the contemplative and God become possible. If Christ is man only, he cannot nourish, cannot inebriate, cannot give life; a man, however loving and however loved, is only a man, finally doomed to lie bloody, dusty, dead. If the anchoress knows Christ only as a man, she has failed to know him at all. These passages, then, continue Aelred's insistence on a Pauline understanding of Christ's dual nature: grace comes through the incarnate God—through God incarnate.

At the same time that Aelred insists on theological orthodoxy in the contemplative's understanding of her journey, he also demands care and intelligence in her reading of his direction for it. He reminds her in these two passages on either side of the passion that if she fails to understand, to de-allegorize, his iconography for spiritual progress, to understand the images, the blood and water, wine and milk, in their reality, as figurative rather than literal in significance, she will also fail to reach the promised union. In this concern he follows Augustine, who says in *On Christian Doctrine*,

> Nor can anything more appropriately be called the death of the soul than that condition in which the thing which distinguishes us from beasts, which is the understanding, is subjected to the flesh in the pursuit of the letter. He who follows the letter takes figurative expressions as though they were literal and does not refer the things signified to anything else.[43]

With the union once achieved, however briefly, during the meditation on the past, the anchoress leaves behind her imaginative meditation on the life of Christ and turns her attention to the second meditation, that on the present. In it she reads Aelred's joyful recounting of the spiritual benefits she has repeatedly received in her life:

[43] Augustine, *De Doctrina Christiana* 3:9; trans. D. W. Robertson Jr. (Indianapolis: Liberal Arts Press, 1958), 84.

> But now consider those gifts of God's goodness which are known only to you. With how glad a face Christ comes to meet one who renounces the world, with what delights he feeds her in her hunger, what riches of his compassion he shows her, what affections he arouses in her, with what a cup of charity he inebriates her. For if he did not leave his runaway and rebellious slave [Aelred himself], called solely in his mercy, without the experience of spiritual consolations, what sweetness shall I not believe he bestowed on a virgin . . . . How often he came to your side to bring you loving consolation when you were dried up by fear, how often he infused himself into your inmost being when you were on fire with love, how often he shed upon you the light of spiritual understanding when you were singing psalms or reading, how often he carried you away with a certain unspeakable longing for himself when you were at prayer, how often he lifted up your mind from the things of earth and introduced it into the delights of heaven and the joys of Paradise.[44]

In essentially the same language as that of the maternal passages but now plainly and unequivocally rather than visually and metaphorically Aelred reminds the contemplative of the mystical joy she has received from her Bridegroom Christ, from her Mother Christ, from her Lord Christ. She is now able to understand rationally and intellectually what she has previously experienced with her heart and body through imaginative meditation. As she was fed with the honeycomb of Christ's body, nourished by the milk of his humanity, and inebriated by the wine of his divinity, so now she recalls the delights, the cup of charity and its inebriation, the spiritual consolations and their sweetness.

Further, her experience in this life truly prepares her for that in the next. Aelred makes it clear that the gladness of Christ's face in meeting her here is merely an anticipation of the same gladness, enhanced by its familiarity, in Paradise. The third meditation, that on the life to come, recalls these joys. First

[44] Aelred, Inst incl 32 (CCCM 1:676; CF 2:96).

Aelred urges the anchoress to anticipate her place at the Last Judgment: "Now turn your eyes to the right and look at those among whom he will place you by glorifying you . . . . Jesus' face shines upon them, not terrible but lovable, not bitter but sweet, not frightening but attractive."[45] Finally, completing his promises to the contemplative with that greatest joy of this life and the next, that vision most to be sought and longed for, he says again:

> What is there further for us to seek? To be sure, what surpasses all these things, that is the sight, the knowledge and the love of the Creator . . . . That lovable face, so longed for, upon whom the angels yearn to gaze, will be seen. Who can say anything of its beauty, of its light, of its sweetness? The Father will be seen in the Son, the Son in the Father, the Holy Spirit in both. He will be seen not as a confused reflection in a mirror, but face to face.[46]

This knowledge and love, this sight of God's face, awaits the contemplative in the life to come, Aelred assures her, but she is not left waiting until that time, for she has seen its beauty, known its sweetness in her life.

Aelred has insisted throughout his work that the contemplative can come to union with God, can receive the infusion of grace in this life, can be introduced into the delights of heaven while yet alive. In the three maternal passages he has guided her along the journey to attain these delights, depicting Christ as a loving, nurturing, and inebriating mother and at the same time as an embracing lover and spouse and so aiding the anchoress to come finally to unmediated knowledge of God, to spiritual union. But in case the reader has remained throughout unable to understand or to believe the promise contained in his metaphor, he spells out in the second meditation in simple, lyrical language the message and truth contained in the maternal passages. Finally in the third meditation he presents the

[45] Aelred, Inst incl 33 (CCCM 1:679; CF 2:99).

[46] Aelred, Inst incl 33 (CCCM 1:680–81; CF 2:101).

glory that waits in the next life, glory familiar already to the contemplative who has followed the path laid out for her.

Aelred embodies his profoundly incarnational understanding of mystical progress and union in the language of metaphor and image rather than in that of abstraction and speculation; through images of the flesh he insists on knowledge of an incarnate God as the goal of the contemplative life. So he leads his readers along the journey to God: Bridegroom, Mother, Lord.

## *Chapter 3*

# Friendship and the Love of God: Augustine's Teaching in the *Confessions* and Aelred of Rievaulx's Response in *Spiritual Friendship*[1]

"I must now carry my thoughts back to the abominable things I did in those days, the sins of the flesh which defiled my soul," writes Augustine at the beginning of book two of the *Confessions*. "And what was it that delighted me except to love and to be loved? But my love did not pause in the affection of one mind for another, going beyond the bright boundary of friendship."[2] In book three, recalling his time in Carthage, he

[1] This chapter is reprinted here by permission from *The American Benedictine Review*, where it first appeared (ABR 56 [2005]: 3–40). I presented an earlier version in the 2000 Summer Ecumenical Institute at Assumption College, whose other participants, especially William Babcock, David Hunter, and Goulven Madec, all contributed to my understanding of Augustine and hence to the final form of this article; I thank them all. For Aelred's teaching on the sacramental nature of human friendship, I am deeply indebted to the late Fr. Charles Dumont, OCSO, many of whose articles on Aelred's *De spiritali amicitia* are collected in *Une éducation du cœur: La spiritualité de saint Bernard et de saint Ælred*, Pain de Cîteaux 3,10 (Oka, Canada: Abbaye Cistercienne Notre-Dame-du-Lac, 1996), 275–373.

[2] Unless otherwise identified, all Augustine citations come from *St. Augustine's Confessions*, ed. P. Knöll, 2 vols., Loeb (Cambridge, MA: Harvard University Press, 1989). English translations are for the most part from *Saint Augustine: Confessions*, trans. R. S. Pine-Coffin (London: Penguin, 1961), with occasional alterations.

revisits his earlier desires: "I did not yet love, but I loved to love . . . . To love and to be loved was sweet to me."[3] In time his discovery of Cicero's *Hortensius*, he explains, converted him to philosophy, though not yet to Christ.[4]

Seven hundred fifty years later, Aelred (1110–1167), abbot of the English Cistercian monastery of Rievaulx, echoed Augustine in the Prologue to his work on the meaning of human friendship, *Spiritual Friendship*:

> When I was a boy at school and the charm of my companions delighted me, amid the ways and vices with which that age is wont to be threatened, I gave my whole mind to affection and devoted myself to love, so that nothing seemed sweeter to me, nothing more enjoyable, nothing more useful than to be loved and to love. So, tossing between fluctuating loves and friendships, my spirit was pulled here and there. Not knowing the law of true friendship, I was often deceived by its likeness.[5]

Fortunately, Aelred explains, during this time Cicero's *On Friendship* came into his hands, offering him a profound and eloquent guide to friendship. In this work he found discipline for his emotional struggles, "a formula for friendship by which I might check the vacillations of my loves and affections."[6] Later, as a monk, he says, he began to think of rewriting Cicero's work in such a way as to season its profundity and eloquence with the salt of Scripture and the honey of Jesus' name.[7]

[3] Augustine, Conf 3.1.

[4] Augustine, Conf 3.4.

[5] Unless otherwise identified, all citations of Aelred come from *De spiritali amicitia*, CCCM 1:279–350. Translations of Aelred are based on *Spiritual Friendship*, trans. Mary Eugenia Laker, CF 5 (Kalamazoo, MI: Cistercian Publications, 1977), but with frequent alterations. {Because of the greater accessibility now of the 2010 CF translation by Lawrence C. Braceland, CF page numbers cited reflect Fr. Braceland's translation instead of Laker's.}

[6] Aelred, Spir am Prol.3 {CCCM 1:287; CF 5:1–2}.

[7] Aelred, Spir am Prol.5 {CCCM 1:288; CF 5:54}. Aelred's comment on the absence of Christ's name from *De amicitia* echoes Augustine's words on *Hortensius*: "this only held me back, that the name of Christ was not there" (Augustine, Conf 3.4).

Although *Spiritual Friendship* presents a definition of friendship only slightly altered from Cicero's and takes the form of Ciceronian dialogue, it owes as much to Augustine as to Cicero. James McEvoy calls attention to its dependence on the *Confessions*: "The direct Augustinian quality is there unmistakably from the very start of this work; much as it will indeed owe to Cicero, its first tones have the vibrant, experiential directness of the author of the *Confessions*, from whom the opening four words are drawn (*Conf.* 1.11.17)."[8] This Augustinian resonance sounds throughout the work, most strikingly in its repeated echo of *amare et amari*, which conveys the essence of Aelred's view of friendship as a route to God.

But while Aelred makes his intellectual and rhetorical debt to the *Confessions* clear throughout *Spiritual Friendship*, he reconsiders rather than recapitulating Augustine's teaching, grounding his own doctrine of friendship in creation and showing it to reach fulfillment in eternity. Whereas Augustine distinguishes between loving one's friend and loving God, Aelred explains human friendship as intended by God, a trace of God's unity implanted in humankind, and therefore a straight way home to God.

[8] James McEvoy, "Notes on the Prologue of St. Aelred of Rievaulx's 'De Spirituali Amicitia,' with a Translation," *Traditio* 37 (1981): 397. Much has been written on changing attitudes toward friendship from Cicero through Augustine and Aelred; besides Dumont's articles in *Une Éducation*, particularly valuable treatments are to be found in Adele M. Fiske, "The Survival and Development of the Ancient Concept of Friendship in the Early Middle Ages," 2 vols., dissertation, Fordham University, 1955, esp. 72–87 (on Augustine) and 672–805 (on Aelred); James McEvoy, "*Philia* and *Amicitia*: The Philosophy of Friendship from Plato to Aquinas," *Sewanee Medieval Colloquium*, Occasional Papers 2 (1984): 1–23; and Pierre Courcelle, "Ailred de Rievaulx à l'école des *Confessions*," *Revue des Études Augustiniennes* 3 (1957): 163–74, and *Les Confessions de saint Augustin dans la tradition littéraire. Antécédents et postérité* (Paris: Études Augustiniennes, 1963), 265–305.

## Aelred's Knowledge of Augustine

Aelred of Rievaulx was born in the north of England in 1110, the last of a long line of priests, just as the Gregorian effort to eliminate clerical marriage was finally achieving success.[9] In 1134, after about ten years at the court of David I of Scotland, Aelred entered the young monastery of Rievaulx, where he served as abbot from 1147 until his death in January 1167. During those years he wrote extensively, producing at least fourteen ascetic and historical works, as well as many sermons and letters.

Nothing is known of Aelred's education, though it seems likely that after his childhood in Hexham he studied briefly in the cathedral school in either Durham or York, probably becoming familiar with Augustine's writings there. Even at court he would have had some exposure to Scripture, the history of the faith, and the teachers of the church: David was the son of Saint Margaret of Scotland, whose piety, along with that of David and his sister Edith, wife of Henry I of England, Aelred celebrated in his *Genealogy of the Kings of the English*.[10] Aelred showed the Scottish court as a place where Christian faith was both lived and taught.

According to Walter Daniel, Aelred's twelfth-century hagiographer, Aelred knew the *Confessions* before his conversion and read it throughout his life. Of Aelred's prayer and meditation in the months before his death, Walter says that "he carried most assiduously in his hands the *Confessions* of Augustine, for he had had these books as a guide when he was

[9] For a comprehensive study of Aelred's life and works, see Aelred Squire, *Aelred of Rievaulx: A Study*, CS 50 (1969; Kalamazoo, MI: Cistercian Publications, 1981); for the effects of Gregorian reform in England on the life and monastic vocation of Aelred, see Marsha L. Dutton, "The Vocation and Conversion of Aelred of Rievaulx: A Historical Hypothesis," in *England in the Twelfth Century*, ed. Daniel Williams (London: Boydell, 1990), 31–49.

[10] Aelred, *Genealogia regum anglorum*, PL 195:711–38 {CCCM 3:1–56}; in Aelred of Rievaulx, *The Historical Works of Aelred of Rievaulx*, trans. Jane Patricia Freeland, ed. Marsha Dutton, CF 56 (Kalamazoo, MI: Cistercian Publications, 2005), 71–122.

converted from the world." He further reports that as Aelred was dying he asked for his Psalter, the Gospel of John, and the *Confessions*, saying: "Behold, I have kept these by me in my little oratory and delighted in them to the utmost while sitting alone there in leisure."[11]

But the best evidence of Aelred's familiarity with the *Confessions* is his own writing, full of Augustine's words and phrases even where apparently characterized by highly personal reminiscence.[12] Aelred incorporated Augustine's regrets for his sinful youth into *The Institution of Anchoresses*, a large portion of which circulated as Augustine's from the thirteenth through the sixteenth centuries.[13] Similarly the conversion narrative in Aelred's earliest work, *Mirror of Charity*, echoes the story of Augustine's conversion in the *Confessions*.[14] Aelred Squire identifies Augustine as the Western doctor who "has the place of predilection among Aelred's sources" and explains the *Mirror of Charity* as reflecting Aelred's devotion to Augustine and the *Confessions* as well as his willingness not only to borrow directly from Augustine but also to recast, rethink, or reject Augustine's positions.[15]

[11] Walter Daniel, *Vita Ailredi Abbatis Rievall'*, ed., trans., and intro. Maurice Powicke (1950; Oxford: Clarendon, 1978), 50, 58; repr. *The Life of Aelred of Rievaulx and the Letter to Maurice*, CF 57 (Kalamazoo, MI: Cistercian Publications, 1994), 128, 135. {Powicke omits *books* from Walter's "illos libros" in the first quotation.}

[12] For the Augustinian and Aelredian parallels, see Courcelle, *Les Confessions*. See also Étienne Gilson, *The Mystical Theology of St Bernard*, trans. A. H. C. Downes, CS 120 (1940; Kalamazoo, MI: Cistercian Publications, 1990), 228 n. 72.

[13] André Wilmart, "Les Méditations VII et VIII attribuées à Saint Anselme: La Série des 21 Méditations," *Revue d'Ascètique et de Mystique* 8 (1927): 276, nn. 63, 65; C. H. Talbot, ed., "The 'De Institutis Inclusarum' of Ailred of Rievaulx," ASOC 7 (1951): 167–69. Migne prints Aelred's Augustinian meditation on the present from that work in the Appendix to Augustine's works in PL 32:1451–52, preceding it with a note identifying Aelred as its author.

[14] See Courcelle, *Les Confessions* 297–98; Squire, *Aelred of Rievaulx*, 38.

[15] Squire, *Aelred of Rievaulx*, 38–50, esp. 38, 42.

The *Confessions'* great themes certainly drew Aelred: the Christian's progress from spiritual infancy through youth to maturity; temptation, sin, and God's loving-kindness to those who struggle and fall; and the sinner's slow journey toward God. Aelred incorporated all of these in his sermons and treatises for the instruction of the monks at Rievaulx.[16] But his works also show his intimate acquaintance with others of Augustine's works, especially his commentary on the Genesis narrative of creation, *On Genesis According to the Letter*.[17] Squire calls particular attention to Aelred's reliance on this treatise: "From the beginning to the end of his career Aelred's use of this book becomes apparent at every important point and there is good reason to think that it meant for his general theological formation all that the *Confessions* meant for his imaginative and devotional life."[18] *On Genesis* pays particular attention to the creation of Adam and Eve and their relationship; Aelred's treatment in *Spiritual Friendship* of the origins and nature of friendship as grounded in the Genesis narrative recalls, though differing from, Augustine's.

Augustine's influence on Aelred as a writer and teacher extended beyond their shared spiritual and theological concerns to genre, form, and rhetoric. From his reading of the

[16] For Aelred as a monastic educator, see esp. the studies of Dumont in *Une Éducation*, and Amédée Hallier, *The Monastic Theology of Aelred of Rievaulx: An Experiential Theology*, trans. Columban Heaney, CS 2 (Shannon, Ireland: Cistercian Publications, 1969).

[17] The two thirteenth-century library catalogues from Rievaulx list forty-four of Augustine's works, including Conf, De bono, De Gen, *De civitate Dei*, *De Doctrina Christiana*, *Epistolae*, and *Soliloquia* (Anselm Hoste, *Bibliotheca Aelrediana: A Survey of the Manuscripts, Old Catalogues, Editions and Studies Concerning St. Aelred of Rievaulx*, Instrumenta Patristica 2 [Steenbruge: Martinus Nijhoff, 1962], 147–76, 201–4). See also David N. Bell, "Lists and Records of Books in English Cistercian Libraries," *Analecta Cisterciensia* 43 (1987): 181–222, and *An Index of Authors and Works in Cistercian Libraries in Great Britain*, CS 130 (Kalamazoo, MI: Cistercian Publications, 1992), 31–38, 250–52.

[18] Squire, *Aelred of Rievaulx*, 131; see 38–39, 159 n. 37.

*Confessions* Aelred knew the power of autobiographical narrative for teaching. As McEvoy says, "Nothing holds an audience or a reading public like a story, as Aelred well knew; and if the story is of the speaker or writer, it is of double value: it is an invitation to relax in the presence of the storyteller, the friend."[19] Augustine's mode of introspective recollection in the *Confessions* complemented the Ciceronian model of teaching through dialogue with which Aelred had already experimented in *Mirror of Charity*. Combining the Augustinian and Ciceronian approaches in *Spiritual Friendship* allowed him to address the least learned of his readers as well as the intellectually sophisticated, to adapt his style to his audience in accord with his words in the *Pastoral Prayer*: "Teach me therefore, sweet Lord, . . . to suit myself to all according to their capacity or simplicity and according to the time and place, in each case as you would have me do."[20]

## *Life and Teaching in Augustine and Aelred*

As both Augustine and Aelred incorporated events and people from their lives into their writing, it is not surprising that both are commonly described in terms of a predisposition for friendship, with their theoretical understanding of friendship subordinated to their experience. McEvoy and Marie Aquinas McNamara explain that predisposition as both genetic and highly individual. McEvoy writes, "Augustine, with his passionate North African temperament and vibrant intellectual curiosity had a profound gift for friendship."[21] And McNamara

[19] McEvoy, "Notes," 396.

[20] *Oratio Pastoralis* 7, ed. André Wilmart, CCCM 1:761; "The Pastoral Prayer," trans. R. Penelope Lawson, *Aelred of Rievaulx: Treatises and the Pastoral Prayer*, CF 2 (Kalamazoo, MI: Cistercian Publications, 1971), 115. Cf. Saint Benedict's advice on this point in his monastic rule, *Regula Benedicti* 64.19; *The Rule of St. Benedict in Latin and English with Notes*, ed. Timothy Fry (Collegeville, MN: Liturgical Press, 1981), 283.

[21] McEvoy, "*Philia*," 14.

says, "Because of his deeply affectionate nature and profound sensibility Saint Augustine was destined to have many friends." Later she notes: "in addition to a natural aptitude for friendship inherited from his parents, Augustine had a special genius for it."[22]

Adele M. Fiske also explains Augustine's views on friendship largely in terms of his own life and experience. As does McNamara, Fiske classifies Augustinian friendships according to the stage of life during which Augustine experienced them: the classical or Ciceronian friendships of his youth, the "enlightened" or "neoplatonic" friendships from before and just after his conversion, and "the Christian friendships of the latter years of his life, which are based on *caritas christiana*."[23] She thus treats Augustine's concept of friendship as based on his own experience and conceptualized in accord with his own intellectual and spiritual development, and she tacitly indicates his view that all friendship between non-Christians is false, with only Christians able to know true friendship. John F. Monagle agrees, commenting that "After his conversion Augustine becomes more and more convinced that no true and virtuous friendship can exist unless it is rooted in the common love of God."[24]

Brian McGuire regards as autobiographical not only Augustine's stories of personal friendship but also his fear of the danger posed by friendship to loving God. He explains Augustine's need for friends as having been so great as to override his desire for God: "However much Augustine wanted to find

[22] Marie Aquinas McNamara, *Friendship in Saint Augustine*, Studia Friburgensia, n.s. 20 (Fribourg: University Press, 1958), vii, 3.

[23] Fiske, "Survival," 74–76; Fiske's treatment of Augustine relies on the study of Augustine's letters by Venantius Nolte, *Augustins Freundschaftsideal in seinen Briefen* (Wurzburg: Rita-Verlag und -Druckerei, 1939).

[24] John F. Monagle, "Friendship in St. Augustine's Biography," *Augustinian Studies* 2 (1971): 85.

rest in God, he could not live without his friends. This makes up an overwhelming part of his existence."[25]

While Aelred's teaching on friendship has received more systematic study than Augustine's, scholars have also tended to focus on Aelred's life and personal experience rather than his thought. Maurice Powicke, for example, emphasizes Aelred's friendships rather than his articulation of the meaning of friendship: "this intensely human monk . . . seems to have found increasing satisfaction in his memories . . . of the friendships which were, he felt, the most precious thing this world had given him."[26] Squire echoes this approach: "it was friendship in the cloister that had sustained and supported and instructed him. . . . Always it had been there . . ., this love of people and this need to be loved, so that in the young Augustine of the *Confessions* Aelred seemed to find himself."[27] McGuire goes still further, making explicit what the others imply when he insists on *Spiritual Friendship* as autobiography: "Aelred's *De spiritali amicitia* . . . is the distillation of Aelred's life experience rather than a set of rules for friendship."[28]

Regarding the subject of friendship, then, both Augustine and Aelred are popularly defined as men who loved to be with other people rather than as thinkers and writers who developed theoretical understandings of the place of human friendship in Christian faith and life and of the relationship between love of God and love of the neighbor. But such an approach is critically naive, privileging the genre and form used by the two men over their rhetorical purpose. Comprehension of Augustine's and Aelred's teaching requires analysis of what they wrote rather than what they may have experienced, a recognition of their use of personal narrative as a vehicle

[25] Brian Patrick McGuire, *Friendship and Community: The Monastic Experience, 350–1250*, CS 95 (Kalamazoo, MI: Cistercian Publications, 1988), 47.

[26] Daniel, *Vita Ailredi Abbatis Rievall'*, xlv.

[27] Squire, *Aelred of Rievaulx*, 99.

[28] McGuire, *Friendship*, 297.

through which to explore the relationship of human beings with one another and with God. Both of these works thus contain within their narratives of apparently candid autobiographical reminiscence narrative *personae*—the first-person narrator in Augustine and the abbot-teacher in Aelred—who articulate their authors' teaching while remaining distinct from those creators. Both *personae* have many friends, but these friendships serve as dramatized explications of the authors' views on friendship.[29]

Scholars have of course already argued against an ingenuous reading of the *Confessions*. Peter Brown notes that in the *Confessions* Augustine appropriates the already familiar convention of using the genres of prayer and autobiography for intellectual purpose: "Prayer . . . was a recognized vehicle for speculative enquiry. . . . The *Confessions* were . . . a prolonged exploration of the nature of God written in the form of a prayer."[30] And Karl Morrison has spoken of the *Confessions* as "a literary genre masquerading as a prayer."[31] Scholars have also recognized *Spiritual Friendship* as a work of speculative inquiry using Ciceronian dialogue to explore the role of friendship in human experience and its relationship to the love of God. Charles

[29] During the 2000 Ecumenical Institute at Assumption College William Babcock noted the presence in the *Confessions* of three Augustines: the young man whose experiences are recalled, the older man who recalls and comments on those experiences, and the author who coordinates the narrative and commentary. For useful discussions of this issue see, e.g., Georges Gusdorf, "Conditions and Limits of Autobiography," trans. James Olney; and Barrett J. Mandel, "Full of Life Now," *Autobiography: Essays Theoretical and Critical*, ed. James Olney (Princeton, NJ: Princeton University Press, 1980), 28–48, 49–72; Thomas J. Heffernan, *Sacred Biography: Saints and Their Biographers in the Middle Ages* (New York: Oxford University Press, 1988), 3–71; and, in the context of imaginative literature, E. Talbot Donaldson, "Chaucer the Pilgrim," PMLA 69 (1954): 928–36.

[30] Brown also refers to the work as "an autobiography in which the author has imposed a drastic, fully-conscious choice of what is significant" (*Augustine of Hippo: A Biography* [Berkeley: University of California Press, 1967], 166, 169).

[31] "The End of Christian Art," 5 May 2000, plenary address at the 35th International Medieval Studies Congress.

Dumont concludes his discussion of Aelred's admiration of patristic authors' use of profane authors for sacred purpose by pointing to the doctrinal effectiveness of the work's revision of Cicero: "if one searches for a doctrinal work on Christian friendship, a theology of that most human reality, there is no work, no finished writing in all of Christian literature which is more to the point than Aelred's treatise."[32]

Both Augustine and Aelred combine central aspects of Ciceronian friendship with Christianity, embodying their teaching in anecdotes of personal experience.[33] They begin with Cicero's definition of friendship, slightly adapted,[34] cite some of his examples of friends and statements about friendship,

[32] Dumont, {"*L'Amitié spirituelle* d'Ælred de Rievaulx," in} *Une éducation du cœur: La spiritualité de saint Bernard et de saint Ælred*, Pain de Cîteaux 3,10 (Oka, Canada: Abbaye Cistercienne Notre-Dame-du-Lac, 1996), 351.

[33] My analysis here of both authors' views is restricted to relationships they define with the word *amicitia* or its derivatives, though Augustine is inconsistent in his terminology, often using *amicitia* for relationships other than true friendships and sometimes using other words in reference to relationships that he may have considered friendships. Monagle notes that Augustine sometimes uses *amicitia* "loosely," i.e., "in a pejorative sense," and sometimes interchanges words such as *amor*, *delectio*, and *caritas*, "which express the union of friendship and affection" ("Friendship," 83–84). Others identify Augustinian passages using terms other than *amicitia*, e.g., *concordia* and *benevolentia*, as describing friendship; see, e.g., Donald X. Burt, *Friendship and Society: An Introduction to Augustine's Practical Philosophy* (Grand Rapids, MI: Eerdmans, 1999), and his earlier study "Friendship and Subordination in Earthly Societies," *Augustinian Studies* 22 (1991): 83–123.

[34] Cicero defines friendship as "omnium divinarum humanarumque rerum cum benevolentia et caritate consensio" (De am 6.20; Cicero, *De senectute, De amicitia, De divinatione*, trans. William Armistead Falconer, Loeb [London: Heinemann, 1923], 108–211). In his letter to Marcianus Augustine slightly alters the phrase and identifies the mutual love of Christ as the necessary "agreement in things divine" (Ep 258, *St. Augustine: Select Letters*, No. 59, Loeb [Cambridge, MA: Harvard University Press, 1980], 491–99). Aelred also begins with the Ciceronian definition following Augustine's phrasing (Spir am 1.11 {CCCM 1:685; CF 5:55}) but finally renders it as "rerum diuinarum et humanarum cum quadam caritate et beneuolentia *summa* consensio" (3.8; emphasis mine {CCCM 1:319; CF 5:90}). Unlike Augustine, Aelred never explains what he understands by "agreement on things divine" or identifies that agreement with Christian faith.

and borrow different aspects of his structure even while explaining friendship as a gift of God and at least sometimes an aid in seeking God. They also insist on the inherent sweetness of friendship, echoing the classical trope attributing sweetness to friendship as well as early Christian writers' association of that trope with God; so they link a classical view of friendship with a Christian understanding of the divine and characterize God as the Christian's friend.[35]

In the *Confessions* Augustine repeatedly contrasts the deceptive sweetness of friendship with God's true sweetness. Of a friend he writes, "there was sweetness in our friendship," a few lines later recalling "a friendship that was sweeter to me than all the joys of life as I lived it then."[36] But he calls God "dulcedo mea sancta" and explains his examination of his life as prompted by the love of God and God's sweetness: "For love of your love I shall retrace my wicked ways. The memory is bitter, but it will help me to savor your sweetness, the sweetness that never deceives, sweetness joyful and secure."[37]

Aelred also uses the language of sweetness for both human and divine love throughout his ascetic works, especially when he writes of the coming together of the divine and the human in the incarnation.[38] In *Spiritual Friendship* he not only defines friendship as "that virtue by which spirits are bound by ties of love of sweetness" but also writes of "the honey of the most sweet name of Jesus."[39] Through such an integrated under-

[35] Fiske, "Survival," 81; Franz Posset, "The Sweetness of God," ABR 44 (1993): 143–47.

[36] Augustine, Conf 4.4.

[37] Augustine, Conf 1.4; 2.1.

[38] E.g., Aelred, Inst incl 29, 31, ed. C. H. Talbot, CCCM 1:663, 668 {CF 2:80, 87}; cf. Dutton, "The Feet and the Face of God: {The Humanity of Christ in Bernard of Clairvaux and Aelred of Rievaulx," in *Bernardus Magister*, ed. John R. Sommerfeldt, CS 135 (Kalamazoo, MI: Cistercian Publications, 1992)}, 203–23.

[39] Aelred, Spir am 1.21 Prol. {CCCM 1:292, 288; CF 5:59, 54}. McEvoy discusses Aelred's use of sweetness in "Notes," 399–400. The association of sweetness with wisdom and with Christ as Wisdom is common in Cistercian

standing of friendship and of God he insists that through friendship one comes to the love and knowledge of Christ, where sweetness is made complete:

> And so in friendship are joined honor and charm, truth and joy, sweetness and good will, affection and action. And all these are begun by Christ, advanced through Christ, and perfected in Christ. Therefore not too steep or unnatural does the ascent appear from Christ as the inspiration of the love by which we love our friend, to Christ giving himself to us as a friend whom we love, so that charm may follow upon charm, sweetness upon sweetness, and affection upon affection.[40]

But a fundamental difference separates Augustine and Aelred in their understanding of friendship and its relationship to God. For Augustine friendship is fundamentally of the flesh rather than of the spirit, something to take pleasure in for a time and then to transcend. Even true friendship he regards as given by God in order that the friends may seek God together; for him friendship is not to be enjoyed in itself but rather used for the enjoyment of God. Like all such gifts, however, friendship may sometimes distract one from loving God.

Aelred, however, consistently expresses confidence in God's gift of friendship as good in itself. He treats it as part of the order of creation and as God's image in his creatures. Furthermore, he says, God sanctified friendship through his incarnation and will perfect it in eternity, when God himself will be the friend of all. Thus for Aelred all friendship, even that which is not yet spiritual friendship, leads to God, manifests God's presence, and anticipates beatitude. Rather than warning that love of a mortal man or woman may interfere with one's progress to God, Aelred explains friendship as sacramental, a way

---

writing; see Edith Scholl, "The Sweetness of the Lord: *Dulcis* and *Suavis*," CSQ 27 (1992): 359–66; Franz Posset, "*Christi Dulcedo*: 'The Sweetness of Christ' in Western Christian Spirituality," CSQ 30 (1995): 245–65, esp. 249–51; cf. Edith Scholl, "Sensing God," ABR 47 (1996): 341–57.

[40] Aelred, Spir am 2.20 {CCCM 1:306; CF 5:75}.

of knowing God now as in time to come.[41] The one who abides in friendship, he says, abides in God, and God in him: *Qui manet in amicitia, in Deo manet, et Deus in eo.*[42]

Finally the two authors differ formally. Augustine makes little effort to specify the place of friendship in human experience, and although the *Confessions* contains the core of his discussion of the subject, he touches on it over and over in his vast corpus, especially in his letters. Aelred is more schematic, devoting all of *Spiritual Friendship* to the topic while elsewhere touching it only in passing.[43] McEvoy is thus right both in

[41] Dumont identifies this position as grounded in incarnational theology and characteristically Cistercian: "C'est la doctrine sacramentelle de l'humanité du Christ, chère aux cisterciens, qui s'applique ici" {"L'amour fraternelle dans la doctrine monastique d'Aelred de Rievaulx,"} in *Une éducation du coeur*, Pain de Cîteaux 3,10 {Oka, Canada: Abbaye Cistercienne Notre-Dame-du-Lac, 1996}, 345. Elsewhere he comments that "C'est surtout dans l'amitié spirituelle, comme dans la dévotion à l'Humanité du Christ, que réapparaît à nos yeux de la foi la beauté de l'image de Dieu" ({"Aelred de Rievaulx, introduction à sa vie et à ses écrits,"} in *Une éducation du coeur*, Pain de Cîteaux 3,10 {Oka, Canada: Abbaye Cistercienne Notre-Dame-du-Lac, 1996}, 221). {See also Marsha L. Dutton, "Eat, Drink, and Be Merry" and "Intimacy and Imitation," chaps. 5 and 6 below.}

[42] Aelred, Spir am 1.70 {CCCM 1:301; CF 5:69}. This altered verse from 1 John 4:16 is a response to a question put to Fr. Aelred, the dialogue's abbot-teacher. When Ivo asks whether it is accurate to say of friendship what John does of charity, i.e., that God is charity, Fr. Aelred offers this substitute, so rejecting the equivalence of God and friendship but emphasizing God's presence in friendship. Aelred thus attempts as an author to ward off readers' misunderstanding of his point here, a misunderstanding that nonetheless plagues discussions of the passage. See, e.g., Squire, who gives the title "'God is Friendship'" to his chapter on Spir am (*Aelred of Rievaulx*, 98–111); and Jean Leclercq, "Friendship and Friends in the Monastic Life," CSQ 24 (1989): 298.

[43] Aelred's *Mirror of Charity* also talks about friendship as part of its exploration of the nature of human relationships in monastic life; see, e.g., Spec 3.39.107–10; ed. C. H. Talbot, CCCM 1:138–59; *The Mirror of Charity*, trans. Elizabeth Connor, CF 17 (Kalamazoo, MI: Cistercian Publications, 1990), 296–99; Kevin M. Long explores the role of friendship in Aelred's historical works in "Echoes of Friendship: *Amicitia* and *Affectus* in the Writings of Aelred of Rievaulx with Special Reference to His Minor Works and the Monastic Foundations of His Theory," dissertation, University of Western Australia, 1993.

noting Aelred's initial dependence on Augustine's ideas and method and in suggesting that Aelred's developed treatment of friendship goes beyond Augustine's: "Despite its systematic character, Augustine's theory of friendship received only episodic expression in his writings. The medieval disciple who best fulfilled the master's programmatic exploration of the theme was undoubtedly St. Aelred."[44]

## Augustine on Friendship and the Love of God

Though Augustine considers friendship throughout his works, his most concentrated discussion occurs in the fourth book of the *Confessions,* the section dealing with his young adulthood.[45] He uses the emotional and structural center of this book to explore the nature of friendship, articulating it in the context of recollected grief for the death of a friend and within a discussion of the impermanence of human life and the necessity of looking beyond things mortal to the eternal God. By placing that discussion so early in the work, well before the narration of conversion in book nine and the portrait of intellectual and spiritual maturity in books ten to twelve, he positions friendship near the center of the spiritual journey, between childish ignorance and adult knowledge of God as eternal Father.[46]

Augustine approaches this discussion of friendship through the narrative of a specific friendship that ends in death. He uses this story both to distinguish between the true friendship given by God and all other friendships and tacitly to acknowledge

[44] McEvoy, "*Philia,*" 16.

[45] For a brief overview of Augustine's teaching on friendship see Joseph T. Lienhard, "Friends, Friendship," *Augustine through the Ages: An Encyclopedia,* gen. ed. Allan D. Fitzgerald (Grand Rapids, MI: Eerdmans, 1999), 372–73.

[46] I have discussed the *Confessions* as the personalized paradigm of that journey in " 'When I Was a Child': Spiritual Infancy and God's Maternity in Augustine's *Confessions,*" in *Collectanea Augustiniana,* ed. Joseph Schnaubelt and Frederick Van Fleteren (New York: Lang, 1987), 113–40.

his theoretical dependence on Cicero. He begins his consideration of friendship by explaining the issues he will confront and defining friendship given by God as *vera amicitia* "true friendship," only then introducing the specific friendship that is his focus. In this approach he follows Cicero, who sets his dialogue on the nature and value of friendship just after the death of a friend of Gaius Laelius, the work's spokesman.[47] Augustine's treatment of friendship through the lens of a friend's death is thus a Ciceronian echo: it considers friendship in light of the certainty that it must end, asks whether with that knowledge one can bear to have friends, and concludes that the anticipation of death is no reason to reject friendship. Like Cicero, he concludes, as McGuire gracefully notes, that "some friends will die, others will betray us, but friendships will remain and persist, despite a world filled with disasters and uncertainties. . . . We cannot run away from the need we have for one another."[48]

### *The Origin and Experience of Friendships*

Augustine uses *amicitia* and its related term *amicus* for all kinds of friendships and friends, but he distinguishes between those friends and friendships that are true and those that are not. The distinction is ontological, determined not by the participants' experience but by a relationship's origin in human affection or in God. Friendships begin, he says, in shared experience and understanding, "in the affection of one mind for the other,"[49] but such grounds are insufficient for true friendship, which only God can create. He then portrays a friendship of his own as formed by shared age, history, and interests. Though such a friendship may be intensely satisfying, he says, it is false if the Holy Spirit is not present:

[47] Cf. Cicero, De am 1.4–5. {For a comparison of Cicero's and Aelred's dialogues, see Marsha L. Dutton, "Antiphonal Learning: Listening and Speaking in the Works of Aelred of Rievaulx," CSQ 54, no. 3 (2019): 273–75.}

[48] McGuire, *Friendship*, 54, 55.

[49] Augustine, Conf 2.2.

> Yet ours was not the friendship that should be between true friends, either when we were boys or at this later time. For no friendship is true unless you bind its members together by the love which is spread in our hearts by the Holy Ghost, who is given to us.[50]

His friendship, Augustine explains, was grounded not in God but in error, for the friend had never held "firmly or deeply to the true faith" until nearly the end of his life, and Augustine himself had in their early years pulled him away from truth.[51] Nonetheless, Augustine uses this relationship to represent all friendships. In Horace's words he defines a friend as the other half of one's soul,[52] and he tells of his own devastation at this friend's death. Of the profundity of the experience Augustine describes here McEvoy writes, "in this friendship, Augustine was confronted with all the mystery of human love for the first time. . . . only a friend . . . could stir the depths which sexual union, family affection and ordinary friendship had hitherto left quite unsuspected."[53]

Despite the deep emotion of these passages, their Ciceronian echoes and Augustine's failure to name the friend combine to make him an abstraction, less a knowable character than a personification of friendship. Perhaps Augustine withholds the friend's name—like that of the mistress a little earlier in the same book—to protect it, but for readers the effect in both cases is a distanced fictionalization, an embodiment of the concept of friend or, in the earlier case, sexual partner rather than a portrait of living beings bound in intimacy with the author. Whatever passionate reality underlies the story of the youthful friendship, Augustine treats it as a Ciceronian convention, an exemplum used to show the power of friendship and to signal the difference between the true and the untrue,

[50] Augustine, Conf 4.4.
[51] Augustine, Conf 4.4.
[52] Augustine, Conf 4.7.
[53] McEvoy, "*Anima una et cor unum*: Friendship and Spiritual Unity in Augustine," *Recherches de théologie ancienne et médiévale* 53 (1986): 51.

emphasizing the inevitable end of the latter and its emotional cost to the survivor.

Such friendships not only fail to lead to God but offend him and result in his chastisement, Augustine goes on, because their sweetness distracts from the eternal. Thus Augustine interprets the friend's death as God's punishment on the survivor, intended to call him back to God: ". . . you took him from this world. For you are the God of vengeance as well as the fountain of mercy. You follow close behind the fugitive and recall us to yourself in ways we cannot understand."[54]

But Augustine insists that even in death friendship may continue to pull the survivor from God. In his case, he says, the deceptive sweetness of grief seemed at first to replace the friend, further delaying his conversion rather than at once drawing him to God. He makes this point by describing his resistance to the impulse to reject mortal attachment and turn to God: "If I said 'Wait for God's help,' [my soul] did not obey. . . . to her, the well-loved man whom she had lost was better and more real than the shadowy being in whom I would have her trust."[55]

Throughout this discussion of death and grief after friendship Augustine insists on this distinction between the mortal and the immortal, the impermanent and the eternal, the friend and God. He also suggests that even as the mourner immerses himself in sorrow he slowly comes to recognize his helplessness and the healing that God offers:

> I lived in misery, like every man whose soul is tethered by the love of things that cannot last and then is agonized to lose them. Only then does he realize the sorry state he is in, and was in even before his loss. . . .
>
> What madness, to love a man as something more than human! What folly to grumble at the lot man has to bear! . . . My soul

[54] Augustine, Conf 4.4.
[55] Augustine, Conf 4.4.

> was a burden, bruised and bleeding. It was tired of the man who carried it, but I found no place to set it down to rest. . . . I had heart only for sighs and tears, for in them alone I found some shred of consolation. I knew, Lord, that I ought to offer it up to you, for you would heal it. But this I would not do, nor could I.[56]

In these passages Augustine makes a point that recurs throughout his writing: that it is wrong to invest one's love in something that will pass away, for the inevitable result of such misplaced affection is grief and resistance to God's love. Indeed he castigates himself less for the excess of his sorrow than for having so loved his friend despite knowing him to be mortal: "The grief I felt for the loss of my friend had struck so easily into my inmost heart simply because I had poured out my soul upon him, like water upon sand, loving a man who was mortal as though he were never to die."[57]

Finally Augustine explains the eschatological significance of human friendships. Loving a friend in God, he says, leads to God. But because only that friendship created by God brings God's peace and joy, failure to love a friend in God means failure to love God, with eternal suffering the certain result:

> Blessed are those who love you, O God, and love their friends in you and their enemies for your sake. They alone will never lose those who are dear to them, for they love them in one who is never lost, in God, our God who made heaven and earth and fills them with his presence, because by filling them he made them. No one can lose you, my God, unless he forsakes you. And if he forsakes you, where is he to go? If he abandons your love, his only refuge is your wrath. Wherever he turns, he will find your law to punish him, for your law is the truth and the truth is yourself.[58]

[56] Augustine, Conf 4.6, 7.
[57] Augustine, Conf 4.8.
[58] Augustine, Conf 4.9.

So Augustine's discussion of friendship in the *Confessions* ends, with God's law, God's truth, God's self—and with the implicit warning that one who loves the friend apart from God will know God's punishment. For Augustine God is the end of true friendship, while the untrue has no end but tears. Only God is to be loved in himself, the God who made it possible for mortals to know and love him by coming to them and drawing them to himself.

### *Friendship and Beatitude*

Augustine offers little hope for the continuation of friendships past death. In the case he recounts in book four, he says that because he loved his friend too much, forgetting his mortality, the friendship was doomed. Having formerly "loved him as though he were never to die," in bereavement the young Augustine doubted even the friend's salvation, fearing that he lived only in memory: "Perhaps this, too, is why I shrank from death, for fear that one whom I had loved so well might then be wholly dead."[59]

But while friendships grounded only in mutual experience and interests end with death, Augustine says, true friendship, between men bound together by God, need not so end. He holds out some possibility of a lasting bond through the story of his friend Nebridius, who "was most persistent in his search for the truth" and "had become a faithful Catholic" before he died, as had Augustine at the time of which he writes. Because this friendship was created by God, filled by the Holy Spirit, and lived for God, Augustine suggests that it may endure despite the friend's death:

> Now he lives in Abraham's bosom, and whatever may be the meaning of that bosom, there Nebridius lives, my very dear friend taken by you to be your son, . . . There he lives. . . . with

[59] Augustine, Conf 4.6.

> the lips of his spirit he drinks in wisdom at your fountain. . . . And I cannot believe that the draught intoxicates him so that he forgets me, for it is you, O Lord, whom he drinks in, and you are mindful of your servants.[60]

Finally Augustine suggests the possibility that by loving God instead of earthly things one may become God's friend, though his use of this phrasing seems a kind of metaphor for faith rather than an expression of intimate relationship. In book eight Ponticianus remembers when one of his friends was "filled with the love of holiness" and made aware of the meaninglessness of his efforts to attain preferment from the emperor. Suddenly the friend recognized the contrast between the vanity of his current life and the ease of turning to God: "Can we hope for anything better at court than to be the emperor's friends? . . . But if I wish, I can become the friend of God at this very moment."[61] Elsewhere Augustine makes this point even more clearly; he suggests in the letter to Marcianus that human friendship may unite the friends with God: "If you hold firmly onto these two [love of neighbor and love of God] with me, our friendship will be true and eternal and will join not only us to one another, but us to God himself."[62]

But mostly in the *Confessions* Augustine examines friendships that exist apart from God, using them to explain the difference between the origins of true friendship in God and all other friendships, with their different ends. While he writes often in his other works of the joys and values of human friendship and insists on the inherent sweetness of all friendships, in the *Confessions* he sees in such sweetness less joy than danger.

[60] Augustine, Conf 9.4.

[61] Augustine, Conf 8.6.

[62] Augustine, Ep 258.4; *St. Augustine: Select Letters*, 496. McEvoy calls this letter "the central statement of [Augustine's] mature views on Christian friendship, its relationship to the classical ideal, and its ambiance of charity" ("*Anima una*," 76).

### *Augustine's Structural Argument*

Augustine uses book four of the *Confessions* to present his views on friendship not only propositionally and narratively but also structurally. In this book as in the work as a whole, he places his discussion of the nature and value of friendship within the larger issue of human movement from the mortal and temporary to the immortal eternal God. Briefly here he considers four topics related analogically and hierarchically: worldly attachments, friendship, language, and the incarnation.[63] The book begins with examples of worldly matters that pull one away from God, including work for money, public speaking, and relationships with women. Although Augustine says that he himself resisted the wrongs inherent in both employment and sexual relationships, trying to teach honesty rather than falsehood and remaining faithful to his mistress, he recognizes in retrospect that while so engaged he wandered from God: "I was led astray myself and led others astray in my turn."[64] Such matters lead only from God and never toward, he suggests.

After these instances of things that are exclusively carnal, distracting one from the eternal, Augustine turns to his lengthy treatment of friendship. Though his discussion presents an untrue friendship as its exemplum, the narrative begins with a statement that true friendship originates in God, continues with Augustine's discovery of God's solace, and concludes with the assurance that those who love their friends in God will know God's blessing. Thus Augustine shows that unlike those things that are sought for self-satisfaction, true friendships come from God and contain within them the love of the

[63] Luc Verheijen offers a different structural analysis of this book in "The *Confessiones* of Saint Augustine: Two Grids of Composition and Reading," in *Collectanea Augustiniana*, ed. Joseph Schnaubelt and Frederick Van Fleteren (New York: Lang, 1987), 189–90.

[64] Augustine, Conf 4.1.

Holy Spirit, suggesting that God may use friendships to draw one to him.

The third and fourth steps in this structural argument consider things belonging inherently to God rather than to humankind: language and the incarnation. While friendships may be false as well as true, all language, however broken, participates in God, who is Logos.[65] Syntactically, Augustine explains, not only individual words but individual sounds move inevitably toward *sententia*, 'meaning': "Our speech appears as significant sounds, with no perfect sentence unless a word, once spoken, gives way so that another may follow."[66] Similarly, while language is incomplete and temporary, falling short of God's eternal perfection, it leads to and is completed in God. Indeed in his later narrative of the vision at Ostia Augustine indicates the link between human language and God's unbroken word by contrasting the two, recalling that after ascending into heaven he and Monica fell back to "the noises of our mouths, where a word has both beginning and ending, unlike your word, our Lord, who remains in himself forever without aging."[67]

Augustine's fourth step from flesh to spirit is the incarnation. While it too involves the human movement from the mortal to the eternal, even in human experience it begins not with human desire or effort but with God. Unlike human language, God's incarnation is complete and perfect, initiated only by God. In the incarnation God assumed human mortality, joining eternity to nature and so transforming it: "Our life descended here and took away our death and killed it out of the abundance of his own life . . . coming first into the Virgin's

[65] I have discussed this theme in "When I Was a Child," 120–22; cf. Ellen C. Caldwell, "The *loquaces muti* and the *Verbum infans*: Paradox and Language in the *Confessiones* of St. Augustine," in *Collectanea Augustiniana*, ed. Joseph Schnaubelt and Frederick Van Fleteren (New York: Lang, 1987), 101–11.

[66] Augustine, Conf 4.10.

[67] Augustine, Conf 9.10.

womb, whence humanity was married to him—in mortal flesh though never mortal—and thence came out like a bridegroom from his chamber."[68]

Augustine thus shapes book four of the *Confessions* so as to show friendship contextually, as superior to human relationships based on the satisfaction of desire—for money, for fame, for sex, for children—but inferior to language and to God's incarnation. The only effective route to God is that which God begins.

### *Friendship and Women in the* Confessions

Many scholars have asserted that Augustine held a view of friendship broader and more inclusive than the classical one, allowing friendship to women as well as men and considering his mistress and his mother to be friends. McNamara writes "Of all his friendships, that with Monica was the truest and deepest." Henry Chadwick calls her his "supreme friend." And Edward C. Sellner interprets as a reference to the mistress Augustine's recollection of "muddying the stream of friendship with the filth of lewdness."[69] Brown even seems to suggest that Augustine considered male-female friendship part of the order of creation; discussing Augustine's comment in *On Genesis* that *amicali quadam beneuolentia* prompted Adam to accept the fruit from Eve in Paradise, he translates the phrase as "the good nature of a friend" rather than the more literal "friendly good will."[70] McGuire develops Brown's translation

[68] Augustine, Conf 4.12.

[69] Augustine, Conf 3.1. McNamara, *Friendship*, 10; Henry Chadwick, *Augustine* (Oxford: Oxford University Press, 1986), 69; Edward C. Sellner, "Like a Kindling Fire: Meanings of Friendship in the Life and Writings of Augustine," *Spirituality Today* 43 (1991): 241–42, 250–53.

[70] Augustine, De Gen 11.42. Peter Brown, *The Body and Society: Men, Women, and Sexual Renunciation in Early Christianity*, Lectures on the History of Religions, n.s. 13 (New York: Columbia University Press, 1988), 402–3.

into a proposition: "In describing the relationship between Adam and Eve, Augustine spoke of their friendship."[71]

In the *Confessions*, however, Augustine tacitly excludes women from friendship, and his other works provide little indication that he ever thought differently. Despite what he portrays as a deep attachment to Monica and devotion to his long-time mistress and mother of his son, he gives no indication that he regards them as friends, and he never identifies any other woman as a friend. Indeed in this work he uses the noun *amica* only for abstractions except when commenting on Monica's ability to arbitrate between a friend and an enemy.[72] He repeatedly explains the relationship of men and women as grounded in the necessity for procreation, in works other than the *Confessions* citing for proof the Genesis account of creation.[73] His consistent position on this matter is perhaps most clearly conveyed in *On Genesis*, when he says that had there been no need for procreation, it would have been better for God to place two men in Paradise, "for living and talking together equally as two friends [*amici*], not a man and a woman. . . . I do not see [*inuenio*] what aid a woman can be to a man, other than for giving birth [*pariendi*]."[74]

[71] McGuire, *Friendship*, 54 n. 39; see also 56. McGuire's view that the classically trained Augustine considered Eve Adam's friend conflicts with his assumption elsewhere that such classical knowledge would have made Aelred unlikely to consider women as friends: "Since [Aelred] was aware of the classical use of this word [*amicitia*] only in terms of male bonds, I think we can rule out the possibility that he was hinting at a relationship with a woman" ("Sexual Awareness and Identity in Aelred of Rievaulx [1110–67]," ABR 45 [1994]: 199).

[72] Augustine, Conf 9.9. For Augustine's vocabulary see *Thesaurus Augustinianus*, curante CETEDOC, Corpus Christianorum, Thesaurus patrum Latinorum (Turnholt: Brepols, 1989).

[73] See, e.g., De bono 1.1, De Gen 9.3–11, and *De civitate Dei* 12.24. For a useful treatment of Augustine's views on women and friendship with particular attention to De bono, see Elizabeth Clark, " 'Adam's Only Companion': Augustine and the Early Christian Debate on Marriage," *Recherches Augustiniennes* 21 (1986): 139–62.

[74] Augustine, De Gen 9.5.

In the *Confessions* Augustine also treats the relationship between men and women as essentially sexual and, intentionally or unintentionally, procreative. When he precedes his discussion of friendship in book four with a statement of the two kinds of relationship possible between men and women, he uses his mistress to exemplify the topic, just as he subsequently uses the friend of his young adulthood for that of friendship. These two figures both personify inappropriate and dangerous kinds of relationship, the woman representing the sexual intimacy that violates God's plan for human procreation and the man representing the friendship that pulls away from God rather than cooperating in seeking him.

Thus just as Augustine offers two patterns of friendship, the one created by God and the other resisting God, so he also offers two patterns of relationship with women, both fundamentally sexual and neither resembling friendship. Marriage, designed by God, has childbearing as its purpose; the other bond, formed by sexual desire, regards childbearing as a misfortune: "I found out by my own experience the difference between the rule of the marriage agreement, contracted for the purpose of having children, and the pact of libidinous love, where even the birth of children is begrudged."[75] He thus insists that such affection as may exist between men and women results from emotional and sensual pleasure, with sex and procreation its only objects.[76]

Augustine's comments about male-female relationships in this book and their placement at the beginning of his graduated movement from self-serving activities to friendship, language, and the incarnation also convey his position that women have no value in a man's search for God. A wife may

[75] Augustine, Conf 4.2.

[76] Cf. Brown, *Augustine*, 62. In De bono Augustine says, however, that a barren marriage should not be dissolved and that all marriages should continue even after the years of childbearing are past, speaking of the natural companionship (*naturalem societatem*) that marriage creates between husband and wife (De bono 3.3).

bear a man's children, so helping to fulfill God's plan for procreation, and an enduring companionship between the husband and wife may result, but that relationship does not help to lead a man to God. And while a woman may draw her child to God by acting on behalf of God's maternity, as Augustine says Monica did for him, that maternal relationship and benefit is not equivalent to friendship but is instead an extension of woman's purpose to aid man through *pariendi*.[77]

Thus despite his intention of adding Christian understanding to classical views of friendship, in this respect Augustine departs little from the classical understanding of friendship's nature and the identity of those able to be friends. He sees in Christianity no reason to redefine friendship to include women. As McEvoy writes, "It took more than Augustine's former flirts, or his mistress, or his mother, to uncover his soul; for these were women."[78]

### *Theory and Life*

"Augustine will never be alone," Peter Brown has famously written.[79] Similarly McEvoy declares the value Augustine placed on friendship: "Friendship remains in Augustine's thought at the centre of human realisation." Augustine's own words from *The City of God*, which McEvoy goes on to cite, bear out the point: "What is there to console us in this human society full of errors and trials, save the genuine trust and mutual love of true and good friends?"[80]

But the very sweetness that Augustine apparently found in his own human relationships troubled him. Although he allowed for God's binding friends in the love of the Holy Spirit

[77] Brown says that Monica "had been the voice of God in his early life" (*Augustine* 30). For an exploration of this theme in the *Confessions* see Dutton, "When I Was a Child," 113–40.

[78] McEvoy, "*Anima una*," 51.

[79] Brown, *Augustine*, 61.

[80] Augustine, *De civitate Dei* 19.8; McEvoy, "*Philia*," 15.

and implied throughout the *Confessions* that friends were God's gift, using phrases like "you found me a friend,"[81] he seems to have viewed his friendships as always likely to keep him from seeking God or to lead him from God. As in this life nothing endures, he says, to love anything mortal is dangerous: one will certainly lose it, perhaps losing oneself as well.

Though Augustine informs Cicero's themes with Christian doctrine, insisting on the role of God in true friendship and the value of true friendship for seeking God, his position is still fundamentally classical: friendship is limited to men, to equals who recognize one another through mental—i.e., rational—affection and through similarities of experience and habits, to those who may seek God in company with one another. Further, despite the joy friendship gives, it is circumscribed by mortality and ends with death. His is always a Ciceronian view of friendship, however transformed by the power of God.

## Aelred of Rievaulx on Friendship and the Love of God

Although Aelred's treatment of friendship in *Spiritual Friendship* depends on Augustine's in many ways, Aelred contests the center of Augustine's teaching, declaring that love of one's friend, man or woman, leads not from but to God. He too says that friendships vary in quality, culminating in the highest and truest, *amicitia spiritalis*, but he insists that God created all friendship when he created the first man and woman. Hence even the lowest of friendships, those that Aelred only reluctantly calls friendship, may lead to the friendship that brings one into the embrace of Christ and so to knowledge of and friendship with God himself. Five times in the work he repeats variations of the same formula of progress to

[81] Augustine, Conf 7.6.

Christ, insisting that friendship "is begun by Christ, continued through Christ, and perfected in Christ."[82]

*Spiritual Friendship* echoes passages about the joys and benefits of human friendship from Aelred's earlier work, *Mirror of Charity*, but *Spiritual Friendship* is more explicit than *Mirror* in responding to Augustine's words and more thorough and systematic about the origins and nature of friendship. The Prologue of *Spiritual Friendship* defines the work as a Ciceronian examination of friendship's origin, nature, and benefits. Developing the argument within the give-and-take of dialogue among an abbot and three monks, Aelred like Augustine uses his work's structure as a dramatic realization of that teaching.

### *The Origin and Nature of Friendship*

Aelred grounds his doctrine of friendship in Paradise, with friendship an essential part of God's plan for his creatures. Indeed for Aelred human love seems to be an aspect of God's image in men and women. He thus articulates his theoretical consideration of friendship not through personal reminiscence but through the story of every human being, the biblical account of creation. Both charity and friendship began, he says, when God shaped creatures with a natural love of the society of their kind.[83] That love of society was God's oneness in them: "he determined . . . that peace should bring together [*componeret*] all his creatures and society unite them. Thus from him who is supremely and uniquely one, all should be allotted some trace of his unity."[84] Desire for the company of others

[82] E.g., Aelred, Spir am 1.8, 2.20 {CCCM 1:290, 306; CF 5:57, 75}.

[83] For Aelred's understanding of friendship as a way of sanctifying partners in marriage see Katherine M. TePas, "Spiritual Friendship in Aelred of Rievaulx and Mutual Sanctification in Marriage," CSQ 27 (1992): 63–76.

[84] Aelred, Spir am 1.53 {CCCM 1:298; CF 5:65}.

like oneself is for Aelred not a matter of individual experience but of God's universal plan.[85]

Further, Aelred explains, God especially extended his original concern for all creatures to the first man and woman. For them he transformed love of society into its human manifestations, charity and friendship, which were in the beginning almost indistinguishable:

> Finally, when God created humankind, in order to commend more highly the good of society, he said, "It is not good for a person to be alone. Let us make for this one a helper like himself." It was from no similar, or even from the same, material that divine might formed this helper, but as a clearer stimulus to charity and friendship he made the woman from the very substance of the man.[86]

Aelred identifies equality as an inherent element of charity and friendship. Moreover, he insists on God's intention that such equality define the relationship between women and men as well as between men:

> How beautiful it is that the second human being was taken from the side of the first, so that nature might teach that all are equal, as it were collateral, and that, as is characteristic of friendship, there is in human affairs neither a superior nor an inferior. So

[85] This discussion reflects Ambrose's treatment of creation in *De officiis ministrorum*, which includes the statement (1.169) that God's gift of *beneuolentia* to the first man and woman explains Eve's confidence in the serpent's words to her, in that she had no awareness of malevolence (ed. Antonio Cavasin, Corona Patrum Salesiana [Turin: Societa Editrice Internazionale, 1938], 5:165–66). (Cavasin comments that "con tutta la riverenza dovuta a saint'Ambrogio, c'è un po' da dubitare se sia persuasiva questa spiegazione della colpa di Eva" [5:166 n. 1].) Aelred's familiarity with Ambrose, especially the first book of *De officiis*, appears throughout Spir am; the Rievaulx catalogues (see n. 17 above) list fifteen of Ambrose's works. On Aelred's use of Ambrose see Squire, *Aelred of Rievaulx*, 48–49 and *passim*; Fiske, "Friendship," 100; {Dutton, "A Model for Friendship: Ambrose's Contribution to Aelred of Rievaulx's *Spiritual Friendship*," chap. 4 below}.

[86] Aelred, Spir am 1.57 {CCCM 1:298; CF 5:66}.

> nature from the very beginning implanted in human minds the desire for friendship and charity, a desire that an interior sense of loving soon increased with a taste of sweetness.[87]

Thus rather than with Augustine suggesting that Adam would have been happier in Eden with a man as a friend, Aelred explains Eve as the direct result of God's wish for friendship and charity among his human creatures and suggests that marriage—and sexual union within marriage—is no barrier to friendship.

Aelred cites Adam and Eve again later in the work when he warns that friendship is no excuse for sin, using them now as an example of inappropriate behavior between friends. Tacitly enlarging on Augustine's saying that Adam took the fruit from Eve out of friendly good will, Aelred says that Adam should instead have rebuked her: "For it is no excuse for sin that you sin for the sake of a friend. The first man, Adam, would have done better had he charged his wife with presumption instead of complying with her request by eating what was forbidden."[88] Thus Aelred uses the first people created by God as his model for both positive and negative manifestations of friendship.

### *Friendship in the Interim*

While in Paradise friendship and charity were essentially identical, Aelred says, after the Fall everything changed. As human morals became corrupted and the natural love that originally bound all people became less and less common, it became necessary for God to command that love as charity, to

[87] Aelred, Spir am 1.57–58 {CCCM 1:298–99; CF 5:66–67}. In De bono Augustine insists on the essential inequality of Eve when explaining that even without sexual congress between the man and the woman there could have been "a certain friendly and familial companionship, the one ruling, the other obeying" (*alterius regentis, alterius obsequentis amicalis quædam et germana conjunctio*) (De bono 1.1).

[88] Aelred, Spir am 2.40 {CCCM 1:310; CF 5:79}.

be exercised even toward those who, Aelred says "are burdensome and grievous to us."[89] But friendship persists still among the good as the remnant of the primitive impulse given by God, and the highest such friendship is that which leads directly to the knowledge and love of God.

Whereas Augustine suggests that friendships in which God binds the friends in the love of the Holy Spirit are rare, the exception rather than the rule, Aelred insists that the presence of God in friendship is the rule itself, an essential piece of what it means to be human. He further affirms God's presence in the personal experience of friendship with the first words of the work, spoken by the abbot-teacher to his young friend Ivo: "Here we are, you and I, and I hope that with us Christ is a third."[90] What is more, in the lived reality of friendship, he says, one may go beyond this confidence in Christ's presence to the intimate experience of Christ's love:

> And thus in praying to Christ on behalf of a friend, and for a friend's sake desiring to be heard by Christ, one directs one's attention with love and longing to Christ. Then it sometimes happens that quickly and imperceptibly the one love passes over into the other, and, as if touching the sweetness of Christ himself, one begins to taste how sweet he is and to feel how delightful. Thus mounting from that holy love with which one embraces a friend to that with which one embraces Christ, one may joyfully partake in fullness of the spiritual fruit of friendship, awaiting the fullness of all things in the life to come.[91]

Because friendship begins in God, Aelred says, it also ends in God, in this life and the next. Jesus is his authority on the

[89] Aelred, Spir am 2.19 {CCCM 1:306; CF 5:75}. Cf. Leclercq, "Friendship," 297.

[90] Aelred, Spir am 1.1 {CCCM 1:289; CF 5:55}. Cf. Matt 18:20. Aelred refers to God [*Deus*] when writing of events outside human history—e.g., creation and beatitude—and to Jesus or Christ when writing of human experience in time.

[91] Aelred, Spir am 3.133–34 {CCCM 1:349; CF 5:125–26}.

point: "Friendship is a stage bordering upon that perfection which consists in the love and knowledge of God, so that from being a friend of other people one becomes a friend of God, according to the words of the Savior in the Gospel: 'Now I will not call you servants, but my friends.' "[92]

Although Aelred rejects Augustine's sharp distinction between friendships that are true because created by God and those not so created, he too distinguishes among different kinds of human relationships. Since the Fall, he says, friendship and charity differ, with charity to be exercised toward all people in obedience to God's command and friendship being instinctive but uncommon. It develops, he goes on, in human experience through reason and affection combined, a kind of prudent chemistry, the mind and heart's collaboration in recognizing a kindred spirit. Charity is difficult but may (and must) be achieved, while friendship is natural, spontaneous, and unachievable through human effort. It is God's gift, grace itself, a survival of Paradise in the postlapsarian world.[93]

Aelred gives repeated instances of the continuation of friendship outside Paradise, showing it to link people of both the same and different sexes and to look toward eternal reunion with God.[94] He names as friends "the girl of Antioch" and the soldier who saved her from the brothel as well as David and Jonathan, and he cites Boaz's kindness to Ruth as exemplifying the way people ought to anticipate and respond to their friends' needs.[95]

But there is a difference, Aelred says, between friendship and other kinds of human associations, such as those grounded

[92] Aelred, Spir am 2.14 {CCCM 1:305; CF 5:73}. See John 15:15.

[93] Aelred, Spec car 3.20ff {CCCM 1:114; CF 17:253–54}. Cf. Spir am 3.54 {CCCM 1:327; CF 5:100}.

[94] Although Aelred gives no instances of friendships between two women in Spir am, the second of the two prefatory stories in *De quoddam mirabile miraculo* shows such a friendship (*De sanctimoniali de Wattun* 1 [PL 195:790] {CCCM 3:137–38; CF 71:111}).

[95] See Aelred, Spir am 1.29, 3.92–96, 3.100 {CCCM 1:294, 337, 339–40; CF 5:61, 111–13, 114}.

in vice or self-interest. Those are neither friendship nor charity: they lack the sweetness of the one and the obedience of the other. Nevertheless, the abbot who is the dialogue's teacher, Fr. Aelred, reluctantly applies to them too the word *amicitia*: "Let us allow that, because of some similarity in feelings, even those friendships that are not true may nevertheless be called friendships, so long as they are judiciously distinguished from that friendship which is spiritual and therefore true."[96] Verbally, then, Aelred identifies a difference between true and untrue friendships and names three types of friendship, two that seek something beyond themselves and the highest, whose reward is itself.[97] As Aelred explains, carnal friendship proceeds from human affection, and worldly friendship is born of desire for temporal advantage or possessions. But spiritual friendship is its own end:

> spiritual friendship, which we call true, is desired not for consideration of any worldly advantage or for any extrinsic cause, but from the dignity of its own nature and the feelings of the human heart, so that its fruit and reward are nothing other than itself. . . . For true friendship advances by perfecting itself and finds its fruit in feeling the sweetness of that perfection. And so spiritual friendship among the good is born of a similarity in life, morals, and pursuits, that is, it is agreement in matters human and divine with benevolence and charity.[98]

This first Aelredian definition of spiritual friendship is fundamentally Ciceronian; it expresses no peculiarly Christian

[96] Aelred, Spir am 1.37 {CCCM 1:295; CF 5:62}.

[97] Though Aelred could not have known Aristotle's treatment of friendship in books 8 and 9 of the *Nichomachean Ethics*, his discussion frequently corresponds closely to Aristotle's; see, e.g., Aristotle's similar distinction between those friendships prompted by utility and pleasure and friendships between the good, whose end is itself (*Ethics* 8.3.1–6).

[98] Aelred, Spir am 1.45–46 {CCCM 1:296–97; CF 5:64}. Cf. Cicero, De am 6.20. Throughout book eight of the *Ethics* Aristotle insists on friendship as restricted to the good, see, e.g., 8.3.6.

understanding. It also recalls Augustine's emphasis on the origin of friendship in shared experiences. Later Aelred provides other explanations of the human beginnings of friendship, as when, again quoting Cicero, he says that true friendship "proceeds from an esteem for virtue."[99] Toward the end of the work, however, he moves from virtue to love as the source of friendship, and finally, using Christ's own words, offers a Christian formulation: "Our Lord and Savior himself has written for us the formula of true friendship, saying 'You shall love your neighbor as yourself.' Behold the mirror."[100] Thus in four steps, while never excluding non-Christians, Aelred develops his explanation of friendship from a fully Ciceronian view to a fully Christian one.[101]

While Aelred is clear in distinguishing between "genuine or spiritual friendship" and those other friendships grounded neither in virtue nor in love, he insists that they too gradually draw one toward God. Four times he makes the point that imprudently formed friendships, even with people not well fitted for friendship, lead to God and that even friendships that begin for the wrong reasons may grow into spiritual friendship. It is in this context that he most sharply signals his disagreement with Augustine's differentiation between the effects of untrue and true friendships, twice identifying as Augustine's the passage from the *Confessions* about the friendships that

[99] Aelred, Spir am 2.38 {CCCM 1:309; CF 5:79}; Cicero, De am 37, 40.

[100] Aelred, Spir am 3.69 {CCCM 1:331; CF 5:104}.

[101] Aelred makes this four-step movement from carnal friendship to spiritual friendship explicit in the passage that ends with his restatement of the Ciceronian definition of friendship: "You see, therefore, the four steps [*gradus*] by which one mounts to the perfection of friendship" (Spir am 3.8 {CCCM 1:319; CF 5:90}). Matt 22:39; see Lev 19:18. Cf. Bernard of Clairvaux's "four degrees of love," which begin with what Bernard calls *amor carnalis*, loving oneself for one's own sake, and culminate in loving oneself for God's sake (Dil 8.23–10.29, ed. Jean Leclercq and H. M. Rochais, SBOp, 9 vols. [Rome: Editiones Cistercienses, 1957–1999], 3:138–44).

consoled Augustine after the death of his friend.[102] Explaining the way all friendship may lead to God, he cites the kind of friendship that Augustine declares untrue as an instance that may lead to spiritual friendship and so to friendship with God:

> This type of friendship belongs to the carnal, and especially to the young people, such as they once were, Augustine and the friend of whom he was then speaking. And yet this friendship, except for trifles and lies, if nothing dishonorable [*inhonestas*] enters into it, is to be tolerated in the hope of more abundant grace, as the beginnings of a holier friendship. By these beginnings, . . . with the growing seriousness of greater age and the illumination of the spiritual senses, one may with purer affections mount higher, as though from a region close by, just as yesterday we said that human friendship could easily change into a friendship with God himself because of the similarity between them.[103]

Thus whereas Augustine makes a sharp distinction between those friendships grounded entirely in mortal pleasure and potentially leading away from God, and those created by God and leading to him, Aelred promises that despite different sources in human experience, even carnal friendship may lead to spiritual friendship and so to God.

[102] Though Aelred presents this passage as referring to the friendship of Augustine and "his young friend," Augustine actually uses these words to describe the friendships to which he turned for solace after his friend's death (Conf 4.8).

[103] Aelred, Spir am 3.87 {CCCM 1:335–36; CF 5:109}. Aelred consistently condemns both heterosexual and homosexual intimacy outside marriage; such a condemnation is probably present in this passage's implication that "*inhonestas*" will prevent immature friendships from developing into spiritual friendship (Spir am 1.44, 3.87 {CCCM 1:296, 335–36; CF 5:63–64, 109}). See Marsha L. Dutton, "Aelred of Rievaulx on Friendship, Chastity, and Sex: The Sources," {CSQ 29 (1994): 121–96}, esp. 151–69, 185–86.

### *A Foretaste of Beatitude*

As friendship reaches its fruition in the life to come, Aelred says, even death is only a temporary interruption. Friendship not only leads to God but also anticipates beatitude, where friendship will be unbroken. *Spiritual Friendship* thus treats beatitude and its foretaste in this life almost indistinguishably. As friendship reaches fruition whenever one enters through love of the friend into the embrace of Christ and into the knowledge and love of God, friends experience that fullness now as in the time to come. For as friends find unity with one another they find it in and with God.

For Aelred the friendship that anticipates beatitude extends beyond two or three friends to the community, which is both the memorial of Paradise and the anticipation of beatitude. Throughout the work he equates friendship with community, calling it "that virtue by which . . . out of many are made one."[104] In the course of the work he slowly expands the community of friends from a few to all the good. After referring to the martyrs as "thousands of pairs of friends," he concludes that the members of the early church were themselves friends: "Were they not . . . strong in the virtue of true friendship, of whom it is written, 'And the multitude of believers were of only one heart and one soul; neither did anyone say that anything was his own, but all things were common to them.'"[105]

Such communities of friends were not limited to the early church but also continue into the present, Aelred says, explicating such a recapitulation of Paradise with two views of monastic community.[106] One of these is the community as seen from ordinary human perspective. Monks come late to meetings, listen to one another with boredom or irritation, wait to

[104] Aelred, Spir am 1.21 {CCCM 1:292; CF 5:59}.

[105] Aelred, Spir am 1:28 {CCCM 1:93–94; CF 5:60}; Acts 4:32.

[106] For a discussion of friendship and monastic community see Leclercq, "Friendship," 298–300, and Dumont, ["Chercher Dieu dans la communauté selon Aelred de Rievaulx," in] *Une Éducation du coeur*, 275–308, esp. 303–7.

get into conversation, backbite, bicker, and joke. Just as a good conversation gets underway it is time to eat. And people die. But the other view of the community is that from the view of eternity, the one that comes only occasionally, a vision of the time when all will love and be loved in fullness:

> The day before yesterday, as I was walking around the monastery's cloister, the brethren were sitting together in a most loving crown. As though among the delights of Paradise, with the leaves, flowers, and fruits of each single tree, I marveled. I found no one in that multitude whom I did not love, and, I felt sure, no one by whom I was not loved. I was filled with such joy that it surpassed all the delights of this world.[107]

As it was in Paradise and as it will be in beatitude, so it is in this life, Aelred says; it all depends on the way one looks at it.

Aelred ends *Spiritual Friendship* by insisting once again that friendship is a blessing in this life and to be enjoyed forever in the next. As the work begins with a pair of friends discussing friendship and continues with another pair in conversation with their abbot, it ends as that abbot recalls two early friendships of his own, friendships that opened to him the way to divine friendship and anticipated it. He then expands this discussion to the community of saints, no longer including just the martyrs and the early church or the monastic community but all the good, proclaiming their union with God. There the work ends, with a promise of eternal friendship in the city of God:

> Then . . . with the destruction of the sting of death together with death itself, whose pangs now often trouble us and force us to grieve for one another, with salvation secured, we shall rejoice in the supreme and eternal good, when this friendship to which here we admitted only a few will be poured out on all and will be poured by all back onto God, when God will be all in all.[108]

[107] Aelred, Spir am 3.82 {CCCM 1:334; CF 5:108}.

[108] Aelred, Spir am 3.134 {CCCM 1:349–50; CF 5:126}; 1 Cor 15:28.

### *Aelred's Structural Argument*

Like Augustine, Aelred uses the structure of his work to reinforce his teaching on friendship, dramatizing his argument through the human interactions that articulate it. Formally the work is a Ciceronian dialogue set in a monastery; brief scenes from monastic life begin each of the three books and end the first two. In the first book an abbot talks with a monk named Ivo who as a youth had read and loved Cicero's *On Friendship*; in the second and third books, Ivo having died, the abbot talks with two other monks, Walter and Gratian.[109] The work thus begins and continues with conversations between friends looking forward to time together rather than, as in Cicero and Augustine, backward with sorrow.

But in Aelred's work too death intervenes: at the beginning of book two Fr. Aelred explains to Walter that the work on friendship he began years before was interrupted by Ivo's death.[110] So Aelred structurally acknowledges the pain caused by a friend's death and the disruption it brings to the survivor's hopes and plans, but only after having first portrayed friendship unclouded by fear of its end. He uses Ivo's death to signal the truth that in this life friendship is always being interrupted while structurally dramatizing the assurance that the survivor of such a death may look happily back on friendship rather than regretting its sweetness or seeing its end as

[109] The abbot of the dialogue is named Aelred; to distinguish this dialogical character equivalent to Cicero's Laelius from Aelred as author of the work I here refer to the abbot as Fr. Aelred.

[110] Aelred, Spir am 2.5 {CCCM 1:303; CF 5:71}. Though McEvoy notes "the literary device of separating the first book from the second and third by a period of many years" ("Notes," 402), the abbot-teacher's explanation that after Ivo's death he left his work on friendship unfinished for some time is generally accepted as a statement of Aelred's own experience, with many scholars assuming on that basis that book one was written some years before books two and three. See, e.g., Squire, *Aelred*, 100. Such a literal reading underlies the common treatment of the work as implicitly autobiographical, a record of actual conversations rather than, as the Prologue explains it, a purposefully Christian revision of Cicero's De am (Aelred, Spir am Prol.5–6 {CCCM 1:288; CF 5:54}).

punishment. He offers the further certainty that in the life to come such separations will be overcome and friendship will endure, perfected and unbroken, forever.

Throughout the work Aelred provides other dramatic reinforcements of the joy of friendship despite constant interruptions, showing the fragmented reality of even on-going human interactions. At the beginning of both books one and two a monk waits impatiently for the abbot to leave other conversations and have private time for him, and in book three only one of two monks arrives on time for a scheduled conversation with the abbot. The conversation of each of the first two books ends abruptly when the abbot is needed elsewhere. The last book concludes, however, not in the brokenness of daily life but in anticipation of beatitude. So Aelred presents his teaching through the embodied experience of friendship, full of interruption in this life but complete and unbroken in the life to come, and the last lines of the work realize all that has been promised of enduring reunion with one's friends and with God.

### *Aelred's Response to Augustine*

Aelred departs from Augustine's teaching on friendship early in *Spiritual Friendship*, confronting their differences by using Ivo not only to raise the topic of friendship, like Cicero's Fannius, but to articulate Augustine's probable objections to the Aelredian view, with the abbot-teacher responding. Later Walter plays the same role, again raising the topic and struggling with some of the abbot's positions. The work's dialogue form thus allows Aelred to distinguish between positions he opposes, often those identified with Augustine, and those he advances, placing the former on the lips of the young monks and the latter on those of the abbot-teacher.

In book one Ivo's questions prompt the first statement of the work's argument, articulated by the abbot. To Ivo's inquiry about the meaning of friendship, Fr. Aelred offers Cicero's definition. When Ivo objects that according to that phrasing anyone at all could be a friend, even "pagans and Jews, and bad Christians,"[111] tacitly recalling Augustine's restriction of friendship to those joined by God, Fr. Aelred responds by mentioning Orestes and Pylades as ancient parallels to the Christian martyrs whom he identifies as friends.[112] He then reiterates Cicero's definition of friendship, only slightly qualifying the inclusiveness that worries Ivo by adding *inter bonos* to the definition: "And so spiritual friendship is born among the good of a similarity in life, morals, and pursuits, that is, it is agreement in matters human and divine with benevolence and charity."[113] Aelred thus confirms and insists on his understanding of friendship as broadly inclusive, God's gift to all humans, and resists Ivo's effort to restrict it to Christians, and good Christians at that.[114]

Having responded to Ivo's objection not by recanting his Ciceronian stance but by reaffirming it, Fr. Aelred explains and supports his position scripturally, through the Genesis narrative of creation. He thus does precisely what the work's Prologue promises: he reconciles the Bible and Christianity with Cicero's teaching.[115] While both Augustine and Aelred insist on God as the originator of friendships, for Augustine that creation occurs case by case, in the life of the individual and apparently only among Christians, but Aelred explains friendship as part of the natural order for humankind.[116]

[111] Aelred, Spir am 1.16 {CCCM 1:291; CF 5:58}.

[112] Cicero and Augustine also identify Pylades and Orestes as archetypal friends (De am 7.24; Conf 4.6).

[113] Aelred, Spir am 1.46 {CCCM 1:297; CF 5:64}.

[114] {See Marsha L. Dutton, "The Sacramentality of Community in Aelred," in *A Companion to Aelred of Rievaulx (1110–1167)*, ed. Marsha L. Dutton (Leiden/Boston: Brill, 2017), 263–67.}

[115] See Dumont, {"L'amour fraternal,"} 351.

[116] Scholars have generally incorrectly assumed that Aelred follows Augustine in restricting friendship to Christians. C. H. Talbot titled his translation of Aelred's work *Christian Friendship* (London: The Catholic Book Club, 1942), and McEvoy summarizes Aelred's view by saying that friendship is

The two authors differ not only regarding the origin of friendship but also on its purpose and value. For Augustine a true friendship requires one to love one's friend in God and for the sake of loving God, as one of the vehicles used in this life of exile to take one home to God.[117] But for Aelred friendship is not merely a matter of loving friends on the way to loving God but also God loving in and through the friend, himself present in his own love. Thus loving one's friend is for Aelred not distinct from loving God and not done for the sake of loving God; it is one result of God's love, one aspect of loving God and being loved by God. One need not avoid the friend or choose between the friend and God or even love the friend for the sake of God, but may simply by loving one's friend experience God's love and love God in return.[118]

### *Amare et amari*

Among the many Augustinian echoes in *Spiritual Friendship*, the one most consistently misunderstood in recent popular representations of Aelred is the phrase *amare et amari* "to love and be loved," which Augustine uses twice in the *Confessions* to describe his youthful obsession with love (2.2; 3.1). In the course of *Spiritual Friendship* Aelred gives the phrase a four-step transformation in form and meaning, so articulating his judgment that human friendship may gradually develop from an adolescent and self-centered desire to receive love into a joyous giving of love to one's neighbor and to God.[119]

---

"within the reach of every Christian" ("Notes" 410). Later, however, McEvoy comments somewhat less decisively that for Aelred, "The way of friendship is open to all who are not submerged in the selfishness of sin" ("*Philia*" 18). {See Dutton, "The Sacramentality of Community in Aelred," 263–67.

[117] Cf. Augustine, *De Doctrina Christiana* 1.4.4. But see also De bono 9.9.

[118] But see Aelred, Spec car 3.39.107–40.111 {CCCM 1:58–60; CF 17:296–300}.

[119] Talbot's critical edition of the work in CCCM 1 indicates no manuscript variation in any instance of this phrase.

Aelred's variations on *amare et amari* acknowledge Augustine's contribution to his thinking on the origin and nature of friendship while also signaling the essential difference between the two men's positions. Initially Aelred echoes the phrase twice in reference to the immature desire for human love, his own as a young man and then Gratian's. In both of these cases, however, he reverses the Augustinian phrasing to *amari et amare* "to be loved and to love."[120] Echoing Augustine, Aelred writes in the first words of the Prologue of his own youthful delight in love; later Walter describes Gratian in much the same words: "I might rightly call him a child of friendship, for his whole study is to be loved and to love. He risks being too avid for friendship and so being deceived by its likeness, taking the false for the true, the imagined for the real, the carnal for the spiritual."[121] Aelred thus tacitly identifies the easily misled human desire for love and friendship with the young Augustine's delight in love, treating it as characteristic of youthful immaturity and so subject to error, but mirroring and anticipating true love.[122]

In the final book of the dialogue Aelred returns to the Augustinian phrase, focusing on the realized relationship between human friendship and the knowledge and love of God, now emphasizing first the giving and then the receiving of love. First, however, he identifies loving and receiving love as necessary acts of reciprocity between those who love one another, using words in which Augustine himself reformulates *amare et amari*; then he returns for a third time to the original phrase,

[120] In Spec car Aelred uses the non-inverted Augustinian phrase to begin his discussion of the various kinds of human love: "Sed amare, inquis, et amari, quid tranquillius?" (Spec car 1.25.71; CCCM 1:42 {CF 17:128}).

[121] Aelred, Spir am 2.16 {CCCM 1:305; CF 5:74}. Cf. Augustine, Conf. 2.1–2; Aelred, Spir am Prol.1–2 {CCCM 1:287; CF 5:53}.

[122] C. S. Lewis refers to this adolescent desire as "Need-love," like Aelred understanding it as an important and necessary preliminary to what he calls "Gift-love" (*The Four Loves* [1960; repr. San Diego: Harcourt, 1988], 1–9 and *passim*).

at last reinverted to Augustine's order. In the first instance, the monk Walter lyrically describes the kind of friendship he enjoys, identifying it with Augustine and using Augustine's own words, which resonate with the biblical call to reciprocate God's love:

> For me and Gratian that friendship suffices that your Augustine describes: namely, to talk and jest together, to humor one another with goodwill, to read together, to discuss together . . . . By these and similar indications emanating from the hearts of those who love and are loved [*amantium et redamantium*] . . . to fuse our spirits by tinder, as it were, and out of many to make but one. This is what we think we should love in our friends, so that our conscience will be its own accuser if we have not loved the one who loves us, or if we have not returned love to the one who loves us.[123]

Although Walter states his preference for carnal friendship, explaining that spiritual friendship is "so sublime and so perfect that I dare not aspire to it,"[124] his words in this passage convey Aelred's rejection of Augustine's fear of human friendship by tacitly linking the mutual and maturing love of human friends to the reciprocal love of God and humankind, echoing Augustine's explanation of the love between friends as essentially identical to the appropriate human return of love to God's gift of love, the one a mirror image of the other. Aelred writes now no longer of friendship as a childish and self-seeking longing to receive love but instead as a desire to return love to those from whom one has received it.

As the work ends Aelred shows the full transformation of the human longing for love into the highest of friendships and so to the knowledge and love of God. Here the abbot-teacher explains spiritual friendship as the joyful culmination of the

[123] Aelred, Spir am 3.85–86 {CCCM 1:335; CF 5:109}. Augustine, Conf 4.9. Cf. 1 John 4:11.

[124] Aelred, Spir am 3.85 {CCCM 1:335; CF 5:109}.

youthful longing for love. Friendship, he concludes, reconciles the love of God and the love of neighbor, opening a way to Christ now and anticipating eternal union with one's friends and with God:

> Was it not a kind of portion of beatitude thus to love and thus to be loved [*amare et amari*], thus to help and to be helped, and so from the sweetness of fraternal charity to wing one's flight aloft to that more sublime splendor of divine love and by the ladder of charity now to mount to the embrace of Christ himself, and then to descend to the love of neighbor, there sweetly to rest?[125]

Thus Aelred in four steps transforms the immature human desire to be loved and to love into Augustine's view of friendship as the human equivalent of and preparation for responding with love to God's love, and finally into his own rich understanding of spiritual friendship as intimacy with Christ in this life and a foretaste of love unbroken in the life to come. At last, he says, when carnal friendship becomes spiritual and achieves fruition in beatitude, when God is all in all, then the youthful hunger to receive love will have become a readiness to give in full, an eager response to God's gift of divine love. For that is God's unity within his creation, God's love for society manifested in human friendship, God's image still present in mortal men and women.

The difference between Augustine's and Aelred's use of *amare et amari* indicates their agreement that friendship has both giving and receiving of love as necessary elements while also reflecting the fundamental difference between their views on the possibility of growing as a friend. When Augustine portrays the adolescent desire to love and be loved as a deceptive desire that overwhelms and overcomes all other desires, he explains it narratively as part of what delayed his own

[125] Aelred, Spir am 3.127 {CCCM 1:348; CF 5:124}. Cf. Aelred's Iesu 3.30–31 {CCCM 1:276–77; CF 2:37–39}.

conversion, drawing him toward human friendship and away from God, though he indicates his confidence that God can use even the consequences of such a friendship to draw one to him. But Aelred suggests that such a hunger for human love, even when it begins as a longing to receive and only later matures into a readiness to give, is merely an incomplete experience of the true love of friend and of God: not bad, but an immaturity that God will transform "with the growing seriousness of greater age and the illumination of the spiritual senses."[126] Neither author wishes anyone to remain at the stage of adolescent desire, but Augustine requires that one replace such untrue friendships with friendships given by God, whereas Aelred regards all friendship, untrue as well as true, as God's gift, manifesting God's presence and leading to friendship with God.

Augustine and Aelred finally agree, however, that in true friendship, in this life and in the life to come, the human desire for love is turned at last the right way round, and that God may draw all who love to himself through their love of one another. Then at last the mature, developed, consciously welcomed desire to love and be loved may be known for what it is: love itself, God present in human friendship, friends abiding in God and God in them. There, in friendship eternal and all-encompassing, the search for God reaches its true end.

[126] Aelred, Spir am 3.87 {CCCM 1:336; CF 5:109}.

*Chapter 4*

# A Model for Friendship: Ambrose's Contribution to Aelred of Rievaulx's *Spiritual Friendship*

*In memory of and gratitude to*
*Père Charles Dumont, OCSO, 1918–2009*

Aelred of Rievaulx pays explicit homage in his great treatise *Spiritual Friendship* to three authors: Cicero, Ambrose, and Augustine. Writing sometime after the April 1164 death of the anti-pope Victor IV, Aelred repeatedly quotes from Cicero's *On Friendship*, Ambrose's *On Duties*, and Augustine's *Confessions*. From time to time he also names the three authors—Cicero eleven times, Ambrose six times, and Augustine three times. While he also cites others, such as Jerome and Terence, it is Cicero, Ambrose, and Augustine who dominate *Spiritual Friendship*.[1]

[1] This paper appears here by permission from *The American Benedictine Review*, where it was first published (ABR 64, no. 1 [2013]: 39–66). It was originally presented at the 2010 Cistercian Studies Conference, celebrating the nine hundredth anniversary of Aelred's death. Citations of *Spiritual Friendship* come from Aelredi Rievallensis, *De spirituali amicitia*, in *Aelredi Rievallensis Opera omnia*, ed. Anselm Hoste and C. H. Talbot, Corpus Christianorum, Continuatio Mediaevalis [CCCM] 1 (Turnhout: Brepols, 1971), 279–350; translations for the most part follow *Spiritual Friendship*, trans. Lawrence Braceland, ed. Marsha L. Dutton, Cistercian Fathers series [CF] 5 (Collegeville, MN: Cistercian Publications, 2010). Citations and quotations of Ambrose come (with occasional slight alterations) from *De officiis*, ed. and trans. Ivor J.

Oddly, Aelred's insistent use of Ambrose's late-fourth-century *On Duties* has largely escaped scholars' attention. Although several people have noted the presence of Ambrosian borrowings throughout *Spiritual Friendship*, few have examined their ubiquity or function, perhaps agreeing with Brian Patrick McGuire's sense that there is simply not much to say: "Aelred's borrowings from Ambrose are so straightforward that they have attracted little attention."[2]

In *Spiritual Friendship* Aelred borrows from Ambrose frequently and often reverentially, calling him both *Beatus Ambrosius* and *Sanctus Ambrosius*, though as Ambrose himself borrows widely from Cicero's *On Friendship* and Aelred does not attribute Ambrosian quotations to Ambrose until book 3 of *Spiritual Friendship*, the immediate source of Aelred's quotations is often unclear.[3] More significant than frequency of citation, though, is the fact that Ambrose's treatment of friendship contributed significantly to Aelred's views on the origin and meaning of human friendship.

Two Ambrosian threads are of particular importance in shaping the theological argument of *Spiritual Friendship*. From beginning to end, Aelred interweaves God's role in creating, modeling, and participating in human friendship with the human experience of friendship, as friends share their every thought and emotion with one another. In both ways Aelred follows Ambrose's lead, insisting on the divine origin and

Davidson, 2 vols. (Oxford: Oxford University Press, 2001) (hereafter Duties). Scholars now agree that the correct title of the work is not *De officiis ministrorum* but *De officiis*. I am grateful to J. Stephen Russell and Fr. Mark Scott, OCSO, for their assistance.

[2] Brian Patrick McGuire, *Friendship and Community: The Monastic Experience (350–1250)*, CS 95 (Kalamazoo, MI: Cistercian Publications, 1988), 126. McGuire calls attention to the borrowings in his note to this sentence, remarking specifically on their neglect by scholars (492 n. 92).

[3] One result and consequent cause of scholarly inattention to Aelred's dependence on Ambrose is that notes to both the critical edition and the various translations of *Spiritual Friendship* cite Cicero much more often than Ambrose, even when both authors make the same point and use the same language.

continuation of friendship and on human friendship as a matter of emotional and intellectual intimacy. But whereas Ambrose keeps the two themes separate, not linking God's role in creating friendship to its human experience, Aelred integrates them, so enunciating unified and sacramental understanding of friendship as both a reminiscence of Paradise and anticipation of beatitude, with the friend, the other half of oneself, known and loved always in Christ. Such a spiritual friendship is the subject of his work; he insists that it is not only its own reward in this life but that it also leads the friends to God now and in time to come. It is Ambrose, however, who provides both the core of Aelred's definition of spiritual friendship and the starting point for Aelred's view of spiritual friendship as sacramental—instituted by God, characterized by intellectual and emotional intimacy in the presence of Christ, and culminating in eternal friendship with God.

## Ambrosian and Aelredian Scholarship

Over the past seventy-five years a number of scholars have explored Ambrose's ethical teaching in *On Duties*, for the most part looking backward to Cicero's influence on Ambrose rather than ahead to Ambrose's influence on later authors. Almost inevitably, then, a central question asked by such scholars has been whether Ambrose reshaped Cicero's teaching with Christian understanding. In 1992, Carolinne White insisted that Ambrose's discussion of friendship remained essentially Ciceronian, mostly uninfluenced by Christianity. Despite the introduction of Christian concepts into Duties, she stated, Ambrose's views remained largely secular: "Ambrose regards human love, even among Christians, as a purely human relationship which, though a support in this life and a source of joy, is not directly connected with a man's love for God."[4]

[4] Carolinne White, *Christian Friendship in the Fourth Century* (Cambridge, UK: Cambridge University Press, 1992), 125–26.

Ambrose's theological works, White went on to say, treated friendship not as a good in itself but merely as a way of making a theological point. Although noting Ambrose's use of friendship as a way of explaining the Trinity, she denied that his use of the parallel had theological implications in his understanding of friendship: "On the occasions when he mentions friendship in his theological works he does not regard it in terms of the human relationship itself but merely as an analogy with the even greater unity of the Trinity."[5]

In a 1994 overview of friendship in medieval and early Renaissance literature, Reginald Hyatte mentioned Ambrose's view of Christ and his Father as model friends and called attention to Ambrose's replacement of Cicero's Roman examples of friendship with biblical ones. Like White, however, he viewed Ambrose's introduction of Christian elements into his discussion of friendship as theologically insignificant: "St. Ambrose . . . adapted to a Christian context . . . many of Cicero's precepts from *On Duties* and *Laelius*, but he did not draw a clear link between Christian friendship based on mutual love of virtue and obligations and the ends of loving God and fraternal charity."[6]

Forty years earlier, Alcuin F. Coyle had argued for Ambrose's having provided a Christian leaven to Cicero:

> St. Ambrose was a pioneer in the field of exposition of Christian ethics. . . . He took from Cicero his general plan, vocabulary, and even at times whole sentences with scarcely any changes in wording. However, his approach was entirely different from that of Cicero—for at the very beginning, he placed his treatise on the spiritual level, by basing it on the truths of faith. . . . [Cicero's *On Duties*] is purely philosophical; the latter [Ambrose's],

[5] White, *Christian Friendship*, 127.

[6] Reginald Hyatte, *The Arts of Friendship: The Idealization of Friendship in Medieval and Early Renaissance Literature* (Leiden: Brill, 1994), 46, 61–68, here 61.

> being essentially based on religion, immediately identifies itself with the highest and deepest motives for human conduct.[7]

Luigi Pizzolato too has argued that Ambrose's discussion of friendship is essentially Christian. In his 1993 book on the history of friendship he stated that Ambrose Christianized the Ciceronian understanding of good will, which Ambrose defined as the source and core of friendship, by turning it from something purely natural to something that "transcends nature and becomes synonymous with grace."[8] Pizzolato called particular attention to Ambrose's statement that good will is of the essence of Christian life: "Good will is enhanced by the communal nature of the church, by our partnership in the faith, by our fellowship as initiates, by our kinship as recipients of grace, and by our communion in the mysteries."[9]

Pizzolato also found a strong Christian element in the Ambrosian description of the relationship between charity and friendship. He called particular attention to charity's role in ensuring friendship's bonding of men and women to God:

> The subordination of friendship to the rule of charity is the guardian of the true nature of friendship, . . . because it assures to friendship the value of a fully human reality, insofar as it unites humans in the context of the union of humankind with God, upon which union humankind ontologically depends.[10]

Pizzolato noted Ambrose's treatment of friendship in *On the Holy Spirit* as a way of understanding the relationships of the

[7] Alcuin F. Coyle, "Cicero's De Officiis and De Officiis Ministrorum of St. Ambrose," *Franciscan Studies* 15 (1955): 256.

[8] Luigi Pizzolato, *L'Amicizia nel mondo giudaico e cristiano antico* (Turin: Giulio Einandi, 1993), 269–76, here 270. Both Latin *benevolentia* and Italian *benevolenza* are translated here as *good will.*

[9] Ambrose, Duties 1.33.170; Pizzolato, *L'Amicizia*, 271.

[10] Pizzolato, *L'Amicizia*, 275.

persons of the Trinity, interpreting that metaphor as an indication of the theological value that Ambrose placed on friendship: "In fact the concept of the *alter ego* permits Ambrose to identify the relationship of friends with the mystery of the union of the Trinity."[11]

Boniface Ramsey mentioned Duties only four times in his 1997 *Ambrose*, referring to its discussion of "the virtue of friendship" merely to comment that it offers no insights about Ambrose's personal life. But while he concluded that "Ambrose's writings are overwhelmingly derivative," he agreed with the view that Duties "gave Cicero an entirely Christian thrust."[12]

Scholarly concern with Ambrose's use of Cicero has militated against investigation of Ambrose's influence on Aelred. Even Ambrosian scholars who have credited Ambrose with contributing to the Christianizing of classical views on friendship have for the most part failed to recognize the contribution of Duties to Aelred's *Spiritual Friendship*. The only significant exception to this widespread neglect of Aelred's dependence on Ambrose is Adele M. Fiske's 1955 Fordham dissertation, "The Survival and Development of the Ancient Concept of Friendship in the Early Middle Ages." This study contains a concise overview of Ambrose's views on friendship and argues for their contribution to Aelred's understanding of the nature of human friendship. Fiske specifically noted Ambrose's explanation of good will as the source of friendship while also suggesting that Ambrose equates good will with both friendship and charity: "*Benevolentia* seems to be identified with *amicitia* in one text" (citing Duties 1.32.167). Again she said, "In the thought of Ambrose, this rather vague quality is transformed into Christian 'good will' that is really love of God, *caritas*." She concluded her evaluation of Ambrose by calling

[11] Pizzolato, *L'Amicizia*, 270; Ambrose, *De spiritu sancto* 2.154; *De spiritu sancto*, ed. Gerhard Crone (Münster: Aschendorff, 1978); Saint Ambrose, *Theological and Dogmatic Works*, trans. Roy J. Deferrari (Washington, DC: The Catholic University of America Press, 1963), 151.

[12] Boniface Ramsey, *Ambrose* (London: Routledge, 1997), 44, 53.

attention to the close relationship he saw between good will, charity, and friendship:

> St. Ambrose is indeed Ciceronian in his thought on friendship, but significant differences appear. The source and nature of friendship is not in the intellect, a *consensio*, but in the will, *benevolentia*. Friendship is implicitly identified with *caritas* and, for all its human qualities, finds its model, *forma*, in Christ.[13]

Fiske called particular attention to two aspects of Ambrose's work that reappear centrally in Aelred's *Spiritual Friendship*: God's gift of good will to Adam and Eve in Paradise, and friendship as a matter of total openness between friends. Of the first she cited Ambrose's explanation of the origin of good will in human life:

> the source of benevolence, for him, is not *amor*, but God. It came out of paradise and has filled the world. It first was placed by God in man and woman, to make them one in spirit as well as body. This text is interesting, for it is perhaps the source of Aelred's citation of Adam and Eve as examples of friendship. Moreover, it applies the scriptural text of the unity of marriage to the concept of friendship, as well as suggesting the "paradisical" character of friendship that links it with the restoration of the image.[14]

Writing of Ambrose's description of friendship, Fiske focused on his treatment of friends' emotional and intellectual unity: "A friend is an *alter tu*; by *caritas* he is embraced in one body; he is one soul, *unanimis*. This oneness is in spirit and mind, unity of soul, undivided in spirit, *individuus spiritus*. . . . A friend hides nothing, if he is a true friend."[15]

[13] Adele M. Fiske, "The Survival and Development of the Ancient Concept of Friendship in the Early Middle Ages," PhD dissertation, Fordham University, 1955, 93–115, here 96–98, 114.

[14] Fiske, "Survival," 100.

[15] Fiske, "Survival," 103.

Fiske's work has had minimal impact on subsequent scholarship, which has discounted or overlooked Ambrose's influence on Aelred. In 1962, writing of *Spiritual Friendship*, Lionel J. Friedman mentioned Ambrose in passing as "a neglected source for medieval theories of love and friendship,"[16] and in 1969, in *Aelred of Rievaulx: A Study*, the great Aelred Squire referred to Ambrose only as one "on whom Aelred certainly depends."[17] Ambrose does not appear in a 1984 survey of early philosophers of friendship by James McEvoy, and when Hyatte discussed *Spiritual Friendship*, he connected it only to Cicero, not mentioning Ambrose.[18] Although McGuire devoted several pages of his 1988 *Friendship and Community* to Ambrose and a chapter to Aelred, citing Fiske in his notes (e.g., 494 nn. 120, 122), he subsumed Aelred within a generalized statement of monastic appreciation of Ambrose, whose contribution he reduced to a moral perspective: "For monastic readers like Aelred, Ambrose provided much of what they wanted and needed to hear about the benefits and duties of friendship." Writing more specifically on Aelred's use of Duties, McGuire suggested that Aelred's borrowings from Ambrose "provide a valuable indication of the common-sense tone Aelred wanted to set for friendship."[19]

Maurice Testard, editor of the 2000 Corpus Christianorum Series Latina edition of Duties, does not mention Aelred in his examination of "instances where we would expect Ambrose's work to be mentioned" or in his discussion of quotations from Duties in the works of eleventh- and twelfth-century authors. Nor does he include Aelred in the volume's Index, although

[16] Lionel J. Friedman, "Jean de Meun and Ethelred of Rievaulx," *L'Esprit Createur* 2 (1962): 139.

[17] Aelred Squire, *Aelred of Rievaulx: A Study*, CS 50 (1969; Kalamazoo, MI: Cistercian Publications, 1981), 49.

[18] James McEvoy, "*Philia* and *amicitia*: The Philosophy of Friendship from Plato to Aquinas," *Sewanee Medieval Colloquium*, Occasional Papers 2 (1984): 1–23.

[19] McGuire, *Friendship*, 45, 326.

his Annotated Bibliography includes the critical edition of Aelred's spiritual works, singling out *Spiritual Friendship* without comment.[20] In the 2001 Oxford edition and translation of Duties, Ivor J. Davidson named book 1 in the *Tractatus de ordine vitae* as "the most extensive twelfth-century reference" of Duties, touching only glancingly on *Spiritual Friendship*: "The English Cistercian, Ælred of Rievaulx . . ., uses Ambrose as well as Cicero in his celebrated characterization of friendship in *De spiritali amicitia*, book 3."[21] The question of Aelred's intellectual debt to Ambrose has thus remained if not quite ignored at least unexplored.

## Ambrose on Friendship

Ambrose had begun thinking about friendship and writing about it as a virtue by at least 377, in *On Virgins*. In this work he included a brief anecdote about two Pythagoreans, Damon and Pythias, who because of their great friendship attempted to die for one another, so bringing about the revocation of their sentence and winning over the one who had condemned them: "Thereupon the tyrant, astonished that friendship was dearer to philosophers than life, asked that he himself might enjoy the friendship of those whom he had condemned. So great was their virtue that it swayed even a tyrant!"[22] Five or six years

[20] Sancti Ambrosii Mediolanensis, Part 5, *De Officiis*, ed. Maurice Testard, CCSL 15 (Turnhout: Brepols, 2000), XIII–XIV, XVI–XVII, XLVI.

[21] Davidson, Introduction to *De officiis*, 1:100. Davidson attributes the *Tractatus de ordine vitae* to Bernard of Clairvaux, but while it was long attributed to Bernard and appears with his works in the Patrologia Latina (PL 184:559–84), its author was the eleventh-century abbot Johannes Homo Dei (Testard, ed., Ambrose, *De Officiis*, XVII, LII). See André Wilmart, "Jean l'Homme de Dieu auteur d'un traité attribué à saint Bernard," in *Auteurs spirituels et Textes Dévots du Moyen Age Latin* (Paris: Études Augustiniennes, 1971), 64–100.

[22] Ambrose, *De virginibus* 2.5.34, ed. Otto Faller (Bonnae: Hanstein, 1933), 59; trans. Ramsey, *Ambrose*, 101.

afterward, in *On the Holy Spirit*, which Ramsey dates to 381,[23] Ambrose compared the oneness found in friendship to the unity of the Trinity: "If, then, man so defines a friend as to say that he was a second self, namely, through oneness of love and friendship, how much more ought we to consider the oneness of majesty in the Father and Son and Holy Spirit, when by the same operation and divinity either oneness or surely that which is more ['sameness'], . . . is expressed?"[24]

Later in that decade Ambrose finally devoted serious attention to friendship at the end of Duties. Though Ramsey says that the work could have been written any time between 377 and 391, Davidson dates it in the late 380s, and Testard places it more specifically between 386 and 389.[25] Writing to instruct the clergy of the diocese of Milan on their duties—their obligation to live lives worthy of their vocation and to serve as examples to the people—Ambrose took Cicero's *Duties* as his model, even appropriating Cicero's title for his own work. In the first book he examined those things that are honorable[26] in human life, identifying four principal virtues: prudence, justice, courage, and temperance.[27] In explaining his love for his spiritual sons, the clergy of Milan, he touches on themes to which he would later return in connection with friendship, specifically that the truest love binds those who will remain together past death and that that best of loves comes from considered choice:

> we ought to have all the greater love for those who, we trust, will be with us forever than we do for those who are with us in this world only. . . . You, though, are loved on the basis of deliberate judgement, and this adds to love's force the great weight

[23] Ramsey, *Ambrose*, 24.

[24] Ambrose, *De spiritu sancto* 2.154.

[25] Ramsey, *Ambrose*, 60; Davidson, Introduction, 1:3–6; Testard, ed., Ambrose, *De Officiis*, VIII.

[26] *Honestum.*

[27] Ambrose, Duties 1.24.115.

> of real affection; it means that you truly approve of those who love, and you truly love those you have chosen.[28]

In book one Ambrose also anticipates his discussion of friendship in book three by defining good will as "bringing people together and uniting them in friendship." He calls it "the source from which friendship springs," notes that it "makes those who were many become one," and points to God's placing the spirit of good will in the man and the woman in Paradise.[29]

The second book considers things expedient[30] for the life to come, rejecting the teaching of the pagan philosophers in favor of knowing God and living well. In this book Ambrose repeatedly writes of the value of friendship, connecting it to the love that he had earlier described:

> It is the greatest possible incentive towards being held in popular affection if a person shows love in return to those who love him, and if he demonstrates that he loves no less in return than he is loved himself, and makes it clear by exemplifying faithful friendship. . . . What instinct is more natural than to show love to someone who shows love to you? What inclination is more deeply implanted and ingrained in human hearts than the urge to devote all your energies to loving a person from whom you want to receive love yourself?[31]

The third book then addresses the relationship of honor and personal benefit, insisting that one must never sacrifice honor to personal advantage. Through the use of many examples, most of them from the Old Testament, Ambrose demonstrates that by seeking what was honorable, both men and women had through the centuries arrived at what was beneficial, even

[28] Ambrose, Duties 1.7.24.

[29] Ambrose, Duties 1.32.167, 172, 173, 169.

[30] *utile*.

[31] Ambrose, Duties 2.7.37.

in cases where their decision to follow honor rather than expediency cost them their mortal lives.

Although the first two books of Duties refer several times to friendship and its origins and meaning, Ambrose does not seem to intend such passages to lead to a fuller discussion of the topic. They indicate, however, that he was already considering the place of friendship within Christian ethics. He treats friendship most fully, though not even then systematically, only at the end of the third book of Duties, beginning with what seems like just one more biblical exemplum of the centrality of honor over personal advantage, citing King Ahasuerus's execution of Haman from Esther 7: "So he sent to the gallows . . . the man he had counted chief among all his friends, for he had seen that by giving him such deceitful advice he had treated him in a dishonourable fashion."[32] Although in both substance and syntax this sentence is an unusual starting point for a discussion of friendship, with its only reference to the topic in a prepositional phrase at the end of a relative clause, it serves as a transition to the new topic, introducing the relationship of friendship and honor:

> Friendship is only commendable, you see, when it preserves what is honourable. Friendship must come before wealth, or honors, or power, certainly, but it is not normal that it should come before what is honourable; rather, it should follow it. . . .[33]
>
> Nothing, therefore, must ever be allowed to come before what is honourable. In case we become so enthusiastic about friendship that we forget this, though, Scripture gives us plenty of reminders on this very point.[34]

Ambrose thus seems to introduce friendship as potentially a danger to both honor and virtue because it is so appealing, so likely to lead away from what is honorable. His topic at this

[32] Ambrose, Duties 3.21.124.

[33] *honourable = honestatum; honors = honoribus.*

[34] Ambrose, Duties 3.21–22.125–26.

point is, after all, still virtue, not the nature or blessings of human friendship. White's evaluation of his attitude toward friendship may be influenced by his apparent hesitance here, a hesitance that she contrasts with what she says is Augustine's more positive view:

> Instead of bringing man closer to God, human love is usually [in Ambrose] seen as potentially destructive of the all-important relationship between man and God. If Ambrose had freed himself from the traditional view of friendship he might have been able to have a more positive attitude to human love, considering the connection between the two parts of Christ's commandment to love (Matt. 22:37–9) on which Augustine, for example, lays so much stress.[35]

Despite expressing caution about friendship, however, Ambrose does not for a moment advise against it. At once he offers a way to protect and indeed strengthen friendship by explaining how to resolve a potential conflict between honor and friendship, insisting that if one's friend is acting dishonorably, one must rebuke the friend: "if you know that there is something wrong in his life, you should rebuke him in secret. If he refuses to listen, you should rebuke him openly. Such friendship rebukes are valuable, and often they are better than the type of friendship that stays silent."[36]

Having addressed and resolved the question of a possible conflict between friendship and honor, Ambrose turns his attention to friendship itself, its nature and joys, no longer expressing any hesitance on the subject. Repeatedly he insists that friends may tell one another anything, that friends should open their hearts and pour all their thoughts into the ears of their friends. Such openness, such an acceptance of one's friend as one's second self, he declares, is the essence of friendship.[37]

[35] White, *Christian Friendship*, 126–27.

[36] Ambrose, Duties 3.22.128.

[37] Ambrose, Duties 3.22.134.

So he defines friendship as a matter of emotional and intellectual intimacy, driving home the point through threefold iteration. First he writes, "Open your heart to your friend, so that he will be faithful to you, and so that you will know joy in your own life from him."[38] Three paragraphs later, he repeats the idea: "It really is a comfort in this life to have someone to whom you can open your heart, someone with whom you can share your innermost feelings, and someone in whom you can confide the secrets of your heart."[39] In a third passage he links this human intimacy to God's own design for human friendship, with Jesus as its exemplar:

> God himself makes us his friends . . . . "I have called you friends," Jesus says, "because I have made known to you everything that I have heard from my Father." A friend hides nothing, then, if he is true: he pours out his heart, just as the Lord Jesus poured out the mysteries of the Father.[40]

It is not clear that Ambrose meant for Duties to culminate with a discussion of friendship. Despite his consideration in book one of the relationship between good will and friendship, here he devotes to friendship only fourteen paragraphs (according to the editorial tradition) and never explicitly links it to the central themes of his work except in his citation of Esther. Even though he argues in general that what is honorable is ultimately beneficial in leading to salvation, he applies neither term—honor or benefit—to friendship. On the other hand, his three books about the obligations imposed on humans by the need for virtue and honor may be read as a rising arc culminating here in the highest of human goods, the ultimate linking of honor and benefit. He has over the course of the work, after all, shown friendship to be the human relationship that was initiated by God in Paradise, that takes its model from Jesus'

[38] Ambrose, Duties 3.22.129.
[39] Ambrose, Duties 3.22.132.
[40] Ambrose, Duties 3.22.136.

relationship with the Father and with the disciples, and that may be identified with charity itself. Duties reaches its climax in its celebration of friendship, as Ambrose brings his treatise on virtues and ethical obligations to a joyous end, Christian rather than Ciceronian in its portrayal of the best aspect of human life.

## Ambrose and Aelred

Surviving medieval monastery library catalogues witness to the general popularity of Ambrose among English Cistercians, with twenty-one of his works found in their houses. Fifteen of them are listed in the thirteenth-century Rievaulx catalogue, including Duties and *On Virgins*.[41] It is not surprising, then, that Aelred was widely familiar with Ambrose's works and incorporated passages from them in several of his treatises. While still a young monk he must have read Ambrose intensively and recognized in his treatment of friendship a focused Christian understanding that he had seen nowhere else. His appreciation of Duties appears in a small but significant way in his first treatise, *Mirror of Charity* (ca. 1142–1144), which incorporates friendship into the second of three loves and of three sabbaths: love of self, love of neighbor, and love of God.[42] In this work Aelred expanded Ambrose's brief lyrical celebration of the comfort offered by friendship into a much longer but still lyrical apostrophe to friendship: "*It is no mean consolation in this life to have someone* with whom you can be united by an intimate attachment and the embrace of very holy love, to have someone in whom your spirit may rest, *to whom you can pour out your soul, . . . to whose most loving breast you may without hesitation confide all your inmost thoughts*, as to yourself and

[41] David N. Bell, *An Index of Authors and Works in Cistercian Libraries in Great Britain*, CS 130 (Kalamazoo, MI: Cistercian Publications, 1992), 24–26.

[42] Aelred, Spec car 3.2.3–5; ed. Anselm Hoste, CCCM 1:106–7; *Mirror of Charity*, trans. Elizabeth Connor, CF 17 (Kalamazoo, MI: Cistercian Publications, 1990), 222–24.

into whose spirit . . . so that you join and attach yourself to him *and blend spirit with spirit, so that out of many you become one.*"[43] In this work he also, Squire and Anselm Hoste have suggested, borrowed from Ambrose's lament for the death of his brother, "De excessu fratis Satyri," in his lament for his monastic friend Simon, and again in his 1153 lament for the death of King David of Scotland.[44] Probably in the early 1160s, he incorporated the exemplum of the young woman of Antioch and her protector in *The Formation of Recluses*, and a few years later he echoed that same passage in "A Certain Wonderful Miracle," about the rape of the young nun of Watton.[45]

About twenty years after Aelred first addressed the question of friendship in *Mirror*, he incorporated the essence of Ambrose's teaching on the subject into *Spiritual Friendship*, his own exploration of the nature of friendship in the life of the Christian. Both Cicero and Augustine contributed extensively to the argument of *Spiritual Friendship*, with Cicero's *On Friendship* providing its structure, form, subject matter, and much of the language,[46] and Augustine's *Confessions* modeling both the personal voice of the teacher and a portrait of youthful friend-

[43] Spec car 3.39.109 (CCCM 1:159; CF 17:29); cf. Ambrose, Duties 3.22.132. Other passages in *Mirror* also recall Ambrose, e.g., Duties 1.18.67–71 and the discussion of Simon as a model of monastic demeanor (Spec car 1.34.107 [CCCM 1:60; CF 17:153]). Italics in Aelredian passages indicate borrowings from Duties, usually directly but occasionally, as here, in paraphrase.

[44] Squire emphasizes Ambrose's influence on Aelred's *Lament for King David* in "Aelred and King David," Coll 22 (1960): 356–76, esp. 360–61; Anselm Hoste, "Aelred of Rievaulx and the Monastic *Planctus*," *Cîteaux* 18 (1967): 387, 395. Hoste also suggests here that Aelred echoes a passage from Ambrose's *De bono mortis* in one of his sermons (392).

[45] {Inst incl 16 (CCCM 652; CF 2:65}; *De sanctimoniali de Wattun* 3 (PL 195:792); {*De Quodam Miraculo Mirabili*, ed. Domenico Pezzini, CCCM 3:140}; *The Lives of the Northern Saints*, trans. Jane Patricia Freeland, ed. Marsha L. Dutton, CF 71 (Kalamazoo, MI: Cistercian Publications, 2006), 114.

[46] {On Aelred's development of Cicero's dialogue form in *De amicitia*, see Marsha L. Dutton, "Antiphonal Learning: Listening and Speaking in the Works of Aelred of Rievaulx," CSQ 54, no. 3 (2019): 273–75.}

ship that Aelred would cite as potentially leading to spiritual friendship. But Ambrose's discussion of the origins of friendship in creation and of the nature and joys of human friendship provided the intellectual and theological insights from which Aelred wove his own rich understanding. Indeed Ambrose's various discussions of friendship function within *Spiritual Friendship* as what John Fleming has called a "supertext": "a secondary literary presence of a specially, and often uniquely, powerful authority."[47]

In *Spiritual Friendship* Aelred quotes Duties over forty times, including passages from all three books of the treatise before first quoting Ambrose's concluding discussion of friendship. For example, when Walter, one of the monks in *Spiritual Friendship*, begins his inquiry about friendship by asking about its fruit, its utility, he tacitly recalls Ambrose's expulsion of utility from friendship and suggests himself, as J. Stephen Russell has shown, to be primarily interested in friendship as rationally justifiable rather than a delightful and affective experience.[48] Later, the teacher Aelredus echoes Ambrose's concern with the human desire to be loved and the value of reciprocal love:

> These and similar signs through lips, tongue, eyes, and a thousand delightful actions well up from the hearts of those giving and receiving love, kindling the spirit and making one out of many. In our friends this is what we believe should be loved, so

[47] John Fleming, *Reason and the Lover* (Princeton, NJ: Princeton University Press, 1984), 69.

[48] Aelred, Spir am 2.8 (CCCM 1:103; CF 5:72); Ambrose, Duties 2.6.26–28. I am indebted to Russell's helpful explication of Aelred's characterization of the two monks Walter and Gratian as respectively narrowly rational and affective in their approach to friendship (J. Stephen Russell, "Cicero, Dialogue, and the Structure of Aelred's *Spiritual Friendship*," paper presented at the 2011 Cistercian Studies Conference, Kalamazoo, MI) {published as "The Dialogic of Aelred's *Spiritual Friendship*," CSQ 47, no. 1 (2012): 59–61}.

that if we did not love one who returned our love or love in return one who loved us, we should have a guilty conscience.[49]

Many of Ambrose's Old Testament examples of friendship recur in *Spiritual Friendship*, especially Ambrose's repeated instances from the friendship of David and Jonathan, with the first of which Ambrose exemplifies the linking of good will and friendship.[50] Ambrose's exemplum of Ahasuerus's valuing his honor above his friendship with Haman also echoes in *Spiritual Friendship*: "Although King Ahasuerus had *considered Haman a friend above all others, he hanged* that haughtiest of ministers *from the gallows*, because he preferred the welfare of the many and the love of his wife to the friendship Haman had injured with his treasonous plots."[51] Aelred also includes such Ambrosian advice as the necessity of banning dishonor or shameful behavior from friendship[52] and of friends' correcting and being corrected by one another.[53]

Particularly significant for Aelred's explanation of the divine origins of friendship is Ambrose's discussion of friendship's beginning in creation. In both authors the development of this theme has three aspects: the love of society shown by all God's creatures, God's placement of his own unity and love of society in the first humans, and the expansion of individual friendships into larger communities.

Ambrose introduces the first element, the love of society shown by creatures, in the first book of *Duties*. In a discussion

[49] Aelred, Spir am 3.86 (CCCM 1:335; CF 5:109); cf. Ambrose, Duties 2.7.37. I follow Russell in calling the abbot-teacher of the work Aelredus, as in manuscripts of the work, to distinguish him from the work's author.

[50] Ambrose, Duties 1.32.167; cf. Aelred, Spir am 2.63 (CCCM 1:314; CF 5:85).

[51] Aelred, Spir am 3.47 (CCCM 1:326; CF 5:98).

[52] Aelred, Spir am 3.87, 3.102 (CCCM 1:336, 340; CF 5:109, 115); cf. Ambrose, Duties 3.21–22.125–26.

[53] E.g., Aelred, Spir am 3.112–13 (CCCM 1:343; CF 5:95); cf. Ambrose, Duties 3.22.127–28.

of the natural presence of prudence in animals, he digresses to consider their social instincts:

> We find that animals of every species are also by nature social creatures: they mix first with those which share their own species and type, and then with others as well. So we see that cattle are happy in herds, horses in droves, and so on—like tends to be happy with like. And think of stags: they stick with other stags—not to say with people, too. As for the desire to procreate and the instinct to produce offspring, or the love that parents feel for their young—what is there to say?[54]

Aelred similarly notes the tendency of animals to group with others of their own kind. But he explains that tendency as reflecting God's eternal purpose for his creatures, he extends it to both insensate creatures and angels, and he twice refers to the relationship among creatures as being similar to friendship itself:

> Since he so planned it eternally, he determined that peace should guide all his creatures and society unite them. Thus from him who is supremely and uniquely one, all should be allotted some trace of his unity. For this reason, he left no class of creatures isolated, but from the many he linked each one in a kind of society.
>
> Let us begin with creatures that lack sensation. What plot of land or what stream turns up only one stone of a single kind? Or what forest produces only one tree of a single species? Thus among non-sentient beings, a kind of love of companionship comes to light, since not one of them is left alone, but each is created and conserved in a kind of society of its own class. But among sentient creatures, who could easily express how great a mirror of friendship and how great an image of a loving society they reflect?
>
> Although in all other respects animals are proven to be irrational, surely in this respect alone they so imitate the human

[54] Ambrose, Duties 1.27.128.

> spirit that they are almost thought to be moved by reason. They so follow the leader, so frolic together, so express and display their attachment in actions and sounds together and so enjoy one another's company with eagerness and pleasure that they seem to relish nothing more than what resembles friendship.
>
> Among angels, too, divine wisdom so provided that not one but several classes should be created. . . . Thus there was a host of angels to banish loneliness and a communion of charity in the various classes to multiply their joy.[55]

After noting the ubiquity of social relationships, both Ambrose and Aelred locate the origins of human friendship in God's intention in creation. Ambrose's passage on the subject comes at some distance from his discussion of the social instincts of animals, and he makes no attempt to link the two ideas. And as he places the passage on creation in his first book, long before the discussion of friendship, he credits God not with creating friendship itself but with placing good will in the man and the woman:

> we could say that good will began in the first place with the personal relations which make up the family . . . then, progressing through different levels of relationship, it completed its circuit in the ties which bind us together in our various cities: having set out from Paradise, it has filled the whole world. So, when he had placed the spirit of good will in the man and the woman, God said: "The two shall be one in flesh," and one in spirit. This was why Eve believed the serpent: having received the gift of good will herself, she simply could not imagine that such a thing as ill-will existed.[56]

Aelred, however, connects the social behavior of animals and angels directly to the natural social attachment of humans,

[55] Aelred, Spir am 1.53–56 (CCCM 1:298; CF 5:65–66).

[56] Ambrose, Duties 1.32.169; see also 1.28.134 for the creation of Eve as a helper (*adiutor*) to Adam.

attributing that attachment to God's eternal purpose.[57] Further, he translates Ambrose's good will into friendship itself as God's gift:[58]

> Finally, when God fashioned the man, to recommend society as a higher blessing, he said, "it is not good that the man should be alone; let us make him a helper like himself." Indeed divine power fashioned this helper not from similar or even from the same material. But as a more specific motivation for charity and friendship, this power created a woman from the very substance of the man. In a beautiful way, then, from the side of the first human a second was produced, so that nature might teach that all are equal or, as it were, collateral, and that among human beings—and this is a property of friendship—there exists neither superior nor inferior.[59]

Although Aelred's insistence here on equality as inherent in God's plan for friendship does not appear in Ambrose's parallel passage, when Ambrose finally discusses the nature of friendship, he too insists that friends must understand themselves as equal: "Friendship is the guardian of loyalty and the teacher of equality; it makes the superior prove himself equal to the inferior, and the inferior equal to the superior."[60]

Finally, both Ambrose and Aelred explain that the friendship begun in Paradise expanded into human communities. For Ambrose, that development is directly tied to God's action in

[57] Ambrose too mentions friendship among angels: "Is there anything more precious than friendship? It is shared by both men and angels" (Duties 3.22.135).

[58] Aelred's recognition of the place of *benevolentia* in friendship also echoes Cicero's definition of friendship (*De amicitia* 6.20; trans. William Armistead Falconer, Loeb [London: Heinemann, 1923], 130–31), quoted with slight variations four times in *Spiritual Friendship*, e.g., *Friendship is agreement in things human and divine, with good will* [benevolentia] *and charity* (e.g., Spir am 1.11 [CCCM 1:291; CF 5:57]).

[59] Aelred, Spir am 1.57 (CCCM 1:298; CF 5:66).

[60] Ambrose, Duties 3.22.133.

Paradise and indeed articulated within the passage where he says that from its beginnings in Paradise "it has filled the world." Aelred, however, ties his discussion of the expansion of individual friendship not to Paradise but to Christ's call to his followers, and he does so not within or after but well before his passage on the divine origins of friendship. Aelred's determination to distinguish between charity and friendship means that he cannot allow friendship to have followed an uninterrupted pattern of growth from Adam and Eve to the present; as God requires charity of all people while friendship persists only among some of them, Aelred explains, friendship initially fell away rather than expanding. Thus he says that although friendship was originally universal, the Fall caused charity and friendship to diverge, with the result that fewer humans continued in friendship than were bound to one another by the obligation of charity: "Therefore friendship, which like charity was at first observed among all and by all people, by natural law lingered among the few righteous."[61] In this way Aelred allows true friendship to continue after the Fall among a few non-Christians.[62]

Later, however, in the new dispensation, Christ's call caused pairs of friends to multiply as they could have from the beginning had there been no Fall, and friendship at last expanded into larger and larger communities, with Christ at their center:

> No wonder the followers of true virtue were rare among the heathen, for they were ignorant of the Lord and giver of the virtues, of whom it was written, the Lord of virtues, he is the king of glory.
>
> In proof of this statement I shall readily present you not with three or four but with a thousand pairs of friends ready to die for each other, thanks to their mutual trust, which people long

[61] Aelred, Spir am 1.59 (CCCM 1:299; CF 5:67).

[62] {See Domenico Pezzini, "Aelred's Doctrine of Charity and Friendship," in *A Companion to Aelred of Rievaulx (1110–1167)*, ed. Marsha L. Dutton, Brill's Companions to the Christian Tradition (Leiden/Boston: Brill, 2017), 245.}

ago celebrated or invented in Orestes or Pylades as a great miracle. According to Cicero's definition, you would agree that those people excelled in the virtue of true friendship, of whom it was said that "the multitude of believers was of one heart and one soul. No one claimed any belonging as his or her own, but all was held in common [Acts 4:32]."

. . . How many martyrs laid down their lives for the brethren? How many spared neither cost nor toil nor their bodies' torture? I suppose that often, not without tears, you have read of that maiden of Antioch who was delivered from among prostitutes by the glorious deceit of a soldier, who became her companion in martyrdom after having found himself the guardian of her virginity in the brothel.[63]

I could cite for you many examples of such heroism, if sheer numbers did not prohibit it and the mass of material impose silence on me. For Christ Jesus preached and spoke, and they were multiplied beyond counting.[64]

Thus Aelred too shows the friendship instituted by God in Paradise to have expanded into human communities, specifically into the early church. This tapestry of interwoven themes, echoes, and borrowings concerning the divine origins of friendship and its expansion throughout the world reveals something of his extensive debt to Ambrose, but transformed to show friendship as not only of the order of creation but perpetuated by Christ.

[63] Ambrose does not define the relationship of the Antiochian woman and her rescuer as friendship but as shared martyrdom; on that basis he contrasts it with the friendship of Damon and Pythias, whose story he inserts within his exemplum of the two martyrs. In passages about the Antiochian woman both here and in *De institutione inclusarum* (Inst incl), Aelred conflates the two pairs, silently eliminating Damon and Pythias while translating their friendship into the other relationship as another instance, showing that friendship includes women as well as men (Ambrose, *De virginibus* 2.4.22–5.35; ed. Faller, Ambrose, *De virginibus*, 53–59; Ramsey, *Ambrose*, 98–102; cf. Aelred, Inst incl 16 [CCCM 1:652; CF 2:65–66]).

[64] Aelred, Spir am 1.27–30 (CCCM 1:293–94; CF 5:60–61).

### *Friendship as Intimacy in Ambrose and Aelred*

While Aelred's cosmological and sacramental understanding of spiritual friendship has a basis in Ambrose's treatment of the origins and development of human friendship, similarly important are other Ambrosian passages defining friendship as a matter of emotional and intellectual intimacy. Like Ambrose, Aelred insists on intimacy as characterizing the truest of human friendships. But he goes further, sacramentalizing that friendship by insisting on Jesus' reliable presence within it and at its heart.

Aelred enunciates the grand theme of his work at the beginning of book one of *Spiritual Friendship*, linking his theological perspective on friendship to Jesus' promise to be present when two or three gather in his name and to Ambrose's focus on the intimacy that characterizes the relationship of friends. At the same time he moves slowly toward a definition of friendship that departs from and contradicts Ambrose's identification of friendship and charity. The dialogue begins as Aelredus, the abbot-teacher of the dialogue, greets the young monk Ivo with a reminder of Jesus' promise: "You and I are here, and I hope that Christ is between us as a third" (cf. Matt 18:20). Almost at once he declares that he and Ivo are friends and explains the nature of their friendship, for the first of ten times in the work issuing an invitation to Ambrosian intimacy: "Yes, most beloved, *open your heart* now and pour whatever you please into the ears of a friend."[65]

Ivo twice echoes this understanding of friendship when he declares his desire to respond as his teacher asks and then expresses his hope that such open-hearted sharing will take place each time the abbot visits his monastery. But whereas Aelredus has spoken only of friendship, Ivo identifies this Ambrosian intimacy with charity: "Nothing but the spirit of charity has opened my mind and its thoughts to you. Would

[65] Aelred, Spir am 1.1 (CCCM 1:289; CF 5:55).

that your kindness might grant me this favor, that whenever you visit your sons who are here I might have recourse to you alone just once, with no others present, and lay bare without interruption the ardor of my heart."[66] A little later, now more clearly echoing Ambrose's identification of charity and friendship, he asks for information about the two, revealing his assumption that they are the same: "Are we not to conclude, then, that there is no distinction between friendship and charity?"[67] Aelredus rejects this identification, relying on the Gospel for his explanation of charity as a requirement of universal obligation and so distinguishing it from friendship as something more restricted. Even as he lays out the difference between the two, however, his explanation echoes Ambrose's insistence on friendship's inherent intimacy: "By the law of charity we are ordered to welcome into the bosom of love not only our friends but also our enemies. But we call friends only those to whom we have no qualm about entrusting our heart and all its contents."[68]

Aelredus later again enunciates the work's two interwoven themes, that friends meet in the presence of Christ and that the core of their friendship is mutual sharing and openness. Although he does not at this point quote Ambrose, he incorporates Ambrose's idea of Christ as the exemplar, adapting it to declare that Christ is not only its model but also himself a friend:

> In friendship, then, we join honesty with kindness, truth with joy, sweetness with good will, and affection with kind action. All this begins with Christ, continues through Christ, and is perfected in Christ. The ascent does not seem too steep or too unnatural, then, from Christ's inspiring the love with which we love a friend to Christ's offering himself to us as the friend whom

[66] Aelred, Spir am 1.3 (CCCM 1:289; CF 5:56).

[67] Aelred, Spir am 1.31 (CCCM 1:294; CF 5:61).

[68] Aelred, Spir am 1.32 (CCCM 1:294; CF 5:61); Ambrose, Duties 3.22.129, 132, 136.

we may love, so that tenderness may yield to tenderness, sweetness to sweetness, and affection to affection.[69]

Later yet, as part of a discussion linking Christ's presence in friendship to the intimacy between friends, Aelred reiterates his earlier distinction between charity and friendship, again explaining that friendship is more restricted than charity. Now, however, he cites Ambrose and quotes him at length:

> With all affection[70] I embrace many whom I do not admit into the intimacies of friendship, which consists especially in communicating all my secrets and aspirations. The Lord says in the Gospel, "I will no longer call you servants, but friends." Then, adding the reason for which friends are considered worthy of the name, he says, "*because I have made known to you everything that I have heard from my Father*" [John 15:15]. And elsewhere, "*you are my friends if you do what I command you*" [John 15:14]. Saint Ambrose comments on this passage: *he gave a model of friendship for us to follow so that we might do the will of a friend, open whatever secrets we have in our hearts to our friend, and not be ignorant of his mysteries. Let us show our hearts to him, and let him open his to us. Indeed a friend hides nothing, if he is genuine. He pours out his spirit, just as the Lord Jesus poured out the mysteries of the Father.*
>
> So says Ambrose. Now how many do I love to whom it would be indiscreet to bare my mind and open my heart in this way, since they are not old enough, mature enough, or discreet enough for such intimacies?[71]

By thus bracketing Ambrose's words on friendship with two statements distinguishing charity's universal requirements from the spontaneous intimacy of friendship and preceding them with the two biblical quotations displaced from within the Ambrosian passage, Aelred tacitly credits Ambrose himself

[69] Aelred, Spir am 2.20 (CCCM 1:306; CF 5:75).

[70] *affectus.*

[71] Aelred, Spir am 3.83–84 (CCCM 1:334–35; CF 5:108–9); cf. Ambrose, Duties 3.22.136.

not only with his core understanding of friendship but with the distinction between charity and friendship.

Immediately after this passage, Aelred further emphasizes his general reliance on Ambrose's views about friendship when he digresses to compare the nature of the spiritual friendship of which he writes with the adolescent friendship that Augustine lamented in the *Confessions*. In this portion of the dialogue the monk Walter rejects the intimacy of Ambrosian spiritual friendship, which Aelredus has been describing, in favor of a friendship that is pleasurable but not too intellectually or emotionally demanding, a friendship that he attributes to Augustine:

> Such friendship is so sublime and perfect that I would not dare aspire to it. For me and Gratian here, the friendship Augustine describes is sufficient: to chat and laugh together, to treat each other kindly, to read or confer together, to be lighthearted or serious together, to disagree at times but without rancor as anyone might argue with himself, and through disagreement now and then to give sparkle to the countless times we agree, to share in turn our experience in teaching or learning, to long for each other anxiously when absent, and gladly to welcome one another's return.[72]

In response, Aelredus distinguishes this kind of friendship from the spiritual friendship of which he has been speaking, saying that the Augustinian friendship that Walter extols is incomplete and immature. Still, he says that so long as it remains free of dishonor (an Ambrosian requirement), it may lead to the truest kind of human friendship, and so to friendship with God:

[72] Aelred, Spir am 3.85 (CCCM 1:335; CF 5:109); cf. Augustine, Conf 4.4; *Sancti Augustini Opera*, ed. Lucas Verheijen, CCSL 27 (Turnholt: Brepols, 1990), 43.

> This is a carnal friendship, especially belonging to adolescents, as were Augustine and the friend of whom we spoke. However, if you avoid childishness and dishonesty, and if nothing shameful[73] spoils such friendship, then in hope of some richer grace this love can be tolerated as a kind of first step toward a holier friendship. As devotion grows with the support of spiritual interests, and as with age maturity increases and the spiritual senses are illumined, then, with affection purified, such friends may mount to higher realms, just as we said yesterday that because of a kind of likeness the ascent is easier from human friendship to friendship with God himself.[74]

By identifying Augustinian friendship here as both carnal and adolescent, needing "the support of spiritual interests" and the illumination of "the spiritual senses," Aelred implicitly defines Ambrosian friendship as spiritual, both mature and sacramental. He also rejects Augustine's view from *Confessions* 4 that such a friendship draws one away from God, explicitly declaring it instead to lead the friend to God. He thus contrasts those who in their immaturity wish only "to be loved and to love," as he has characterized both his own young self and the monk Gratian,[75] with those who rejoice in the full intellectual and emotional maturity of spiritual friendship, delighting in the ability to reciprocate in loving, "so to love and so to be loved."[76]

[73] *inhonestas.*

[74] Aelred, Spir am 3.87 (CCCM 1:335–36; CF 5:109).

[75] Aelred, Spir am Prol.1, 2.16 (CCCM 1:287, 305; CF 5:53, 74).

[76] Aelred, Spir am 3.127 (CCCM 1:348; CF 5:124). See Marsha L. Dutton, "Friendship and the Love of God: Augustine's Teaching in the *Confessions* and Aelred of Rievaulx's Response in *Spiritual Friendship*," chap. 3 above, 75–120. Aelred's emphasis on the desire to be loved echoes Augustine's confession that as a young man in Carthage he sought only to love and be loved (Conf 2.2.2, 3.1.1) as well as Ambrose's passage on the natural desire of all humans to be loved: "there is nothing more beneficial than to be loved, and nothing more devoid of benefit than not to be loved" (Duties 2.7.29–39, here 29).

One consequence of the intimacy that friends share is for both Ambrose and Aelred (as also for Cicero and Augustine) a growth into emotional and intellectual oneness. As Ambrose approaches the end of his discussion in book three, he returns to this point: "What is a friend, in fact, but a partner in love? You unite your soul to his, you join your spirit to his, you blend so thoroughly with him that you wish to become one out of two. You entrust yourself to him as to another self, from whom you fear nothing."[77] Six times in *Spiritual Friendship* Aelred echoes this thought, writing for example, "And what is more delightful than so *to unite spirit to spirit* and so *to make one out of two*?"[78] Again, "*Since a friend is the partner* of your soul, *to whose spirit you join and link your own and so unite yourself as to wish to become one out of two, to whom you entrust yourself as to another self*, from whom you conceal nothing, *from whom you fear nothing*."[79]

While both Ambrose and Aelred consider this unity a characteristic of friendship in this life, modeled on Jesus' friendship with the Father, Aelred regularly also links it to his theological project—to the extension of human friendship into beatitude, into the embrace of Christ, into the eternal sight of the face of God. Relying on the words of both Scripture and Jerome, he insists that no true friendship—no friendship in which two have become one—can end:

> Hence even the philosophers of this world placed friendship not among the accidents of mortal life but among the virtues that are eternal. Solomon seems to agree with them in this verse from Proverbs 17: "a friend loves always." So he obviously declares that friendship is eternal if it is true, but if it ceases to exist, then although it seemed to exist, it was not true friendship. . . . And as our Jerome says, "A friendship that can end was never true."[80]

[77] Ambrose, Duties 3.22.134; cf. Ambrose, *De spiritu sancto* 2.154.

[78] Aelred, Spir am 2.11 (CCCM 1:304; CF 5:72). Ambrose, Duties 3.22.132.

[79] Aelred, Spir am 3.6 (CCCM 1:318; CF 5:89). Ambrose, Duties 3.22.134.

[80] Aelred, Spir am 1.21, 24 (CCCM 1:192, 193; CF 5:59).

Later, when Aelred returns to this point, he quotes Ambrose, though now without naming him, as additional support for the enduring nature of such a friendship: "*For friendship should be steadfast*, and by being *unwearied in affection*, it should present an image of eternity."[81]

As a practical exemplification of the eternal endurance of such friendship, Aelredus testifies to his own experience. He tells Walter that although his friend Ivo died some years before, Ivo is still present to him in spirit:

> the remembrance of my beloved brother—or rather his untiring affection and embrace—are always so fresh in my mind that in spirit he seems never to have departed. For there he is always with me, there his devout countenance beams upon me and his gentle eyes smile. There his joyful words have so much flavor for me that it seems that either I have passed over with him to a better life or he still shares this humbler one with me.[82]

Later he says the same of two other friends from the monastery, now also both dead: "I recall now two of my friends, who although no longer among the living are still alive for me and always will be."[83] Thus whereas in *Confessions* 4 Augustine recalls his grief at the death of the friend of his youth and blames himself for doing so, Aelred declares that his friendships, however broken in human experience, endure.[84]

## Aelred's Sacramentalizing of Friendship

Throughout *Spiritual Friendship*, Aelred makes it clear that he found in Ambrose the essence of his portrait of human friendship. That portrait provides the bridge between Aelred's explanation of the way humans experience friendship, with

[81] Aelred, Spir am 3.6 (CCCM 1:318; CF 5:89); Ambrose, Duties 3.22.128.
[82] Aelred, Spir am 2.5 (CCCM 1:303; CF 5:71).
[83] Aelred, Spir am 3.119 (CCCM 1:345; CF 5:121).
[84] Augustine, Conf 4.6–10 (CCSL 27:42–45).

Christ both present among those gathered in his name and being himself a friend, and his cosmological theology of friendship as created by God and culminating in God. The result is a profound and sacramental understanding of the friendship men and women experience within the daily reality of human life, of the mutual love that binds the community within which one lives, and of the way this love transcends this life and reaches into the life to come.

Such friendship is sacramental because God is always present within it, having placed his own unity in the first man and woman and remaining present in the person of his Son whenever the friends meet; such friendship becomes complete in beatitude, where God will be all in all. So Aelred writes, "God himself acts to channel so much friendship and charity between himself and the creatures he sustains . . . . The true and eternal friendship that begins here is perfected there."[85] In such friendships, which originate in God's action and persist past the Fall, revivified by Christ's call, friends share all their thoughts with one another, participating in true intimacy. These friendships have Christ as initiator and participant, though in this life his presence is still a matter of hope rather than a felt or tasted experience. But from time to time even in this life they lead to the unmediated experience of his love. These friendships reach their end and find their fruit in the eternal friendship of God.

As dependent as Aelred is on Ambrose in his explanation of the human intimacy that defines such friendships, he goes much further than Ambrose in extending those characteristics into a sacramental theology that explains the intimacy characterizing the best of human friendships as both instituted by God and reaching without effort or interruption into the eternal presence of God. For although Ambrose insists that equality is essential between friends, in writing of the friendship

[85] Aelred, Spir am 3.79–80 (CCCM 1:333; CF 5:107).

between God and humans, he assumes an essential inequality: "God himself makes us his friends, though we are really the very lowliest of his servants." Indeed he articulates even friendship with God as a matter of obedience: "Now you are my friends, if you do what I command you."[86] Ambrose goes somewhat further than this when he briefly shows Jesus to be not only a model of friendship but a friend to his disciples, having shared with them all that God had shared with him and so having become one in spirit with them.[87] But as that sharing took place in the past, it functions in Duties like all of Ambrose's biblical examples, as an instance, not a present reality. In his understanding, Christ is essentially a model for imitation rather than a participant in the friendship of men and women in the present time.

Aelred's theological understanding of friendship is not only explicitly sacramental but also much more systematically developed than Ambrose's. James McEvoy has written of Aelred's "programmatic exploration" of the theme of friendship,[88] and Fr. Charles Dumont eloquently proclaimed its theological clarity and power: "if one searches for a doctrinal work on Christian friendship, a theology of that most human reality, there is no work, no finished writing in all of Christian literature which is more to the point than Aelred's treatise."[89] Aelred declares that friendship originated in creation, points to its expansion through Christ's call not merely to the world but to the birth and growth of the church, repeatedly states its continuation through Christ, and ends by proclaiming its end in beatitude. So he insists on friends' unity at each stage with God and with God's Son. For Aelred the intimacy of human

[86] Ambrose, Duties 3.22.136; John 15:15; cf. Aelred, Spir am 3.83 (CCCM 1:335; CF 5:108).

[87] Ambrose, Duties 3.22.136–37.

[88] McEvoy, "*Philia*," 16.

[89] Charles Dumont, "*L'Amitié spirituelle* d'Ælred de Rievaulx," in *Une éducation du cœur: La spiritualité de saint Bernard et de saint Ælred*, Pain de Cîteaux 3,10 (Oka, Canada: L'Abbaye Notre-Dame-du-Lac, 1996), 351.

friendship leads directly into intimacy with Christ in this life and the next.

The link between friendship and eternity need not be delayed until beatitude, Aelred insists. It may be experienced here, now, for it includes Christ within it. The friendship that Aelred and Ivo share is Ambrosian, a mutual sharing of one another's hearts and a oneness of spirit. But it goes beyond what Ambrose defined, for Aelred insists that it always includes Christ's presence. Christ is necessary to this friendship: his presence defines it, preserves it, and fulfills it. That reality makes friendship sacramental, for the unity the friends share in this life is also a realized unity with Christ.

Aelred twice declares that in loving one's friend one need no longer merely hope for the presence of Christ or look forward to it in time to come but may enter now into Christ's embrace. The first such statement comes as Aelredus recalls the second of his good friends from monastic life:

> Was that not like the first fruits of bliss, so to love and so to be loved, to help and to be helped, and from the sweetness of brotherly love to fly aloft toward that higher place in the splendor of divine love, or from the ladder of charity now to soar to the embrace of Christ himself, or, now descending to the love of one's neighbor, there sweetly to rest?[90]

Again as he approaches the end of the dialogue he promises that from prayer for the friend one may ascend to Christ:

> Thus praying to Christ for a friend and desiring to be heard by Christ for a friend, we focus on Christ with love and longing. Then sometimes suddenly, imperceptibly, affection melts into affection, and somehow touching the sweetness of Christ nearby, one begins to taste how dear he is and experience how sweet he is.[91]

[90] Aelred, Spir am 3.127 (CCCM 1:348; CF 5:124).

[91] Aelred, Spir am 3.133 (CCCM 1:349; CF 5:126).

This final promise comes just at the end of the work, pointing again to the unbroken nature of such love and unity. The distinction between being one in spirit with one's friend and enjoying the embrace of Christ has finally disappeared, as the truest of human friendships becomes complete, eternally realized, tasted and enjoyed for its sweetness:

> Thus rising from that holy love with which a friend embraces a friend to that with which a friend embraces Christ, one may take the spiritual fruit of friendship fully and joyfully into the mouth while looking forward to all abundance in the life to come. . . . then with the beginning of relief from care we shall rejoice in the supreme and eternal good, when the friendship to which on earth we admit but few will pour out over all and flow back to God from all, for God will be all in all.[92]

Ambrose has vanished from the scene here, for this piece of the argument is entirely Aelred's, though grounded in Ambrose's own teaching. Ambrose probably gave Aelred the idea of friendship as originating in creation, and Ambrose certainly gave Aelred the concept of and language for the intimacy that defines the best of friendships, with friends sharing everything between themselves, being partners of one another's souls, and so becoming one. But to what he received from Ambrose Aelred added a sacramental vision of the relationship between human experience and God's love, now and forever, in this world and the next, world without end. He might have done it without Ambrose, but as it happens, he did not have to.

## Cistercian Intimacy

The search for intimacy with God is a hallmark of twelfth-century Cistercian spirituality. As it emerges naturally from the incarnation, from God's becoming a man, it is a present response to God's initiation of love. Cistercian spirituality is pro-

[92] Aelred, Spir am 3.134 (CCCM 1:349–50; CF 5:126).

foundly sacramental, grounded in the meeting of the worshiper with Christ on the altar, in Christ's revelation of himself there through the gift of the Holy Spirit, and in Christ's presence when two or three meet in his name.[93] Elizabeth Freeman has intimately linked Cistercian spirituality to the incarnation:

> Since God chose to participate in human history, this endorsed human time and human activity by the power of association. . . . It means that, in so far as one can detect a distinctive Cistercian spirituality, it is characterized first by its endorsement of human experience and second by its resultant emphasis on community life. That is, God is sought through the experiences *of* others and through experiences *with* others.[94]

It is not surprising, then, that Aelred consistently declares God's gift of friendship to be good in itself, treating it as part of the order of creation and as God's image in his creatures. Furthermore, he says, God sanctified friendship through his incarnation and will perfect it in eternity, when God himself will be the friend of all. Thus for Aelred all friendship, even that which is not yet spiritual friendship, leads to God, manifests God's presence, and anticipates beatitude. Rather than warning that loving a mortal man or woman may hinder one's progress to God, Aelred explains friendship as a way of knowing God now as in time to come.[95] Although he repeatedly

[93] Marsha L. Dutton, "Intimacy and Imitation: The Humanity of Christ in Cistercian Spirituality," chap. 6 below, 193–236. {See also Marsha L. Dutton, "The Sacramentality of Community in Aelred," in *A Companion to Aelred of Rievaulx (1110–1167)*, ed. Marsha L. Dutton, Brill's Companions to the Christian Tradition (Leiden/Boston: Brill, 2017), 246–63.}

[94] Elizabeth Freeman, *Narratives of a New Order: Cistercian Historical Writing in England, 1150–1220* (Turnhout: Brepols, 2002), 14.

[95] Dumont identifies this position as grounded in incarnational theology and characteristically Cistercian: "It is the sacramental doctrine of the humanity of Christ, dear to the Cistercians, that applies here" ("L'amour fraternel dans la doctrine monastique d'Ælred de Rievaulx," in *Une éducation du coeur: La spiritualité de saint Bernard et de saint Ælred*, Pain de Cîteaux 3,10 [Oka, Canada: L'Abbaye Notre-Dame-du-Lac, 1996], 345).

rejects the identity of charity and friendship, he declares an essential similarity in the way they bind one to God: "The one who abides in friendship," he says, "abides in God, and God in him."[96]

This theology of divine and human intimacy, central to Aelred's treatise on friendship, is drawn at least in its human beginnings from Saint Ambrose's *Duties*. If in the fourth century Ambrose remained hesitant about the ultimate theological value of human friendship, eight hundred years later Aelred recognized the sacramental implications of Ambrose's teaching on human friendship and, by making them part of his own thought, also made them a fundamental piece of the theological and philosophical history of friendship.

[96] *Qui manet in amicitia, in Deo manet, et Deus in eo*, altered from 1 John 4:16. Aelred, Spir am 1.70 (CCCM 1:301; CF 69).

*Chapter 5*

# Eat, Drink, and Be Merry: The Eucharistic Spirituality of the Cistercian Fathers[1]

William of Saint-Thierry says,

> The sight for seeing God . . . is charity. There are, however, two eyes in this sight, always throbbing by a sort of natural intensity to look toward the light that is God: love and reason . . . . One of them—reason—cannot see God except in what he is not, but love cannot bring itself to rest except in what he is . . . . Reason . . . seems to advance through what God is not, toward what God is. Love, putting aside what God is not, rejoices to lose itself in what he is.[2]

With these two eyes the Cistercian fathers look into the Eucharist for the sight of God, attempting with the eye of reason to

[1] I first presented this chapter at the Cistercian Studies Conference as part of the International Medieval Studies Congress at Western Michigan University in 1985; it was published in *Erudition at God's Service: Studies in Medieval Cistercian History, XI*, ed. John R. Sommerfeldt, CS 98 (Kalamazoo, MI: Cistercian Publications, 1987), 1–32. It appears here by permission of Cistercian Publications.

[2] William, Nat am 3.21 (PL 184:393; CF 30:77–78) {abbreviated titles of the Cistercian works appear in the abbreviations, pp. xix above}. Occasionally the translation in the text varies from the CF 30 translation, as I have attempted to allow the common eucharistic vocabulary of the Fathers to appear in the English. Any unattributed translation is my own.

understand the presence of Christ's body and blood in the bread and wine—to see God in what he is not—and with the eye of love to rest in union with him, to lose themselves in what he is. This attempt to do two things at once, to understand God rationally and love him intimately, results for them in an understanding that is love, a transformation of the two eyes into a single vision of God's face, a contemplation that manifests itself in a spirituality centered in the sacred humanity of Christ.

The real presence of Christ in the Eucharist, of the substance of his body and blood in the sacrament, increasingly occupied twelfth-century Christians anxious to ascertain the way in which he was present there, the relationship between the *res*—the substance of the Eucharist—and the *sacramentum*—the species of bread and wine. As such questions ramified, the Cistercian fathers began seriously to explore them. If the Eucharist was the food of salvation, they needed to understand what it was and what were its effects. The eye of reason had plenty of work to do.[3]

At the same time, the fathers longed to know God now, in this life, to love him and join with him in mutual embrace. While his presence in the Eucharist ensured that embrace, their rational hesitance to relax into a solution theologically but not emotionally satisfying restrained them from easily acquiescing to it. Their unsatisfied longing to know and love God led the Cistercians of the twelfth century finally to a new way of understanding him and to intimate love shaped by that understanding. So they created a eucharistic and incarnational spirituality,

[3] An excellent study of the Eucharist in the Middle Ages is Gary Macy, *The Theologies of the Eucharist in the Early Scholastic Period* (Oxford: Oxford University Press, 1984). My brief summaries of the various eucharistic questions explored by the Cistercian fathers are generally derived from Macy's thorough treatment. A valuable compendium of the development of eucharistic theology from the primitive church forward is Darwell Stone, *A History of the Doctrine of the Holy Eucharist*, 2 vols. (New York and London: Longmans, Green, 1909). Chapters 5 and 6 of vol. 1 are those relevant to the medieval period.

one that was within a century to turn medieval Christianity toward the humanity of Christ and so to direct the attention of Western Christianity from that time on to the incarnate God, Jesus of Nazareth.

Three of the early Cistercians, William of Saint-Thierry, Baldwin of Ford, and Isaac of Stella, wrote theological treatises on the Eucharist.[4] But as the fathers were not men of the schools, their inquiry into eucharistic theology emerged not by and large in theological treatises but in their affective works, treatises and sermons concerned with knowing God through love. At the same time they were intellectual men, insisting that reason, however alienated from God, must seek him out and understand him before the heart can love him. William so defines the route to God and the Cistercian inquiry into the Eucharist, urging, "Therefore let us strive as far as possible to see, by seeing to understand, and by understanding to love, so that by loving we may possess."[5]

The Cistercian fathers' approach to the Eucharist begins, then, in two places with two different questions, one rational, the other affective. From them two lines of inquiry develop, but as the one engenders the other and exists for its sake, the two cannot long stay separate. They overlap and intertwine almost at once, uniting in one spirituality centered in Jesus. Although William, for example, allows them to be distinct for a time, he suggests that at last "Love gives life to reason and reason gives light to love; thus their gaze becomes simple as the dove's in contemplation and prudent in circumspection."[6]

[4] William, *De sacramento altaris* (PL 180:341–66); Baldwin of Ford, *De sacramento altaris* (PL 204:641–774); *Baudouin de Ford: Le sacrement de l'autel*, ed. John Morson and trans. E. de Solms, SCh 93–94 (Paris: Cerf, 1963); Baldwin of Ford, *Tractatus de sanctissimus sacramento eucharistiae* (PL 204:403–14); *Baoudouin de Ford, Traités*, ed. and trans. R. Thomas, Pain de Cîteaux 35–40 (Chimay: OEIL, 1973–1975); Isaac of Stella, *Epistola and Joannem Episcopum Pictaviensem de officio missae* (PL 194:1889–96).

[5] William, Ep frat II.194 (SCh 223:302; CF 12:77).

[6] William of Saint-Thierry, Cant I.8.92 (SCh 82:212; CF 6:74).

This paper attempts to keep the two strands separate, to speak of the fathers' approach to the Eucharist through reason and through love, but the distinction is artificial and unsustainable. I here first establish the framework for a complete study of the Cistercians and the Eucharist, then examine the questions asked of the Eucharist by reason and the Cistercian responses to them. The other half of the scheme, which emerges from the questions asked by love, is developed separately.[7]

## The Eye of Reason

Three large questions shape the Cistercians' rational exploration of the Eucharist: (1) Which body of Christ is found in the species of bread and wine? (2) What in this life is the significance of finding that body? and (3) What in the life to come is the effect of the Eucharist?

While the three great Cistercian fathers Bernard of Clairvaux, William of Saint-Thierry, and Aelred of Rievaulx agree in finding the answers to these questions and related ones in the sacred humanity of Christ, the differences among the three, especially between Bernard and William on the one hand and Aelred on the other, reveal an idea in the process of being shaped, a new attitude emerging and culminating in Jesus as the center of Christian devotion. Between Bernard, who urges love toward the infant and crucified lord as a means to the spiritual love of God, insisting on "that other love which does not know the Word as flesh so much as the Word as wisdom, as justice, truth, holiness, loyalty, strength,"[8] and Aelred, who marvels that "He who fills heaven and earth is enclosed in a manger; he who owns the earth and the fullness thereof has

[7] See Marsha L. Dutton, "Intimacy and Imitation: The Humanity of Christ in Cistercian Spirituality," chap. 6 below, pp. 193–236.

[8] Bernard, SC 20.8 (SBOp 1:120; CF 4:154). {My discussion of Bernard here is based almost entirely on his Sermons on the Song of Songs.}

no room in an inn,"[9] a new element has entered Christian spirituality.

## The Eye of Love

The eye of love, like the eye of reason, begins its inquiry with the Eucharist. It is concerned not with rational questions about the nature and effects of the Eucharist, but rather with one much more immediate: "Who can love what he does not see? How can that be lovable that is not in some way visible?"[10] William asks that question in the person of Moses, longing to see God's face, and Moses' sight of God's back answers William's question as well: both are able to love the God whom they are allowed to see in the flesh, the incarnate God.

The question addressed to the Eucharist by the Cistercians is the same: "Given that I cannot see Christ in the sacrament, how can I love him there?" The inevitable answer to the question for them as for all Christians is "You cannot." And from the evidence of the incarnation, they infer that God agrees: in the fullness of time he became man and dwelt among men.

But after the ascension, Jesus, who had showed God to humankind because humans cannot love what they cannot see, was no longer visible to human sight. Aelred asks, "What then are we to say, brothers, for he is not physically present on earth and we are not able to receive him physically: must we then despair of his coming?"[11] Unwilling finally either to accept that hopelessness or to attempt to love by faith alone, the Cistercians found an answer in what they could see and physically receive, the sacrament of Christ's body and blood. Aelred

[9] Aelred, S. in nativitate Domini; in *Sermones inediti beati Aelredi abbatis Rievallensis*, ed. C. H. Talbot, Series S. Ordinis Cisterciensis I (Rome: Curia Gen, O.Cist., 1952), 37; {Aelred, S 49.2; CCCM 2B:22; CF 80:28}.

[10] William, Contemp 3 (SCh 61:17; CF 3:40).

[11] Aelred, S. in assumptione b. Mariae, PL 195:303; trans. Anthony Storey, "The Castle of the Soul," *The Tablet* 198 (1951): 91; {Aelred, S 19.3; CCCM 2A:147; CF 58:263–64}.

explains in the words of Paschasius Radbert, "An impatient love considers difficulty only an excuse and does not yield before impossibility."[12]

The humanity of Christ, already discovered by the eye of reason, solves the central question of the eye of love as the Cistercian fathers come to see that they can love God by loving the man they meet in the Eucharist and that by loving him in his humanity they can come to union with him in this life and the next. Further, they provide the method, declaring that by imitating those who once lived in intimacy with Jesus, men and women may be intimate with him even now in his crucifixion, his body and blood.

While the meeting with Jesus may be accomplished by meditation or in metaphor, it is, the Cistercians insist, certain in the Eucharist. So the Cistercian fathers bring their new knowledge of and love for God as man full circle, again to its natural end in the Eucharist, where it is not necessary to imagine or allegorize, but merely to eat and drink of Jesus' body and blood, in *sacramentum* and in *res*.

## The Single Eye of Charity

When the communicant has eaten of the sacrament and received its substance, when both eyes have seen the man whose body and blood constitute the sacrament, the yearning soul has become one with him. The eyes at last are one, "illumined by grace" and "of great mutual assistance," as William promised all along, transformed in love "into a certain spiritual and divine understanding that transcends and absorbs all reason."[13] It is no longer necessary to inquire or even to receive

[12] Aelred, S. in natale apostolorum Petri et Pauli; in *Sermones inediti B. Aelredi abbatis reivallensis*, ed. C. H. Talbot, Series Scriptorum S. Ordinis Cisterciensis (Rome: Curia gen., O.Cist., 1952), 135; {Aelred, S 71.35 (CCCM 2B:230; CF 80:289–90)}. Charles Dumont, *Saint Aelred de Rievaulx* (Namur, Belgium: Soleil Levant, 1960), 135, attributes this sentence to Paschasius.

[13] William, Cant I.8.92 (SCh 82:212; CF 6:74).

in blindness, unable to understand the God who lay in the manger and on the cross and lies now on the altar, for love itself is understanding.

## Which Body?

For the Cistercians the first question prompting reason's search into the Eucharist concerned the presence of Christ within it: "Which body of Christ is present in the Eucharist?" Medieval theologians agreed by and large that Christ was truly present in the Eucharist in his body—but precisely which body that was was a greater problem. Was it the body born of Mary and hung on the cross, or the body glorified and sitting at the right hand of God? Or was it perhaps the body of the church itself? Such questions led the Cistercians toward a new concern with Jesus, born of Mary and crucified under Pontius Pilate.

This concern with Jesus had of course formed the life and kerygma of Christianity, but in the post-biblical writings of the early church Jesus is hidden in the manger, more significant in what he is to become than what he is, a human baby.[14] With the Cistercians, however, that baby began slowly to make himself known.

Bernard, the first of the Cistercian fathers, is often credited with originating the medieval devotion to the humanity of Christ and the affective piety that accompanied it. W. R. Inge wrote in 1899, "[Bernard's] great achievement was to recall devout and loving contemplation to the image of the crucified

[14] In Homily 24 on 1 Corinthians John Chrysostom, "Doctor Eucharistiae," had said, "This body even when lying in a manger the Magi reverenced. These heathen foreigners left home and country and went on a long journey, and came and worshipped him with fear and great trembling. We are citizens of heaven: let us imitate these foreigners. For they approached with great awe when they saw him in the manger and in the cell and saw him in no way such as you see him, not in a manger but on an altar, not with a woman holding him but with a priest standing before him, and the Spirit descending upon the offerings with great bounty" (Stone, *History of the Doctrine*, 55).

Christ, and to found that worship of our Saviour as the 'Bridegroom of the Soul,' which in the next centuries inspired so much fervent devotion and lyrical sacred poetry."[15] In 1927 Pierre Pourrat agreed, saying that Bernard "excelled in bringing into relief the touching aspects of the lives of the Saviour and of the blessed Virgin . . . . he contributed more than anyone to the giving of an affective character to the piety of the Middle Ages."[16]

The eucharistic ground of Bernard's devotion to the humanity of Christ appears in any reading of his works. Eating and drinking appear throughout his sermons and spiritual treatises as the central metaphor for coming to the understanding of God. In the first of his sermons on the Song of Songs he presents God as him who is seen in the breaking of the bread and who himself breaks it, biblical language for understanding the Eucharist itself.[17] Defining the Song of Songs as a loaf of "splendid and delicious bread," he asks,

> But who is going to divide this loaf? The Master of the house is present; it is the Lord you must see in the breaking of the bread. For who else could more fittingly do it? . . . For I myself am one of the seekers, one who begs along with you for the food of my soul, the nourishment of my spirit . . . . O God most kind, break your bread for this hungering flock.[18]

[15] W. R. Inge, *Christian Mysticism* (London: Charles Scribner's Sons, 1899), 140 n. 2.

[16] Pierre Pourrat, *Christian Spirituality*, vol. 2, *The Middle Ages*, trans. S. P. Jacques, 4 vols. (1927; Westminster, MD: Newman Press, 1953), 2:20. Pourrat here rejects the common assumption of Franciscan originality in such devotion, saying, "St Francis of Assisi was not the first to pour forth lamentations before the crucifix, nor to weep with pity when contemplating the infant God in the manger. Before him, St Bernard had let his grief burst forth while meditating on the passion of Christ, and was moved to tears when speaking of Christmas night."

[17] See Luke 24:35.

[18] Bernard, SC 1.4 (SBOp 1:4; CF 4:3).

Bernard again speaks, in Sermon Twelve on the Song of Songs, of the Lord known in the breaking of bread, but more concretely, with more attention to the question of the body of Christ present in the bread and wine. Here Bernard addresses, though without resolving, the difficulty of distinguishing between the two bodies of Christ, that born at Bethlehem and crucified at Golgotha, and that which is the church, his bride:

> It will thus be clear that you abound with the best ointments, that you have undertaken to care not only for the head or feet of the Lord, but, as far as in you lies, for his whole body which is the Church. It was perhaps for this reason that the Lord Jesus would not allow the mixture of spices to be used on his dead body: he wished to reserve it for his living body. For that Church which eats the living bread which has come down from heaven is alive: she is the more precious Body of Christ that was not to taste death's bitterness, whereas every Christian knows that his other body did suffer death.[19]

In another sermon Bernard speaks explicitly of eating and drinking of the crucified Jesus, now with no mention of the sacrament: "They pierced his hands and his feet, they gored his side with a lance, and through these fissures I can suck honey from the rock and oil from the flinty stone—I can taste and see that the Lord is good."[20] In this abstract and allegorical eating of Jesus' flesh the combination of the words from Deuteronomy 32:13 with those from the Gospel narrative of the passion insists on the human—and crucified—Jesus tasted in the Eucharist, responding to reason's question: "Which body?"

Although Bernard repeatedly shows that it is Jesus, the son of Mary, who is present in the Eucharist, he usually presents him not historically but symbolically, liturgically, and spiritually, as the bread of heaven, the fruit of salvation. Explaining Song 2:3—"As an apple-tree among the trees of the wood, so is my beloved among the sons"—he says,

[19] Bernard, SC 12.7 (SBOp 1:65; CF 4:83).

[20] Bernard, SC 61.4 (SBOp 2:150; CF 31:143).

> Justly "as an apple tree," since after the manner of a fruit-bearing tree he casts a refreshing shadow and yields excellent fruit. . . . Christ alone, the Wisdom of God, is the tree of life, he alone the living bread which comes down from heaven and gives life to the world. . . . His shadow is his flesh; his shadow is faith. The flesh of her own Son overshadowed Mary; faith in the Lord overshadows me. And yet why should his flesh not overshadow me too, as I eat him in the sacrament?[21]

While Bernard, then, finds and loves the Jesus present in the Eucharist, he is always less concerned with the man than with what his flesh provides, in this life, faith—the evidence of things not seen—and in the next, salvation.

Like Bernard, William writes of Jesus with less attention to his humanity than to its significance and the salvific effects of his crucifixion. He too finds in the Eucharist the body of Christ, and in that crucified body he finds the sacrament: "Open to us your body's side, that those who long to see the secrets of your Son may enter in and may receive the sacraments that flow therefrom, even the price of their redemption."[22]

Further, William defines this sacrament as that through which the communicant remembers both Jesus' redemptive deed and his command so to remember:

> This is what happens when we eat and drink the deathless banquet of your body and your blood. As your clean beasts, we there regurgitate the sweet things stored within our memory and chew them in our mouths like cud for the renewed and ceaseless work of our salvation. That done, we put away again in that same memory what you have done, what you have suffered for our sake.[23]

But for William Jesus is more often allegorically or dogmatically conceived—as the bridegroom who feeds his bride or as

[21] Bernard, SC 48.5–6 (SBOp 2:70; CF 31:16–17).
[22] William, Med 6.12 (PL 180:226; CF 3:131).
[23] William, Med 8.5 (PL 180:230–31; CF 3:142).

the second person of the Trinity, the Son of the Father, more nearly half God and half man than wholly God and wholly man: "Let me . . . pour [the perfume] out upon your head, whose head is God, and upon your feet, whose lower part is our humble nature."[24]

In fact William sees the humanity of Christ in the Eucharist as the door to the reality of God, but not as essentially important in itself. He sometimes, even while specifying that the species of the Eucharist are indeed Jesus' flesh and blood, denies their importance there: "To those fretting about the sacramental mystery of his Body and Blood he says: It is the Spirit who gives life; the flesh, however, does not profit anyone."[25]

In the writings of Aelred, however, the humanity of Jesus discovered in the Eucharist by Bernard and William is fully developed and welcomed. In Aelred's sermons and contemplative works the humanity of Jesus emerges from inquiry into the Eucharist, but for him Jesus is rarely the Logos or an allegorically conceived bridegroom; rather he is wholly man, a man of flesh and blood. And not only does Aelred not hasten to distinguish between the man Jesus and the Godhead in this life; he understands even beatitude in terms of Jesus, there indeed glorified, sitting to judge the quick and the dead, but showing the same face to the blessed as to his friends during his human life: "Jesus' face shines upon them, not terrible but lovable, not bitter but sweet, not frightening but caressing."[26] In his writings Aelred progresses from a tentative attention to Christ's humanity like that he has met in Bernard and William to a fully developed devotion to the man Jesus.

Like his predecessors, Aelred explicitly associates the humanity of Christ with the Eucharist, sometimes in language full of the symbolic and eucharistic significance of the infant

[24] William, Med 5.9 (PL 180:221; CF 3:123).

[25] William, *Speculum fidei* 60 (SCh 301; CF 15:46).

[26] Aelred, Inst incl 33 (CCCM 1:679; CF 2:99). This is the only use of the name "Jesus" in Aelred's meditation on the future; elsewhere he is called judge (*iudex*), Christ, Son (*Filius*), or Lord (*Domine*).

Jesus. He says in *On Jesus as a Boy of Twelve* that God led him to a city that "abounds in bread and is called the House of Bread, Bethlehem . . . . You have filled [the hungry soul] with that bread indeed which came down from heaven and was laid in the manger to become the food of spiritual animals."[27] He continues, explaining not only the nativity but the incarnation itself in the language of the Eucharist:

> For bread made from fine wheaten flour is pure, clean, without ashes, without leaven, without husks—"In the beginning was the Word, and the Word was with God, and the Word was God." But who is capable of assimilating this? It is the bread of angels, whose palate has not been dulled by tasting sour grapes. Therefore they taste and see fully and perfectly that the Lord is sweet. But in order that men might eat the bread of angels, the Bread of Angels became man, taking upon him the husks of our poverty, the ashes of our mortality, the leaven of our infirmity. He who is great became a little child.[28]

Aelred writes again in *On Reclusion*[29] of the body of Christ as the food of those who love him, allowing to the eucharistic symbols the literal and physical reality of the crucifixion. When the soldier pierces Jesus' side, Aelred urges the contemplative, "Hasten, linger not, eat the honeycomb with your honey, drink your wine with your milk. The blood is changed into wine to inebriate you, the water into milk to nourish you."[30] In this

[27] Aelred, Iesu 3 (CCCM 1:252; CF 2:16).

[28] Aelred, Iesu 11–12 (CCCM 1:259; CF 2:16).

[29] Although this work, *De Institutione inclusarum,* is better known by its title in the CF 2 translation of M. P. Macpherson, *A Rule of Life for a Recluse,* I here use a direct translation of the Latin title that better defines the work.

[30] Aelred, Inst incl 31 (CCCM 1:671; CF 2:90). The language and eucharistic insistence of Aelred's passion scene recalls Berengar's Oath at the Synod of Rome in 1079, the culmination of the great eucharistic controversy of the age: "The bread and wine which are placed on the altar . . . are changed substantially into the true and proper vivifying body and blood of Jesus Christ our Lord and after the consecration there are the true body of Christ which was born of the virgin . . . and the true blood of Christ which flowed from his

passage the wine of the Eucharist is certainly Jesus' blood: the recipient drinks of Jesus himself. It is not, Aelred suggests, that the substance of the wine is changed into blood during the Mass, but that it was blood in the first place.

Immediately after receiving Jesus' blood, the contemplative enters the wound in his side to become one with him in his flesh. Within the wound the blood is not wine, but blood, and she is to kiss it until her lips are stained with it, "become like a scarlet ribbon." As she then helps to carry Jesus to the tomb she is to "gather up carefully the drops of the precious blood as they fall one by one."[31] The blood becomes wine for her who will drink of it, but it remains primarily and always Jesus' precious blood.

Although all three of the fathers describe the sacraments as flowing from Jesus' side, Aelred here is the most explicit of them in identifying the eucharistic wine with Christ's blood, concretely and visually substantiating eucharistic doctrine, like contemporary paintings of the passion with angels receiving directly into chalices the blood that pours from Jesus' wounds.

Aelred's explanation that at the crucifixion the blood and water are transformed into wine and milk to inebriate and nourish the lover of Christ may also be regarded as a response to one of the continuing eucharistic questions, the relationship between the accidents and the substance of the eucharistic species, between the *sacramentum*, the bread and wine, and the *res sacramenti*, Christ's body and blood. For centuries the church had struggled to explain why and how in the Mass, at the prayer of consecration, the bread and wine are transformed in substance into body and blood; why the sensible characteristics, their accidents, remain those of bread and wine; and why when one eats Christ's body it looks like, smells like, and tastes like bread.

---

side, not however through sign and in the power of the sacrament, but in their real nature and true substance" (Macy, *Theologies*, 37).

[31] Aelred, Inst incl 31 (CCCM 1:671, 672; CF 2:91).

From the time of Ambrose the church had explained that the accidents persist "so that there shall be no horror of the blood" (*horror cruoris*).[32] That is, the body and blood retain the appearance of bread and wine as a comfort to the sensibilities of the communicants, and through these accidents the species indeed both nourish and inebriate. When Aelred argues that the true transformation took place once for all at the crucifixion,[33] turning body and blood into bread and wine to nourish, inebriate, and, moreover, comfort through avoidance of the *horror cruoris*, he echoes the church's various explanations for the fact of and the reason for the concurrent presence in the Eucharist of substance and species.

Having emerged from the Eucharist, risen in the flesh from the manger, the cross, the tomb, and the altar, Jesus for Aelred is always fully human, fully flesh, but at the same time he is also always divine, his humanity always sacred. In *On Reclusion* the infant Jesus is no longer the bread of spiritual animals, but has become a real child to be caressed and loved in all humanity. Aelred says to the contemplative,

> When the infant is laid in the little manger break out into words of exultant joy together with Isaiah and cry: "A child has been born to us, a son is given to us." Embrace that sweet manger, let love overcome your reluctance, affection drive out fear. Put your lips to those most sacred feet, kiss them again and again.

Again he asks, "Do you not think you will gain some devotion by contemplating him at Nazareth as a boy among boys, obedient to his mother and helping his foster-father with his work?"[34]

[32] Ambrose, *De sacramentis* iv.20 (PL 16:443A).

[33] Aelred here addresses another enduring eucharistic controversy, whether the sacrifice on the cross took place once for all (see Heb 10:10) or recurs in each Mass. His statement that the blood is changed to wine at the crucifixion itself argues one sacrifice, not replicable but recallable.

[34] Inst incl 29 (CCCM 1:663–64; CF 2:81, 82).

This emphasis on Jesus' human body and work culminates for Aelred at the passion, when the contemplative is to "lick the dust from his feet" in the Garden of Gethsemane and on the road to the tomb.[35] The new devotion to the God-man budding in the spirituality of Bernard and flowering in William has come to fruit in Aelred's dusty-footed Jesus.

## What Does It Signify?

Neither the nativity nor the crucifixion is self-explanatory, and their mystery becomes for the fathers identical with the mystery of the Eucharist. Just as they look into the manger to find the infant Lord and into the crucifixion to find the God who hangs there dead, so they search with the eye of reason into the Eucharist to pierce beyond the *sacramentum* and find out the *res*, the humanity of Christ, and would go yet beyond, to the divinity with the humanity. For as the significance of the nativity and crucifixion is within, not apparent to the onlooker, so too is that of the Eucharist. What for this life is the significance of the Eucharist and, specifically, of the humanity of Christ discovered there?

This is the second of the great questions raised for the fathers by the search of the eye of reason into the Eucharist, for when it has found the sacred humanity of Christ, what then? If they find there only Jesus, a man bleeding and dead, then surely they have found nothing. Is it possible in the man they have found in the Eucharist to reach God as well, to know Christ's divinity with his humanity? Or is it true that as the communicant cannot with bodily senses see or taste the bread and wine as other than bread and wine, so the eye of reason cannot find out the divinity within the dead Lord?

On this question too Bernard, William, and Aelred's positions present an overlapping development, culminating in Aelred's greater incarnationalism and fuller, more confident,

[35] Inst incl 31 (CCCM 1:669, 672; CF 2:88, 90).

devotion to Jesus. As for both Bernard and William the humanity of Christ leads the Christian onward past him to the Godhead, for them concentration on his humanity endangers the Christian, for he may in his fallen state rest there, in carnal love, never continuing to Christ's divinity.

For both William and Aelred, however, it is possible sometimes even in this life to know the divinity of Christ, though only through his humanity. Where all three of the fathers understand the sacrament to emerge from Jesus' wounds, only these two allow the worshiper to enter the wound itself. For them the risk is not only worth the reward but the only way to it. In fact, Aelred sees little risk in loving Jesus; for him Jesus is always God as well as man, man as well as God, and while one would linger in loving him if one could, "in this wretched life nothing is stable, nothing eternal."[36] The risk is slight because impossible; the Christian needs more often to be urged to overcome timidity, reluctance, and fear than to be restrained and warned.

The fathers' exploration of this second question sometimes seems to leave the Eucharist far behind, as for all three of them the question and the answer arise in the midst of meditation on Christ's humanity, not in eucharistic commentary. But as his humanity is comprehended by the crucifixion, in the breaking of his body and the spilling of his blood, they are unable long to contemplate that humanity without coming again to the body and blood. The humanity emerges for them in the first place from the Eucharist and coexists with the Eucharist, so for them to meditate on Christ's humanity is to contemplate the Eucharist.

Bernard is most unwilling to rest for any time in contemplation of Jesus. For him, the Eucharist is in this life to be eaten primarily in faith and to produce faith. While the eucharistic feast is made up of the body and blood of Jesus, Bernard's attention is rather on the feast and its salvific benefits than on

[36] Inst incl 31 (CCCM 1:673; CF 2:92).

Jesus himself. Bernard eats of Jesus' flesh in order to be overshadowed with faith in his divinity. For him devotion to Jesus and his human activity is always somewhat suspect, certainly only an intermediate stage, valuable in this life for drawing worshipers onward to love him spiritually:

> Notice that the love of our heart may be carnal when it has as its object the flesh of Christ; that which Christ did or taught in the flesh specially touches our human heart. The faithful soul . . . meditates on nothing more sweetly than the life of Christ . . . . To the Christian who prays the image presents itself of the God-man being born, fed with milk, or teaching, dying, rising from the dead or ascending to heaven . . . . For my part, I think that the chief reason which prompted the invisible God to become visible in the flesh and to hold converse with man was to lead carnal men, who are only able to love carnally, to the healthful love of his flesh and afterwards, little by little, to spiritual love.[37]

Bernard warns that even to the contemplative God does not appear in his humanity:

> For I believe that in this vision images of his flesh, or of the cross, or any other suggestions of physical frailty were not imprinted on [the bride's] imagination, since the Prophet tells us that under these forms he possessed neither beauty nor majesty. But as she now contemplates him, she declares him both beautiful and majestic, making it clear that her present vision transcended all others . . . . She must have glimpsed something of the beauty of his higher nature, something that wholly transcends our vision, that eludes our experience.[38]

For Bernard, as Dom Cuthbert Butler points out, "When the bride is the soul of the devout individual man, the Bridegroom is not Jesus Christ in His Humanity, but the Divine Word, the

[37] Bernard, SC 20.6 (SBOp 1:118; CF 4:152). The four references to Christ's flesh in this passage are all variants of *caro*.

[38] Bernard, SC 45.6, 10 (SBOp 2:45; CF 7:236, 239).

Logos, the Second Person of the Holy Trinity—in more than one place He is called 'the Bridegroom-Word,' 'Verbum Sponsus' (*Cant* lxxiv.3)."[39] Indeed Bernard will not allow his Bridegroom-Word to be understood as the human Jesus: "And when you consider the lovers themselves, think not of a man and a woman, but of the Word and the soul."[40]

Bernard understands meditation on the humanity of Christ rather than on the allegorically conceived Bridegroom of the soul as essentially an aid to virtue, food for spiritual beginners:

> I have said that wisdom is to be found in meditating on these truths [of the "anxious hours and bitter experiences of my Lord"]. For me they are the source of perfect righteousness, of the fullness of knowledge, of the most efficacious graces, of abundant merits . . . . For anyone traveling on God's royal way, they provide safe guidance amid the joys and sorrows of life, warding off impending evils on every side . . . . This is my philosophy, one more refined and interior, to know Jesus and him crucified . . . . I do not ask where he rests at noon, for I see him on the cross as my Savior. What [the bride] desired is the more sublime; what I experience is the more sweet. Her portion was bread that satisfies the hunger of children; mine is the milk that fills the breasts of mothers.[41]

For Bernard, then, Jesus illuminates the way to the Godhead but does not himself manifest the Godhead:

> Even now he appears to whom he pleases, but as he pleases, not as he is. Neither sage nor saint nor prophet can or could ever see him as he is, while still in this mortal body; but whoever is found worthy will be able to do so when the body becomes immortal. Hence, though he is seen here below, it is in the form that seems good to him, not as he is.[42]

[39] Cuthbert Butler, *Western Mysticism* (London: Constable, 1922), 97.
[40] Bernard, SC 61.2 (SBOp 2:47; CF 31:141).
[41] Bernard, SC 43.4 (SBOp 2:38; CF 7:222–23).
[42] Bernard, SC 31.2 (SBOp 1:220; CF 7:125).

William too sees Jesus as showing the way to God, frequently defining his humanity as a door to knowledge of God, but he is torn between a longing to enter that door, anxiety that it may be closed to him, and fear that once he has entered, it will close behind him, trapping him there apart from the joy of salvation. William of the three fathers is most aware of Paul's warning that he who partakes of the Eucharist without discerning the Body "eats and drinks judgment on himself,"[43] yet he fears that in discerning the Body one may know no more of Christ than that.

Repeatedly William insists that the crucified Jesus is necessary for the Christian, the only and efficacious door to God:

> For he labors who would go up some other way, but he who enters by you, O Door, walks on the smooth ground and comes to the Father, to whom no one may come, except by you . . . . In sweet meditation on the wonderful sacrament of your passion she muses on the good that you have wrought on our behalf, the good that is as great as you yourself are great, the good that is yourself. She seems to herself to see you face to face when you thus show her, in the cross and in the work of your salvation, the face of the ultimate Good. The cross itself becomes for her the face of a mind that is well-disposed toward God.[44]

But William sometimes finds himself stopped short of the fullness of God even when approaching him through that door, whether in meditation or in the sacrament:

> But when in my eagerness I would approach him and . . . like Thomas, that man of desires, I want to see and touch the whole of him and—what is more—to approach the most holy wound in his side, the portal of the ark that is there made, and not only to put my finger or my whole hand into it, but wholly enter into Jesus' very heart, into the holy of holies, the ark of the covenant, the golden urn, the soul of our humanity that holds within itself

[43] 1 Cor 11:29.

[44] William, Med 10.7 (PL 180:236; CF 3:154).

> the manna of the Godhead—then, alas! I am told: "Touch me not!"[45]

Elsewhere, however, he offers more hope of finding God there:

> Those unsearchable riches of your glory, Lord, were hidden in your secret place in heaven until the soldier's lance opened the side of your Son our Lord and Savior on the cross, and from it flowed the mysteries of our redemption. Now we may not only thrust our finger or our hand into his side, like Thomas, but through that open door may enter whole, O Jesus, even into your heart, the sure seat of your mercy, even into your holy soul that is filled with the fullness of God, full of grace and truth, full of our salvation and our consolation.[46]

William sometimes promises not only knowledge of Christ's humanity and divinity, but unity with him and the Father:

> When you say to the longing soul, "Open your mouth wide and I will fill it," and she tastes and sees your sweetness in the great Sacrament that passes understanding, then she is made that which she eats, bone of your bone and flesh of your own flesh. Thus is fulfilled the prayer that you made to your Father on the threshold of your passion. The Holy Spirit effects in us here by grace that unity which is between the Father and yourself, his Son, from all eternity by nature, so that, as you are one, likewise we may be made one in you.[47]

For William meditation on the humanity of Christ is in fact equivalent to receipt of the sacrament; it effects a spiritual knowledge of and union with the body and blood of the Lord. He promises through it full possession of the spiritual presence

[45] William, Contemp 3 (SCh 61:64; CF 3:38).
[46] William, Med 6.11 (PL 180:225–26; CF 3:131–32).
[47] William, Med 8.5 (PL 180:231; CF 3:142).

of Christ, the *res* of the sacrament, without necessary sacramental reception of the body and blood:

> Anyone who has the mind of Christ knows also how profitable it is to Christian piety, how fitting and advantageous it is to God's servant, the servant of Christ's redemption, to devote at least one hour of the day to an attentive passing in review of the benefits conferred by his passion and the redemption he wrought, in order to savor them in spirit and store them away faithfully in the memory. This is spiritually to eat the Body of the Lord and drink his Blood in remembrance of him who gave to all who believe in him the commandment: "Do this in remembrance of me."
>
> The sacrament without the substance brings death to the communicant, but the substance of the sacrament, even without the visible species, brings eternal life.
>
> Now if you wish, and if you truly desire it, this is at your disposal in your cell at all hours both of day and of night. As often as you stir up sentiments of piety and faith in recalling to mind him who suffered for you, you eat his body and drink his blood. As long as you remain in him through love and he in you through the sanctity and justice he works in you, you are reckoned as belonging to his Body and counted as one of his members.[48]

While Aelred does not directly address William's question of whether meditation on the humanity is equivalent to receipt of the Eucharist, he allows the contemplative full knowledge of and full union with the humanity and divinity of Jesus in meditation on his passion, and he seldom speaks of the sacrament except through moments in the life of Jesus. The center of Aelred's theology is Jesus, not the church or its sacraments.

However, like both Bernard and William, Aelred recognizes the danger of receipt of Christ's flesh without the spirit. In a sermon on the Assumption he comments of Mary and Martha that

[48] William, Ep frat 30.115, 117–19 (SCh 223:234–38; CF 12:49–51).

> These two women were blessed in receiving him physically, but much more blessed because they received him in spirit. Many in those days received him physically and ate and drank with him, but not having received him in the spirit, they remained in their misery.[49]

The Jesus who appears in Aelred's works is indeed true God and true man. Aelred consistently tells of a Jesus who is fleshly and human rather than allegorical or metaphorical, but who is also divine. He does not allow Jesus' divinity to be severed from his humanity, and his crucified Christ does not merely lead from earth to heaven, but links heaven and earth: "The Mediator of God and men hangs midway between heaven and earth, unites the depths with the heights and joins the things of heaven to the things of earth."[50]

For Aelred as for William Jesus' humanity appears in his feet, but for Aelred his divinity rests there as well. At Jesus' birth Aelred directs the contemplative to kiss "those most sacred feet,"[51] later she sees the paralytic let down "before his feet, where kindness and power came to meet one another,"[52] and finally she hears Jesus keep Mary Magdalene "at a distance from [his] most sacred and most desirable feet," but only for a time.[53] In Aelred's works Jesus' feet and head as well show forth both man and God in Christ, and both are to be adored by the Christian: "Break then the alabaster of your heart and whatever devotion you have, whatever love, whatever desire, whatever affection, pour it all out upon your bridegroom's head, while you adore the man in God and God in the man."[54]

[49] Aelred, S. in assumptione b. Mariae; PL 195:303; Storey, "Castle," 191; {Aelred, S 19.3–4; CCCM 2A:147; CF 58:264}.

[50] Aelred, Inst incl 31 (CCCM 1:670; CF 2:89).

[51] Aelred, Inst incl 29 (CCCM 1:663–64; CF 2:81).

[52] Aelred, Inst incl 31 (CCCM 1:666; CF 2:84).

[53] Aelred, Inst incl 31 (CCCM 1:672; CF 2:92).

[54] Aelred, Inst incl 31 (CCCM 1:667; CF 2:85).

Aelred argues, however, that one comes to the divinity through the humanity, kissing the feet in order to know their sacredness, loving the man and so discovering the love of God; in that he has no disagreement with his predecessors. He identifies Christ's two natures with milk and wine in his meditation on the Last Supper and indicates the order in which they are known: "If you are not capable of greater things, leave John to inebriate himself with the wine of gladness in the knowledge of the Godhead while you run to feed on the milk which flows from Christ's humanity."[55]

And when in meditation on the crucifixion the contemplative is to receive the two combined, Aelred is careful again to explain them as distinct though indistinguishable: "Then one of the soldiers opened his side with a lance and there came forth blood and water. Hasten, linger not, eat the honeycomb with your honey, drink your wine with your milk. The blood is changed into wine to inebriate you, the water into milk to nourish you."[56]

Throughout his meditation on the humanity of Christ Aelred is more confident in assuring knowledge of Christ's divinity in union with Christ than either Bernard or William. Although he, like William, shows the risen Jesus sending Mary Magdalene away, saying, "Do not touch me," for him these words do not suggest a barrier to knowledge of Christ's divinity in this life. Rather, Aelred allows Mary to engage in reasoned conversation with Jesus, to raise a theological question calling attention to his new state, and to receive an answer typically divine.

Mary asks Jesus, "Are you less gentle than usual because you are more glorious?" Jesus' answer, like God's to Job, is tangential, experiential, and affective rather than speculative, but it is the right one for Mary and her companions: "'Fear not, this boon is not refused you but kept until later.' . . . And

[55] Aelred, Inst incl 31 (CCCM 1:668; CF 2:87).

[56] Aelred, Inst incl 31 (CCCM 1:671; CF 2:90).

notice, the boon is now given which had previously been kept until later, for they came close and clasped his feet."[57]

Aelred understands Christ's rejection of Mary to be temporary, not absolute, even in this life, and although Mary is sent away by the risen Lord, he welcomes her back to physical embrace. She recognizes him, questions him, and finally with her companions is allowed once again, in his resurrection as in his life, to clasp his feet.

Aelred argues not only that one may know Christ's divinity in this life, but that one may come into physical and spiritual unity with him here. He directs the contemplative to eat and drink of his body, then to enter into the wound in his side, "in which, like a dove, you may hide." In this union the worshiper becomes not only physically one with her Lord but like him, her lips stained with his blood and her word sweet. Seeing her inability to stay there, Aelred urges, "But wait yet awhile until that noble councilor comes to extract the nails and free his hands and feet."[58] After Mary Magdalene is allowed to clasp the feet of the risen Christ, he says again,

> Linger here as long as you can, virgin. Do not let these delights of yours be interrupted by sleep or disturbed by any tumult from without. However, since in this wretched life nothing is stable, nothing eternal, and man never remains in the same state, our soul must needs, while we live, be fed with a certain variety.[59]

Jesus is fully God and fully man, and the one who loves him is spirit and flesh as well. Jesus both feeds and is fed by Mary and Martha:

> If only Mary had been in that house, no one would have been there to feed the Lord, and if only Martha, no one would have

[57] Aelred, Inst incl 31 (CCCM 1:672–73; CF 2:92).

[58] Aelred, Inst incl 31 (CCCM 1:671; CF 2:91). See also Dutton, "Christ Our Mother: Aelred's Iconography for Contemplative Union," chap. 2 above, 45–74.

[59] Aelred, Inst incl 31 (CCCM 1:673; CF 2:92).

> been there to delight in the sermons and presence of the Lord . . . . Mary signifies the rest that frees a man from bodily works that he may delight in the sweetness of God.[60]

Similarly, the contemplative both washes his feet and allows him to wash hers, "because the man whom he does not wash will have no part with him."[61] Thus the union with Christ in the sacrament is for Aelred not merely physical ("We become part of Christ because we eat him"[62]), but spiritual as well: "The man who unites himself with him becomes one spirit with him, passing into that unity which is always the same and whose years do not come to an end."[63] The union for Aelred in the meditation on Christ's humanity and in the Eucharist is real, present, and joyful.

For Aelred the body available to Christians is the same after the resurrection as before; not only is the body received in the Eucharist both the body crucified and the body resurrected, but it may in this life, however briefly, be known as the person of God himself. For Aelred one finds God in the divinity of Christ whenever one finds his humanity, whether before the crucifixion, in the crucifixion, or in the resurrection.

## What Effect?

The last of the great eucharistic questions asked by the fathers is really only a variant of the second: what in the life to come is the effect of the Eucharist? Specifically, what is the relationship of the feast of Christ's body and blood to the heavenly banquet? Where the first question of the eye of reason

[60] Aelred, S. in assumptione b. Mariae; PL 195:306; Storey, "Castle," 92. {Aelred, S 19.18–19; CCCM 2A:151; CF 58:269.}

[61] Aelred, Inst incl 31 (CCCM 1:668; CF 2:86).

[62] Paschasius Radbert, *De corpore et sanguine Domini* (*passim*; see, e.g., IX:111–18); ed. Bede Paulus, CCCM 16:56; Macy, *Theologies*, 70. Paschasius refers to this as "natural" union.

[63] Aelred, Inst incl 26 (CCCM 1:659; CF 2:74).

discovered the humanity of Christ in time past and the second considered the experience of the worshiper in time present, the third inquires into the things to come in beatitude.[64]

In the twelfth century the salvific benefits of the Eucharist were a matter of general agreement, but as the fathers emerged from their new and reasoned understanding of the humanity of Jesus they came to a new understanding of the Eucharist. No longer was receiving the species merely an act of faith, a blind tasting in unquestioning acceptance of what that tasting promised; now it meant feasting with both eyes open. Indeed, each of the fathers came to see the Eucharist and its eternal benefits much as they saw the Jesus they had come to know there. As his flesh was the sacrament, it was not surprising that their new conception of him shaped their conception of the sacrament.

Thus, as Bernard and William see Christ's humanity as essentially a door to the Godhead and fear that lingering there will keep them from eternity, so they understand the Eucharist itself as an invitation, a foretaste, a transitory table at which one dare not linger. They see that God invites them to him through these gifts of his grace but argue that the one who considers those gifts the feast rather than the invitation will eat and drink to judgment. And as Aelred knows Jesus' humanity to be one with his divinity and encourages those who would know him to hasten to him and linger at his feet, so he considers the Eucharist itself a feast of delight, certainly a foretaste of what is to come, but no less an occasion of joy in this world.

At the same time, in this third step in understanding the Eucharist, the fathers move again away from the humanity of Christ, into eating and drinking, banquets, milk, oil, bread, and wine. As the writers turn to the eucharistic banquet and to the foretaste it offers of the heavenly banquet to come, of

[64] These are the subjects of Aelred's three meditations in *On Reclusion*, though he does not suggest them as eucharistic or eschatological categories.

salvation itself, they turn increasingly toward the face of God or the vision of Christ coming in glory. Jesus the man is now left far behind, become in the writings of the fathers once again almost symbolic.

The Cistercian fathers agree that the goal of the pilgrim in this world is beatitude, the heavenly Jerusalem, the eternal banquet of the vision of God: "Taste and see how sweet is the Lord."[65] Their regular repetition of these words, surely the biblical verse most frequent in the works of the fathers, enforces the interrelated themes that God is to be tasted to be known and that one tastes in this world in order to dine in the world to come. As knowing leads to love, so tasting brings eternal vision.

This apparently mixed metaphor present in the Psalm and used by the fathers exemplifies their common understanding of the effects of the Eucharist for all time, in time to come. That effect is the salvation of believers, the redemption of all who eat of the body and blood, restoration to the sight of God's face lost in the Fall. As Adam and Eve in eating of the tree of the knowledge of good and evil brought about expulsion from the Garden and hence from the sight of God, so those of their descendants who eat of God himself are restored eternally to his sight. It is not surprising that, for the Cistercians, eating brings vision, tasting allows one to see.

All three of the fathers indicate this understanding of the Eucharist when they speak of Jesus in the words of Genesis: "The Lord God made trees spring from the ground, all trees pleasant to look at and good for food; and in the middle of the garden he set the tree of life and the tree of the knowledge of good and evil."[66] Bernard enunciates the reversal of the Fall and the Christian's experience of the reversal in the Eucharist: "Christ alone, the Wisdom of God, is the tree of life, he alone the living bread which comes down from heaven and gives

[65] Ps 34:9.

[66] Gen 2:9.

life to the world . . . . [He alone] produces a life-giving food . . . the enduring fruits of salvation."[67]

William too brings together humankind's Fall and restoration through eating of God:

> For when of old in your paradise you created me, and gave me the tree of life for my possession, as of abiding right, you willed—or at least you allowed me to reach my hand out also for the fruit of the tree of the knowledge of good and evil. . . . I tasted of the fruit and saw not your sweetness but my own shame . . . . And now, Desire of my soul, my soul desires to wait on you a little space, and to taste and see how sweet you are, O Lord.[68]

Aelred too links taste and sight, Fall and Redemption, explaining humankind's loss of the enduring sight and taste of God through Adam's eating in the Garden. For Aelred Jesus' life and crucifixion are a rectification of the Fall; when Christians next eat, now of his body, they will at last taste of God and see him without error. In a sermon on the nativity Aelred says that Jesus was born to restore what Adam lost:

> [In creation man's] memory was like a thread of the soul, retaining God without ever forgetting him: his reason was like a look which saw God without possibility of error; his love was a tasting of God in the interior of his heart, which made him desire no other.
>
> Oh unhappy Adam! What more did you want? O ingrate! Here you are considering your crime: "No, I will be like God." O ingrate! . . . O intolerable pride! You were just made from clay and mud, and in your insolence you wish to be like God. It is very possible that the devil, seeing this foolish thought in your spirit, said, "I will show you a way: eat and you will be like the gods."[69]

[67] Bernard, SC 48.5–6 (SBOp 2:70; CF 31:16–17).

[68] William, Med 4.4, 9 (PL 180:215–16; CF 3:112, 115).

[69] Aelred, S. in nativitate Domini, in Talbot, ed., *Sermones Inediti*, 38; {Aelred, S 49.5; CCCM 2B:23; CF 80:29–30}.

For the Cistercian fathers the Eucharist above all redeems the fallen and restores to them what was lost in Adam's eating from the tree, the vision of God in eternity. The feast of Christ's body is at last the fruit of the tree of life for Adam's heirs, the food of salvation and of eternal life.

The fathers differ, however, in their degree of emphasis on the Eucharist as preliminary, partial, anticipatory. Of the three, Bernard most systematically uses the language of eating and drinking to define the stages to the eternal vision of God: he insists that the union with God in the sacrament, while real and substantial enough, is incomplete, a help along the way to beatitude. Much as he speaks of meditation on Christ's humanity as "safe guidance on God's royal way,"[70] he explains Jesus' words from John 14:6, "I am the way, the truth, and the life," as meaning finally "I am the food, the viaticum, to sustain you on the way."[71]

Bernard repeatedly defines the journey to God in three steps, at least three times in the eucharistic language of the Song of Songs: "Eat, my friends, and drink: be inebriated, my dearest ones."[72] He explains that although bread and wine are available at all stages along the way to God, beginners are restricted to the bread of sorrow and the wine of compunction. Elsewhere Bernard insists that the highest step, with the purest wine, is available only to the blessed, seated already at the heavenly banquet:

> Then at last, the soul is admitted to the wine-bowl of wisdom, of which it is said, "How good is my cup, it inebriates me! . . . Eat before death, drink after death, be inebriated after the resurrection. It is right to call them dearest who are drunk with love;

[70] Bernard, SC 43.4 (SBOp 2:38; CF 7:223).

[71] Bernard, Hum I.1 (SBOp 3:17; CF 13:30). Bernard clearly does not use *viaticum* here in its current sense. He is consciously engaging in word play throughout this passage: "Ego sum vita, id est viaticum, quo sustenteris in via."

[72] Song 5:1.

> they are rightly inebriated who deserve to be admitted to the nuptials of the Lamb, eating and drinking at his table in his kingdom."[73]

The same scheme appears briefly in a sermon, where Bernard again defines the Eucharist as foretaste, saying that in this world and while "in the corruptible flesh" one eats what one will later drink, now eating in faith, later drinking in contemplating the face of the Lord, seeing him face to face.[74]

Repeatedly Bernard emphasizes that eating Jesus "in the memory of his Passion" prepares one for salvation:

> In the meantime memory is sweet for those who seek and long for God's presence, not that they are satisfied but that they may hunger all the more for him that they might be satisfied. Thus he testifies that he himself is food: "Who eats me will hunger for more." Whoever is nourished by him says, "I shall be satisfied when your glory appears."[75]

While Bernard consistently speaks of knowing God now only in anticipation and by faith, only as he wills to be known, William occasionally allows real unity with God in this life in the Eucharist, however briefly, promising that "when [the soul] tastes and sees your sweetness in the great Sacrament that surpasses understanding, then she is made that which she eats, bone of your bone and flesh of your own flesh. The Holy Spirit effects in us here by grace that unity which is between the Father and yourself, his Son, from all eternity by nature; so that, as you are one, likewise we may be made one in you."[76]

[73] Bernard, Dil 33 (SBOp 3:146–47; CF 13:123–24).

[74] Bernard, *Sermones Diversi* 87.4 (SBOp 6:331; CF 68:329).

[75] Bernard, Dil 11 (SBOp 3:127; CF 13:103); Sir 24:21, where Wisdom speaks: "Those who eat of me will still hunger; those who drink of me will still thirst." See Jesus' words in John 4:13-14. I have discussed Aelred's use of Wisdom's self-introduction in Inst incl 14 (CCCM 1:650; CF 2:63), in "Christ Our Mother: Aelred's Iconography for Contemplative Union," chap. 2 above, 51–52.

[76] William, Med 8.5 (PL 180:231; CF 3:142).

Elsewhere, however, after quoting from Jesus' prayer in the Garden—"I in them, and you in me, that they may be made perfect in oneness"—he acknowledges that

> [t]his unity of course transcends the limits of our human nature, but falls short of the unity that belongs to the being of God . . . . Moreover, the likeness of God will be conferred on us by the sight of God, when we see not only that he is, but see him as he is; that is the likeness that will make us like to him.[77]

William argues finally that while unity with Christ is possible in this life, it is rare and incomplete; real and enduring union with the Father and the Son comes only in beatitude, and the Eucharist is primarily an anticipation of that vision and that union rather than an eternal verity:

> Then just as in the past the new sacraments of grace put an end to the old sacraments, so the Reality of all the sacraments [*res ipsa sacramentorum omnium*] will utterly put an end to all sacraments. In the sacraments of the New Testament, it is true, the day of new grace began to break, but in that end of perfect consummation will come the full noonday when glass and riddle and that which is in part shall be done away, but there shall be the vision face to face and the plenitude of the highest Good.[78]

Like Bernard, William writes frequently of the grace of God that makes itself known in food and drink to beginners on the road to God, but warns against accepting that grace as a stopping place rather than as a help along the way:

> When [the soul], like a person raised in the country, nourished on and accustomed to country cooking, has begun to taste these affections of which we spoke, it is like her first entrance to a royal court. When she is ignominiously chased away and violently thrown out, she can hardly consent to return again to the house

[77] William, Med 6.8 (PL 180:224; CF 3:129).
[78] William, Cant II.4.176 (SCh 82:360; CF 6:142).

> of her poverty. She returns time after time to the door, importunate, persistent, and eager, as one in need. As a beggar, hoping, sighing, she looks up to see if anything is going to be offered to her whenever the door is opened. And sometimes by her shamelessness and importunity she has so overcome and overstepped all hurdles that, leaping along in her desire even up to wisdom's inmost table, she may impudently take a seat, a guest sure to be turned out again, and may hear, "Eat, friends, drink! Drink freely, my dearest friends!"
>
> At this stage, unless one is on his guard, the grave hindrance of temptation occurs . . . . What one has received for the journey from his dutiful Father, to prevent him from succumbing on the way, he begins to consider adequate, and setting up a milestone of his journey there, where he fails to advance, he really begins to fail! . . .
>
> The psalmist says, "The enemies of the Lord lied to him and their time shall be forever. And he fed them with the finest wheat and satisfied them with honey from the rock." Notice: they are fed; yet notice: they are enemies! Notice: they are satisfied; yet, notice: they are liars! Notice: not only with wheat but with the finest wheat, not just the rock but honey from the rock, that is, the hidden and divine grace of the sacraments . . . . Anyone who is satisfied seeks no longer what he has received, for he is full; what he has is enough for him.[79]

Like William, Aelred sees both the union with God in Christ here and the Eucharist as promises of the fullness to come, but while he agrees in regarding them both as temporary, his incarnational certainty renders them both less transitory, more satisfying in themselves than is true for Bernard and William. Where Bernard repeatedly preaches that the wine that inebriates is to be found only in beatitude, for Aelred the Christian may obtain it here, from Jesus himself, and where both Bernard and William argue that the Jesus one meets here is only the back of, the door to, his Father, for Aelred he is true God, in whom the worshiper may find union.

[79] William, Nat am 2.10–11 (PL 184:386; CF 30:64–66).

Aelred appears to see little risk that the worshiper may be tempted to stay in the fleshly delights of either the embrace of Jesus or the eucharistic banquet. One is at more risk by holding back, ashamed of "that insolent serving girl, my flesh"[80] or needing to be urged forward. Over and over in his meditation on Jesus' humanity Aelred says, "Hasten, run!" or "Do not delay to claim for yourself some portion of this sweetness."[81]

So too the Last Supper described by Aelred is both a meal producing salvation and one of delights in itself. He says to the contemplative:

> Now then go up with him into the large upper room, furnished for supper, and rejoice to share the delights of the meal which brings us salvation. Let love overcome shyness, affection drive out fear, so that he may at least give you an alms from the crumbs of that table when you beg for something. Or stand at a distance and, like a poor man looking to a rich man, stretch out your hand to receive something, let your tears declare your hunger.[82]

This concrete and biblical variant on the parable told by William is for Aelred not followed by a warning against lingering there, but quite a different question: "Why are you in such a hurry to go out now? Wait a little while." And at once the contemplative is directed to see the disciple John receiving the wine of the knowledge of the Godhead and being inebriated by it, just as she herself is to do at the crucifixion. For Aelred the Eucharist, like Jesus the God-man, is both a promise of things to come and complete in itself, to be eaten and enjoyed in assurance of what is to come but also as a present delight.

But Aelred too insists that this meal is primarily a foretaste, provided as an appetizer for what is to come:

[80] Aelred, Inst incl 31 (CCCM 1:669; CF 2:88).

[81] Aelred, Inst incl 31 (CCCM 1:668; CF 2:87).

[82] Aelred, Inst incl 31 (CCCM 1:668; CF 2:86).

> Love is the heart's palate for him who knows that you are sweet . . . . This is that abundance of your house, by which your lovers are inebriated, passing out of themselves that they may pass over into you. And how, Lord, unless in loving you? . . . I beg, Lord, that some small portion of this great sweetness of you may descend into my soul, by which the bread of its bitterness may become sweet. Let it experience in this little draught the foretaste of what it desires, what it longs for, what it sighs for in this its pilgrimage. Let it have its foretaste in hungering, its drink in thirsting. For those who eat of you hunger still, and those who drink you thirst still. They will be sated, however, when your glory appears, when that great abundance of your sweetness is shown.[83]

Aelred speaks similarly of "those gifts of God's goodness" known only to the contemplative, but suggests in using the word *debriauit* rather than his more usual *inebriauit* that for him as for Bernard the inebriation of the contemplative is different in quality from that experienced in beatitude:

> With how glad a face Christ comes to meet one who renounces the world, with what delights he feeds her in her hunger, what riches of his compassion he shows her, what affections he arouses in her, with what a cup of charity he inebriates [*debriauit*] her . . . . How often he lifted up your mind from the things of earth and introduced it into the delights of heaven and the joys of Paradise.[84]

Aelred is less concerned than Bernard and William to warn against stopping short with the Eucharist, the taste of God's sweetness in the world, assuming apparently that the delights

[83] Aelred, Spec car 1.1.2 (CCCM 1:13; CF 5:88). See Paschasius, *Epistola ad Fredugarum* II.105–9 (CCCM 16:148): "Just as in the present 'we know in part' whatever we know of God, and 'in part' by the testimony of the Apostle, 'we prophesy' of the future and of the kingdom of heaven, so it is in part that we pre-taste, not with the palate of our mouth, but with the palate of our heart, and by faith we believe it to be the body and blood of Christ."

[84] Aelred, Inst incl 32 (CCCM 1:676; CF 2:96).

of the taste will be sufficient to draw one onward, but he is no less clear than the others that it is the heavenly banquet for which one longs, the joy of beatitude and of eternal sweetness. For while Christians may delight in the food of the Eucharist or in meditation on the humanity of Christ, it is more common that they will eat their bread in the sweat of their face, like all the descendants of Adam.

The fathers' shared understanding of the relationship between the things of this life and those to come appears in Aelred's conclusion to his meditations on things past, things present, and things to come:

> Meditation will arouse the affections, the affections will give birth to desire, and desire will stir up tears, so that your tears may be bread for you day and night until you appear in his sight and are received by his embrace and say to him what is written in the *Song of Songs*: "My Beloved is mine and I am his."[85]

The Cistercians agree finally that Christians must wait in darkness, loneliness, and hunger for that day when they will come to "the sight, the knowledge and the love of the Creator," when "that lovable face, so longed for, upon which the angels yearn to gaze, will be seen."[86] Then they may rejoice with all those who are "glad with the ceaseless glory of the sight of [God], voided of all that could distract from feasting forever on [his] face."[87]

For the Cistercian fathers the eye of reason has moved from the bread and wine within which the body of Christ is hidden to that body of Christ itself and, finally, now in faith reformed through experience, back to the Eucharist, understood not as an end in itself, but as an anticipation, a foretaste of the vision of God to come in the heavenly Jerusalem.

[85] Aelred, Inst incl 33 (CCCM 1:681; CF 2:102). The phrase "and are received by his embrace" [*et suscipiaris ab amplexibus eius*] does not appear in CF 2, though Talbot indicates its absence in no MS.

[86] Aelred, Inst incl 33 (CCCM 1:681; CF 2:101).

[87] William, Med 6.2 (PL 180:222; CF 3:125–26).

*Chapter 6*

# Intimacy and Imitation: The Humanity of Christ in Cistercian Spirituality[1]

The incarnation represents the intimacy of the human state with God, says Gregory of Nyssa,[2] and the works of Cistercian spirituality echo that understanding. In his sermons on the Song of Songs, the great book of intimacy between the divine and the human, Bernard of Clairvaux lays a foundation for an incarnational and sacramental spirituality of just such intimacy, explaining the incarnation, the Holy Spirit, and the soul's reception of God's power and knowledge all in terms of a kiss:

> The mouth that kisses signifies the Word who assumes human nature; the nature assumed receives the kiss; the kiss, however, that takes its being from both the giver and the receiver, is a person that is formed by both, none other than "the one mediator between God and mankind, himself a man, Christ Jesus."[3]

[1] First presented at the Cistercian Studies Conference at Western Michigan University, May 1986. Originally published in *Erudition at God's Service: Studies in Medieval Cistercian History XI*, ed. John R. Sommerfeldt, CS 98 (Kalamazoo, MI: Cistercian Publications, 1987), 33–69. Reprinted here by permission from Cistercian Publications.

[2] *De virginitate* 2 (PG 46:323); Gregory of Nyssa, *Dogmatic Treatises*, trans. William Moore and Henry Astin Wilson, Nicene and Post-Nicene Fathers, 2nd series, 5 (New York: Wipf and Stock, 1893), 344.

[3] Bernard, SC 2.3 (SBOp 1:9–10; CF 4:10).

And again:

> Then look at Jesus in the presence of his Apostles: "He breathed on them," according to St John, "and he said: 'Receive the Holy Spirit.'" That favor, given to the newly chosen church, was indeed a kiss. That? you say. That corporeal breathing? O no, but rather the invisible Spirit, who is so bestowed in that breath of the Lord that he is understood to proceed from him equally as from the Father, truly the kiss that is common both to him who kisses and to him who is kissed . . . . It is by giving the Spirit, through whom he reveals, that he shows us himself; he reveals in the gift, his gift is in the revealing. Furthermore, this revelation which is made through the Holy Spirit not only conveys the light of knowledge but also lights the fire of love.[4]

William of Saint-Thierry expands this understanding, saying, "The soul in its happiness finds itself standing midway in the Embrace and the Kiss of Father and Son."[5] And Aelred of Rievaulx defines three spiritual significations of marriage, of which "the first was accomplished in Bethlehem, when like a bridegroom coming forth from his chamber, emerging from the virginal womb, the Word in our nature brought forth unity with men."[6]

## The Origins of Cistercian Spirituality

The spirituality of the Cistercian fathers is profoundly incarnational, centered in the love of God made known in his intimate union with humanity and participating in the mutual love of the Father and the Son through the Holy Spirit. As it is

[4] Bernard, SC 8.2, 3, 5 (SBOp 1:37–38; CF 4:46, 48).

[5] William, Ep frat 263 (SCh 233:354; CF 12:96).

[6] Aelred, S. in Epiphania de tribus generibus nuptiarum, in *Sermones inediti B. Aelredi abbatis Rievallensis*, ed. C. H. Talbot, Series Scriptorum S. Ordinis Cisterciensis (Rome: Curia gen., O.Cist., 1952), 39; {Aelred, S 50.2; CCCM 2B:26; CF 80:32}.

always a present response to God's initiative of love both past and present, it is in essence willed, active, and intimate.

Another way of expressing the same idea is to say that Cistercian spirituality is in essence sacramental, grounded in the meeting of the worshiper with Christ on the altar and in Christ's revelation of himself there through the gift of the Holy Spirit. God channels his grace in the sacrament as in the incarnation, through the sensible, leading humankind through creatures of bread and wine to his son, begotten, not made, and so to himself. For Cistercian spirituality, far from being rooted in a desire to escape the flesh and the world, begins and ends in God known in the flesh in this world. Rather than attempting to bypass the incarnation on its way to God, it never leaves the eucharistic feast behind in its hunger for the heavenly banquet, nor does it turn away from the feet of Jesus in its yearning for the eternal sight of the face of God.

The spirituality of the Cistercian fathers must then be understood through the incarnation and its sacramental mirror, the Eucharist. There it begins and ends. Moreover, it participates in the Eucharist and takes on its likeness, always both loving and showing forth the humanity of Jesus. In their sermons and spiritual treatises the fathers insist that one becomes one with Christ by finding his humanity in his body and blood on the altar, joining him in his human life, and finally coming to physical and spiritual oneness with him by partaking of his body and blood once again.[7]

[7] Gary Macy says that Lanfranc included "contact with the humanity of Jesus as one of the principal results of the reception of the Eucharist" (*The Theologies of the Eucharist in the Early Scholastic Period* [Oxford: Oxford University Press, 1984], 47). Macy adds: "The devotion to the Eucharist in the twelfth and thirteenth centuries was one expression of a whole movement toward a more personal love for the Human Christ. Despite the manifold forms that the devotion to the Eucharist manifested in the early scholastic period, however, the two consistent features of that devotion appear to be a strong belief in a real, nearly sensual, presence of Christ in the sacrament, and a growing interest in the Human Christ so present" (95). See Dutton, "Eat, Drink, and Be Merry: The Eucharistic Spirituality of the Cistercian Fathers," chap. 5 above, 157–91.

But the search for Christ that culminates in eucharistic spirituality also arises from the Cistercians' insistent sense that they live in exile in this world, seldom vouchsafed even a foretaste of the glory to come, in a land of unlikeness cast out from their Father's face. And in that exile they long for nothing so much as the presence of God. Recalling Paul's lamenting promise that "here we see in a glass darkly, but there face to face,"[8] Aelred titles his first known work, apparently at Bernard's bidding, *The Mirror of Charity*, so signaling its recognition that in this life love is always obscure, darkened, distorted.[9]

Repeatedly the fathers mourn their separation from the feast of the Lord, the embrace of the Lord, the face of the Lord. Aelred speaks of Lent as representing the time between the Fall and "the last day, when we shall be finally liberated from this exile of ours," and of the fasting in Lent as a reminder "that in this life our desire for the heavenly bread can never be fully satisfied."[10] And William considers this life his hell "till I appear before your presence and behold your glory, and the eternal feast day of your face has shone upon my soul."[11]

The longing for that face in glory drives the Cistercian fathers on in unremitting yearning to see God now, to have him here, to love him in this world as in heaven. For just as the Eucharist provides a beginning and end for Cistercian spirituality, the fathers' longing for beatitude defines its necessity and its approach. As they long for God's embrace, the "feasting for ever on [his] face,"[12] they seek some temporary and partial measure of satisfaction.

[8] 1 Cor 13:12.

[9] Bernard, "Ep. ad Aelredum" (SBOp 8:486–89; see Lawrence C. Braceland, "Bernard and Aelred on Humility and Obedience," in *Erudition at God's Service*, ed. Sommerfeldt), 149–59.

[10] Aelred, Inst incl 11 (CCCM 1:647; CF 2:58).

[11] William, Med 3.4 (PL 180:212; CF 3:104). William's longing for the face of God dominates his spiritual works, especially the *Meditations*.

[12] William, Med 6.2 (PL 180:222; CF 3:126).

As their goal is love, their route must be love, and as their goal is sensuous and intimate—dining, drinking, embracing, and looking at last on him whom they love, now at last face to face—so too must their journey be sensuous, intimate, comprised of eating and drinking, of loving and embracing, of seeing the face of God in the familiar face of a man.

Indeed, the face for which they yearn in glory is already known to them here as the face of Jesus, and Aelred insists that it is the same face. When in his meditation on the Judgment he speaks of Christ the Judge, who comes "in anger, his fury all ablaze and his chariot like a storm," at the left the damned drop their eyes.[13] But as the blessed stand on his right, "Jesus' face shines upon them, not terrible but lovable, not bitter but sweet, not frightening but attractive."[14] In fact in the third meditation of *On Reclusion*, Aelred uses the name Jesus only here, insistently identifying the Judge as the Jesus whose loving and gentle gaze has been known on earth. For Aelred God in glory is identical to the God known here in Jesus.

So the fathers kiss the feet of Jesus in order to come to the vision of God's face. Bernard says, "Prostrate yourself on the ground, take hold of his feet, soothe them with kisses";[15] William: "Anyone may see me lying with the sinful woman at your mercy's feet, washing them with the tears of my heart and anointing them with the perfume of heartfelt devotion!"[16] Aelred's *On Reclusion* is full of the kissing of Jesus' feet, in the manger, at the Last Supper, before and after the crucifixion, but Aelred often suggests a more direct link between them and the vision than do the others: "Surely you would not advise Mary to leave those feet which she is kissing so sweetly, or to

[13] William too acknowledges that that face for which he longs will be terrible to the damned, saying: "In your face an enemy, by contrast, finds a fiery oven; a sinner finds the portion of his cup, fetters and flames, sulphur and stormy winds" (Med 8.6 [PL 180:231; CF 3:143]).

[14] Aelred, Inst incl 33 (CCCM 1:678; CF 2.98–99).

[15] Bernard, SC 3.2 (SBOp 1:15; CF 4:17).

[16] William, Med 5.9 (PL 180:221; CF 3:123).

turn her eyes away from that most beautiful face which she is contemplating, or to stop listening to the sweet words with which he regales her."[17]

This historical, physical approach to God through Jesus is combined with a metaphorical and at the same time eucharistic one as the fathers speak of entering to God through Jesus, "the way, the truth, and the life."[18] William also speaks of Jesus as the door and as a bridge, even a ramp:

> He who enters by you, O Door, walks on the smooth ground and comes to the Father, to whom no one may come, except by you . . . . For what better preparation, what happier arrangement could have been made for the man who wanted to ascend to his God . . . than that, instead of going up by steps to the altar, he should walk calmly and smoothly over the level of his own likeness, to a Man like himself, who tells him on the very threshold: "I and the Father are one." And he is forthwith gathered up to God in love through the Holy Spirit and receives God coming to him and making his abode with him, not spiritually only but corporeally too, in the mystery of the holy and life-giving body and blood of our Lord Jesus Christ. This, Lord, is your face towards us and our face towards you, full of good hope.[19]

The desire of the fathers is not only to be assisted in their loneliness and separation in this world, but to come to God in the next. Eucharistic theology is always essentially concerned with salvation, of course, not contemplative union; the Cistercian fathers in seeking to see God through the Eucharist hope primarily through the Eucharist to reach salvation. Their longing to see God here is not a desire for quick thrills, temporal and temporary pleasure, but a means of enabling them to continue in the love of God.

[17] Aelred, Inst incl 31 (CCCM 1:667; CF 2:86).

[18] John 14:6; Bernard, Hum 1.1 (SBOp 3:17; CF 13:30); William, Contemp 12 (SCh 61:110; CF 3:60).

[19] William, Med 10.7 (PL 180:236–37; CF 3:154).

For in the exile of this life, it is not a simple thing to keep one's eyes—and heart—set on the goal. The great difficulty, for the fathers as for all Christians, is that voiced by William: "Who can love what he does not see? How can that be lovable that is not in some way visible?"[20] And Aelred's Mary Magdalene voices the inevitable Cistercian anxiety to the risen Jesus: "Are you become less tender because more glorious?"[21] If they will come in love to God finally, they must find a way to remain in love with him now, but the difficulty seems insurmountable.

If Cistercian spirituality develops through the yearning that combines loneliness, anxiety, unwillingness to accept absolute exile in this life, and the desire to dwell in eternity within God's love, to "so pass through things temporal that we lose not the things eternal,"[22] that yearning is far from despair. It consists of love not hopeless but hopeful, and that love is the means to love. William says:

> He . . . who desires loves always to desire, and he who loves desires to love always. And for him who desires and loves, O Lord, you make what he desires so to abound that the desirer is vexed by no anxiety, nor does he who has plenty ever have too much . . . . To travel always thus is to arrive.[23]

As no true lover can peacefully acquiesce to separation from the beloved, Cistercian love is not peaceful, passive, experienced as merely a wait for God's longed-for but unsought visits. Rather, it is on the road, active, urgent, importunate.

Bernard and Aelred both cite Peter as the prototype for such importunity, and Aelred explicitly defines him as the great lover of Jesus among the disciples, applauding his unwillingness to wait for the sight of him whom he loves. A man of

[20] William, Contemp 3 (SCh 61:67; CF 3:40).
[21] Aelred, Inst incl 31 (CCCM 1:672; CF 2:92).
[22] Proper collect 12, Book of Common Prayer (1979), 231.
[23] William, Contemp 6 (SCh 61:76–82; CF 3:46–47).

violent, impetuous love, who fully clothed races the boat through the Sea of Galilee to greet his risen Lord cooking breakfast on the shore, Peter is compelled to hasten by his hunger to see, to touch, to eat and drink with his Lord:

> O admirable ardor! . . . Only Peter, like a hart burning with thirst, devoured by internal fire, fears neither the stares nor the waves, thinks only of him whom he sees afar on the beach . . . . Our Spirit asks which of our fathers surpasses the others in the love of God. Now we know—our Lord said it himself—that Peter loved him more than the other apostles.[24]

The importunity of Cistercian spirituality, the refusal to give up the flesh of Christ, prompts some anxiety among the fathers. Both Bernard and Aelred speak of the love of Jesus' flesh that binds the hearts of the disciples, and especially of Peter. Both declare that love to be immature, characterizing beginners in faith. But while Aelred praises it, Bernard blames it. He reminds his listeners that "the love of the heart . . . is sweet indeed, but liable to be led astray if it lacks the love of the soul," then cites the example of Peter:

> When [Jesus] was speaking in the same way about his approaching death, Peter who loved him so dearly tried to stand in the way. When, as you remember, [Jesus] rebuked him, what was it

[24] Aelred, "S. in natale apostolorum Petri et Pauli," in Talbot, ed., *Sermones inediti*, 132–33; {Aelred, S 71.20, 22 [CCCM 2B:225, 226; CF 80:284]}. Aelred even lauds Peter's cutting off the ear of Malchus, saying in the same sermon: "If the zeal of Peter was perfect when he brandished his sword, his charity had not yet attained the perfection of wisdom . . . . And however, it is necessary to praise the ardor of Peter, my brothers, and admire his devotion to the Lord. An immense love had seized his spirit and inspired him against the persecutors of Christ" {S 71.35 (CCCM 2B:230; CF 80:289)}. It is not accidental, then, that Peter is one of those granted in life the loving gaze of Christ to be seen in glory. In his meditation on the life of Christ Aelred says of Jesus: "See with what a loving gaze, how mercifully, how effectually, he looks at Peter who has thrice denied him" (Aelred, Inst incl 31 [CCCM 1:669; CF 2:88]).

> but his imprudence that he was correcting? Finally, what did he mean in saying, "You do not mind the things of God" except you do not love wisely, you are following your human feeling in opposition to the divine plan . . . . Taught to love with his whole soul, Peter was still weak. He was well instructed but not well prepared, aware of the mystery but afraid of being witness to it.[25]

Bernard insists throughout his works that such love of the flesh is carnal, restricted, potentially dangerous, and in fact no longer possible since the ascension.

Although Aelred applauds Peter's impetuosity, he agrees with Bernard that to love Christ only in the humanity is to be a spiritual infant, that the mature Christian must advance to knowledge and love of his divinity:

> One may note, however, that the love of Peter exercises itself with more tenderness toward the humanity of the Savior while Paul is more eager to contemplate the mystery of the divinity . . . . Both [Peter and Paul] knew and loved perfectly the strength of his divinity and the mystery of the Incarnation, especially after the glorification of Jesus and the reception of the fullness of the Holy Spirit. However, one may say that in the affection of Peter is the milk of doctrine offered to infants, and in the love of Paul, the solid nourishment of contemplation.[26]

[25] Bernard, SC 20.5 (SBOp 1:117–18; CF 4:151).

[26] Aelred, S. in natale, in Talbot, ed., *Sermones inediti*, 133 {S 71.24; CCCM 2B:226–27; CF 80:285}. In "Christ Our Mother: Aelred's Iconography for Contemplative Union," chap. 2 above, I have discussed Aelred's treatment of the progression from knowledge of the humanity to knowledge of the divinity, there conceived as milk and wine. But not only does Aelred not suggest that adults should in going forward to the wine of inebriation leave behind the milk of nourishment, but he insists on their mutual reception, saying: "Hasten, linger not . . . drink your wine with your milk. The blood is changed into wine to inebriate you, the water into milk to nourish you" (Aelred, Inst incl 31 [CCCM 1:671; CF 2:90–91]). In *Mirror*, however, Aelred associates wine with compunction for beginners and milk with consolation for proficients: "And when they have been torn from the milk, they will become guests at the banquet of the coming of his glory" (Aelred, Spec car 2.12.30 {CCCM 1:79; CF 5:183}).

William agrees:

> When the faithful soul has been taught by such things, however, she should begin not to need them and pass from physical to spiritual things and from spiritual things to the Maker of the spiritual and physical. Truly, then, she shall leave her baggage behind! For having left the body and all bodily cares and hindrances, she forgets everything except God.[27]

But despite their fears, despite their general sense that the mature lover of God may and must move beyond the flesh, Bernard, William, and Aelred recognize that carnal humankind, animal souls, novices, unschooled anchoresses, all the spiritual babes to whom they preach and for whom they write, continue to need God made man as fully after the glorification of Jesus and the reception of the fullness of the Holy Spirit as before. Bernard muses:

> I think this is the principal reason that the invisible God willed to be seen in the flesh and to converse with men as a man. He wanted to recapture the affections of carnal men who were unable to love in any other way, by first drawing them to the salutary love of his own humanity, and then gradually to raise them to a spiritual love . . . . So it was only by his physical presence that their hearts were detached from carnal loves.[28]

And William says:

> It was not the least of the chief reasons for your incarnation that your babes in the church, who still needed your milk rather than solid food, who are not strong enough spiritually to think of you in your own way, might find in you a form not unfamiliar to themselves. In offering of their prayers they might set this form

[27] William, Nat am 44 (PL 184:417; CF 30:107–8).

[28] Bernard, SC 20.67 (SBOp 1:118; CF 4:152).

> before themselves, without any hindrance to faith, while they are still unable to gaze into the brightness of the majesty of your divinity.[29]

For spiritual beginners love temporal is the only route to love eternal; the kiss of Jesus' feet is the route to the eternal vision of the face of God.

## The Work of the Eye of Love

But the difficulty in loving Jesus begins with Paul's statement, echoed repeatedly by Bernard: "If we once knew Christ in the flesh we know him thus no longer."[30] And William asks, How is it possible to love him here when we cannot see him here? How does one love what one cannot see? And where in this post-ascension time, in this life, does one look for his sight?

Having posed the question, William gives its solution: One must see; having seen, one will love and, what is more, possess the beloved: "For to see the good things of the Lord is to love them, and to love them is to have them."[31] William points those who would see toward the Eucharist, insisting that it is the Eucharist that allows the sight of God even here:

> Not that divinity may be seen by physical eyes, but that glorification of the body by some grace manifested through it will point out the presence of divinity. Even in this life the religion of the physical sacraments is effective for this. Since we understand scarcely anything besides bodies and physical things while we are passing through as an image, we are bound by the physical sacraments lest we draw away from God.[32]

[29] William, Med 10.4 (PL 180:236; CF 3:152–53).

[30] 1 Cor 2:14; e.g., Bernard, Hum 8.23 (SBOp 3:34; CF 13:52).

[31] William, Ep frat 2.194 (SCh 223:302; CF 12:77).

[32] William, Nat am 44 (PL 184:417; CF 30:107).

William even explains the mechanism of that sight:

> The sight for seeing God . . . is charity. There are, however, two eyes in this sight, always throbbing by a sort of natural intensity to look toward the light that is God: love and reason . . . . One of them—reason—cannot see God except in what he is not, but love cannot bring itself to rest except in what he is . . . . Reason . . . seems to advance through what God is not toward what God is. Love, putting aside what God is not, rejoices to lose itself in what he is. From him love has come forth, and it naturally aspires to its own beginning. Reason has the greater sobriety; love the greater happiness.[33]

Elsewhere he explains further, now insisting on the eyes' mutual action through grace:

> One of these eyes searches the things of men, according to knowledge; but the other searches divine things, according to wisdom. And when they are illumined by grace, they are of great mutual assistance, because love gives life to reason and reason gives light to love . . . . Often when these two eyes faithfully cooperate, they become one; in the contemplation of God, where love is chiefly operative, reason passes into love and is transformed into a certain spiritual and divine understanding that transcends and absorbs all reason.[34]

So William defines the scheme of Cistercian spirituality, its basis in the Eucharist, and its method: the eye of reason looks into the bread and wine, the *sacramentum*, what God is not, and finds the *res*, God in Christ, in the Eucharist; the eye of love on seeing him there loves him, loses itself in what he is, and so possesses him. The two eyes then work together to see God, in this life and the next.

[33] William, Nat am 21 (PL 184:393; CF 30:77–78).
[34] William, Cant 1.8.92 (SCh 82:212; CF 6:74).

The work of the eye of love is parallel to that of the eye of reason. The eye of reason begins by looking into the Eucharist, finds Christ's humanity there, and so develops a new understanding of his humanity, of the eucharistic meal itself, and of its relationship to beatitude and the heavenly banquet. Finally it returns to the Eucharist with a newly integrated understanding become faith. Bernard says of Christ, "the tree of life . . . the living bread": "His shadow is his flesh; his shadow is faith. The flesh of her own Son overshadowed Mary; faith in the Lord overshadows me. And yet why should his flesh not overshadow me too, as I eat him in the sacrament?"[35] So too the eye of love begins and ends in the Eucharist, meeting and loving Christ therein.

When the eye of love looks into the Eucharist, however, it does not, like reason, ask speculative questions, probe, analyze, or discriminate, but rather works actively to seek out the beloved and to enter into intimacy with him. Its action is an imaging forth of Jesus, remembering his life, meditating on the various ways of uniting with him, and rediscovering the continuing possibility of that remembering, meditating, and uniting in this life, in the eucharistic meal itself. Love of his humanity not only begins in the Eucharist but leads inevitably to his passion; there his body crucified and pouring forth blood returns the beholder, the lover, the worshiper once again to the altar, to the bread that is his body, the wine that is his blood. There the two eyes become one again in unity, in charity, in the sight of God. And the fruit of that charity is the sermons and treatises of Cistercian spirituality. The process is then a circle, longing for God, seeking him, loving him, becoming one with him, and leading others to begin the search again.

Although the eye of love is synthetic rather than analytic in its working, analysis may aid in understanding that synthesis. Just as charity, the sight of God, can be divided into its two

[35] Bernard, SC 48.5–6 (SBOp 2:70; CF 31:16–17).

parts for fuller understanding of each, so may the love of God in Christ be schematized for better understanding, for the eye of love loves Jesus in many ways, in all the ways that humans are loved.[36]

## The Humanity of Christ

The Gospel accounts furnish the ground for the Cistercians' knowledge of the humanity of Christ, and the fathers remain close to those accounts, rarely wandering into apocrypha or blurring the distinctions between Gospel characters. Aelred, who provides the fullest life of Jesus, concentrating on the humanity[37] and not skipping from nativity to passion but detailing the principal events of Jesus' human experience, only once tells an apocryphal story, which he identifies as such, saying that it is included "in order to kindle love,"[38] and maintains the Gospel distinction between Mary of Bethany, the woman taken in adultery, and Mary Magdalene.[39]

The biblical narrative of Jesus' life lends itself naturally to Gregorian allegoresis,[40] as Aelred demonstrates in his use of

[36] Aelred provides a precedent for the analytical approach here and below to unity, saying: "Now charity has two divisions, love of God and love of neighbor. Further, love of one's neighbor has two subdivisions . . . . There are two elements in the love of God, interior dispositions and the performance of works" (Inst incl 27, 28 [CCCM 1:659, 662; CF 2:74, 79]).

[37] Aelred is so faithful to the events of Jesus' life as reported in the Gospels that he includes almost no events revealing the divinity of Christ. For example, although he reports Jesus' mourning the death of Lazarus, he does not mention his raising him. I have discussed this point in Marsha Dutton Stuckey, "Two Middle English Translations of Aelred's *De institutione inclusarum*," PhD dissertation, University of Michigan, 1981, 51–52.

[38] Aelred, Inst incl 31 (CCCM 1:664; CF 2:81–82).

[39] Aelred, Inst incl 28, 31 (CCCM 1:660–61, 665, 667, 672; CF 2:75, 79, 83, 91).

[40] Gregory I, *Moralia in Job*, Ep 3 (PL 75:513). {Marcus Adriaen, ed., *Moralia in Iob*, CCSL 143, 4–5; Gregory the Great, *Moral Reflections on the Book of Job, Volume One, Books 1–5*, trans. Brian Kerns, CS 249 (Collegeville, MN: Cistercian Publications, 2014), 51–53.}

historical, allegorical, and moral units in the story of Jesus at twelve. At the first level the Cistercians are concerned historically with Jesus' life as a man of Nazareth. At the allegorical level, they understand him in a series of human examples of union, as infant, lover, and mother, typologically as the bridegroom of the Song of Songs and as Wisdom, "the mother of fair love and of fear and of knowledge and of holy hope."[41] Finally, at the moral level, they consume him in the Eucharist and so become one with him. The stages move from the fleshly and literal to the spiritual and then back to the flesh, now known through the spirit rather than apart from it.

At the literal level Jesus is loved as an infant, child, and man, and the soul loves him as did those who loved him in his human life. It is Aelred who most commonly presents Jesus simply and clearly as a man because he is least anxious, most clear that being wholly man, Jesus is wholly God: "You adore the man in God and God in the man."[42] However, passages of devotion to Jesus in his manhood also appear throughout the works of Bernard and William.

At the historical level the soul is encouraged to involve herself intimately in the human life of Jesus, either with or in imitation of those who lived with him. All who knew Jesus—as infant, child, or adult; before, during, or after the passion—are models for his modern-day lover. His family, disciples, friends, followers, and even strangers show the contemplative soul how to love Jesus.

Both Bernard and Aelred direct the listeners' attention to the greeting of Elizabeth and John to the unborn Jesus, Bernard saying, "[by hastening to visit Elizabeth, Mary gave] opportunity to the little prophet to offer the first fruits of his office to his still smaller Lord. And while the mothers ran to greet each other, affection was roused in the babes from womb to

[41] Sir 24:24-25. See Dutton, "Christ our Mother," chap. 2 above, 51–52.

[42] Aelred, Inst incl 31 (CCCM 1:667; CF 2:85). See Dutton, "Eat, Drink, and Be Merry," chap. 5 above, 178.

womb."[43] And he says of Joseph's love for the child Jesus, "To him it was given not only to see and to hear what many kings and prophets had longed to see and did not see, to hear and did not hear, but even to carry him, to take him by the hand, to hug and kiss him, to feed him and to keep him safe."[44]

William also directs his audience to intimacy with Jesus, leaping in one sentence from infancy to the resurrection: "You will allow [the soul], for example, to embrace the manger of the newborn babe, to venerate the sacred infancy, to caress the feet of the crucified, to hold and kiss those feet when he is risen, and to put her hand in the print of the nails and cry: 'My Lord and my God!' "[45]

Aelred's works are full of people clamoring to be with, to embrace, to love Jesus. Of those who traveled to Jerusalem with Jesus he says: "See, I beg, how he is seized upon and led away by each and every one of them. Old men kiss him; young men embrace him; boys wait upon him. And what tears do the boys shed when he is kept too long by the men? How do the holy women complain when he lingers a little longer with his father and his companions? Each of them, I think, declares in her inmost heart: 'Let him kiss me with the kiss of his mouth.' "[46]

While Bernard and William occasionally allude to incidents in the life of the adult Jesus and to the love of those who knew him between his birth and his passion, only Aelred lingers there, directing the anchoress through scenes with strangers as well as intimates: the woman taken in adultery, the paralytic let down through the roof, the disciples, and especially Mary, Martha, and Lazarus: "But we must leave this scene and come to Bethany, where the sacred bonds of friendship are consecrated by the authority of our Lord. For Jesus loved Martha, Mary, and Lazarus. There can be no doubt that this was on

[43] Bernard, Miss 4.6 (SBOp 4:52; CF 18:51–52).
[44] Bernard, Miss 2.16 (SBOp 4:27; CF 18:29).
[45] William, Med 10.4 (PL 180:235; CF 3:152).
[46] Aelred, Iesu 5 (CCCM 1:253; CF 2:9).

account of the special friendship by which they were privileged to be more intimately attached to him."[47]

The anchoress is also directed to accompany the disciples to the Last Supper, to Mount Olivet, to the courtyard of the High Priest, to Pilate, and to the crucifixion and then to assist those who bear him to the tomb:

> But wait yet a while until that noble councillor comes to extract the nails and free his hands and feet. See how in his most happy arms he embraces that sweet body and clasps it to his breast . . . . It is for you to follow that precious treasure of heaven and earth, and either hold the feet or support the hands and arms, or at least gather up carefully the drops of the precious blood as they fall one by one, and lick the dust from his feet. See also how gently, how solicitously blessed Nicodemus handles his limbs, rubbing ointments on them, and then with holy Joseph wraps them in the shroud and lays them in the tomb.[48]

In a concern wholly appropriate for their purposes, the fathers show the friends and followers of Jesus clinging to his flesh in love even after the resurrection, through Mary Magdalene, Peter, and Thomas. Both Bernard and William speak of Thomas's doubt as an image of their own; hence, he becomes a model for their love for Christ and for those spiritual babes for whom they write. Bernard identifies him with Joseph, whose love for the infant Christ he remarks:

> Mary's engagement is to be explained in the same way as Thomas's doubting . . . . Thus, just as Thomas, putting out his hand in doubt to touch the Lord, was to become a stout witness to the resurrection, so Joseph, in engaging himself to Mary, watched over her reputation by his protection and thus became a faithful witness to her modesty. Thomas's doubt and Mary's engagement fit beautifully together . . . . And sure enough I, weak man that

[47] Aelred, Inst incl 31 (CCCM 1:667; CF 2:85).

[48] Aelred, Inst incl 31 (CCCM 1:671–72; CF 2:91).

> I am, I find it easier to believe in the Son's resurrection when I see Thomas doubtfully touching him than when I see Cephas believing on simple hearsay.[49]

And Aelred's Mary Magdalene is an essential model for the contemplative in her yearning for the embrace of Christ, now as then:

> Do not fail subsequently to keep Magdalene company; remember to visit with her your Lord's tomb, taking with you the perfumes she has prepared. If only you might be found worthy to see in spirit what she saw with her eyes . . . . With what affection, I ask, with what desire, with what fervor of mind and devotion of heart was it that you cried "Master"? . . . She runs quickly [to tell the disciples], anxious to run quickly. She returns, but together with other women. These Jesus comes to meet with affection, restoring their spirits and banishing their sadness. And notice, the boon is now given which had previously been kept until later, for they came close and clasped his feet. Linger here as long as you can, virgin.[50]

The historical stage, however, does not allow true physical union. The women who embrace Jesus or clasp his feet remain separate from him, able to be sent away precisely as they may be welcomed back. Only a more allegorical understanding may allow imagery of physical union to represent the spiritual.[51]

[49] Bernard, Miss 2.12 (SBOp 4:29; CF 18:24).

[50] Aelred, Inst incl 31 (CCCM 1:672; CF 2:91–92).

[51] It is no doubt a rational anxiety about eliciting an erotic response to Jesus that causes the fathers generally to maintain a distinction between the literal and allegorical levels of devotion to the humanity. Bernard and William essentially avoid the historical Jesus as they use the inherently erotic texts, language, and imagery of the Song of Songs, concentrating on the allegorical in their treatises of love for Christ, while Aelred concentrates on the historical stage and the man Jesus while generally avoiding erotic language, even when speaking of Christ as bridegroom. Caroline Walker Bynum, *Jesus as Mother: Studies in the Spirituality of the High Middle Ages* (Berkeley and Los Angeles: University of California Press, 1982), 141, says that "*Brautmystik* (the use of

At the allegorical stage Jesus is understood not as a man fixed in time and space, but metaphorically, in the ways humans love one another most intimately. This conception appears more often in the works of Bernard and William, who frequently leave Jesus the man behind as they turn to the bridegroom of the soul. For them in fact it is not always, or for long, clear that that bridegroom is Jesus, as he almost always clearly is for Aelred. But Bernard too sometimes integrates them, as when in *On Loving God* he moves rapidly from the passion to the love of the bride and bridegroom and back to the passion:

> The faithful, on the contrary, know how totally they need Jesus and him crucified . . . . The Church sees King Solomon with the diadem his mother had placed on his head. She sees the Father's only Son carrying his cross, the Lord of majesty, slapped and covered with spittle; she sees the Author of life and glory pierced by nails, wounded by a lance, saturated with abuse, and finally laying down his precious life for his friends. After she beholds this, the sword of love transfixes all the more her soul, making her repeat: "Cushion me about with flowers, pile up apples around me, for I languish with love." These fruits are certainly the pomegranates the bride introduced into her Beloved's garden. Picked from the tree of life, they changed their natural taste for that of heavenly bread, their color for Christ's blood.[52]

The times in human experience when two people become most nearly one are three, closely related to one another; indeed, two of the three are identical except for the perspective. They are moments of physical and spiritual union, of participation in one another, of becoming one flesh. They are the

nuptial and erotic imagery to describe the soul's union with God), the use of maternal names for God, and devotion to the Virgin did not occur together in medieval texts." While that statement is largely not true of the works of the Cistercian fathers, they allow significantly little blurring of the exegetical levels.

[52] Bernard, Dil 3.7 (SBOp 3:124–25; CF 13:98–99).

union of the unborn child with his mother, the sexual union of lover with beloved, and the union of the mother with her unborn child. The Genesis account of the man's joyful recognition of the partner God has given him resonates in such passages: "This at last is bone of my bones and flesh of my flesh; . . . Therefore shall a man leave his father and his mother and cleave to his wife, and they shall be one flesh."[53]

For Jesus is bone of humankind's bone, flesh of the soul's flesh as one finds union with him as mother, bride, and babe and as he reciprocally becomes that person's unborn child, her lover and groom, and her mother. As the soul and Jesus become one, the divine and the human become one in mutual interpenetration. The two become one in imaginative union as sacramentally and spiritually they will be one in the Eucharist.[54]

While all the fathers devote most of their allegorical attention to Christ the lover and bridegroom of the soul, they also speak of his being a child within the soul and as conceiving, bearing, or nursing the soul as a mother. Aelred says to the

[53] Gen 2:23, 24.

[54] This is a more difficult stage than the first because it depends on metaphors so intimate in their functioning in Cistercian spirituality that twentieth {and twenty-first}–century readers resist them. Additionally, while in two of the three Jesus appears usually as male, in the third he appears as female; in this fact too the metaphors are less comfortable for modern audiences, but perhaps more accessible for the monks for whom he is so defined as an object of union in his flesh, as Bynum suggests: "For if the God with whom they wished to unite was spoken of in male language, it was hard to use the metaphor of sexual union unless they saw themselves as female . . . . But another solution was of course to see God as a female parent, with whom union could be quite physical (in the womb or at the breast)" (161). She also points out that for the Cistercians "conceiving and giving birth, like suckling, are . . . images primarily of return to, union with, or dependence upon God, not images of Christ's sacrifice or of human alienation . . . . Thus the most frequent meaning of mother-Jesus to twelfth-century Cistercians is compassion, nurturing, and union" (150–51). While Bynum's attention to the maternal passages is broad and thorough, her primary concern is historical. My paper, "Christ Our Mother," chap. 2 above, deals extensively with the contemplative significance of such passages in Inst incl.

soul: "For just as the Lord Jesus is born and conceived in us, so he grows and is nourished in us, until we all come to perfect manhood, that maturity which is proportioned to the complete growth of Christ."[55] Conversely, William sees the soul as borne within Christ:

> Lord, where do you draw those whom you thus embrace and enfold, save to your heart? The manna of your Godhead, which you, O Jesus, keep within the golden vessel of your all-wise human soul, is your sweet heart! Blessed are they whom your embrace draws close to it. Blessed are the souls whom you have hidden in your heart, that inmost hiding-place, so that your arms overshadow them from the disquieting of men and they only hope in your covering and fostering wings. Those who are hidden in your sweet heart are overshadowed by your mighty arms; they sleep sweetly.[56]

All of the fathers, however, present Jesus more frequently in terms describing a mother nursing rather than conceiving, carrying, or giving birth, perhaps because of greater ease in identifying the milk with the level of instruction and devotion appropriate for those whom they are teaching. So Bernard says, "Too often we must interrupt the sweet kisses [of contemplation] to feed the needy with the milk of doctrine."[57] William says: "It is your breasts, O eternal Wisdom, that nourish the holy infancy of your little ones . . . . Since that everlasting blessed union and the kiss of eternity are denied the Bride on account of her human condition and weakness, she turns to your bosom, and not attaining to that mouth of yours, she puts her mouth to your breasts instead."[58] And Aelred explicitly associates the milk of Jesus with his humanity: "Leave John to cheer himself with the wine of gladness in the knowledge of

[55] Aelred, Iesu 4 (CCCM 1:259; CF 2:8).
[56] William, Med 8.4 (PL 180:230; CF 3:141).
[57] Bernard, SC 41.56 (SBOp 2:32; CF 7:208).
[58] William, Cant 1.38 (SCh 82:122; CF 6:130).

the Godhead while you, {running to the breasts of the humanity, press out the milk by which you may be nourished}."[59]

Bernard and William's sermons on the Song of Songs consistently present Christ as the bridegroom, the lover, to the bride who is the church or the soul. Aelred too shows Jesus as bridegroom to the contemplative bride, urging her to prepare her nuptial robe of virtues with borders of gold, "that is, of charity in all its brilliance," "a many-colored robe in which your Bridegroom will delight to see you."[60] And he describes her groom to her: "See who it is you have chosen as your Bridegroom, who it is you have made your friend. He who is the most comely of the sons of men, more resplendent even than the sun and than the stars in all their beauty . . . . He it is who has already chosen you as his bride."[61]

Aelred speaks of Simeon's embrace of Jesus at the Presentation in the Temple as not merely a boon of personal intimacy, but an example of the third spiritual signification of marriage, the daily union of the soul with the Word:

> [Simeon] had received the promise that he would not die before seeing the Christ, and that loving soul today embraced his Savior in his arms. Look, if you will, how the attraction wakened that love, how the desire made the ardor grow, and how, finally, it reached perfection through consent . . . . He received him in his arms and his love was overwhelmed by that embrace. Ah! brothers, the tongue here can only be still, that tongue which has until this moment spoken as well as it could. But now there is only silence. These are the secrets of the nuptial couple and their intimate joys that a third person cannot share. "My secret is my own, my secret is my own." What is your secret, O bride, who alone have known the joy of this spiritual kiss in which the created spirit and the uncreated spirit merge to become two in one,

[59] Aelred, Inst incl 31 (CCCM 1:668; CF 2:87). {The Macpherson translation here reads "while you run to feed on the milk that flows from Christ's humanity."}

[60] Aelred, Inst incl 27, 25 (CCCM 1:659, 657; CF 2:74, 72).

[61] Aelred, Inst incl 15 (CCCM 1:650; CF 2:63).

> that is, no longer to be more than one, justifying and justified, sanctifying and sanctified, deifying and deified.[62]

At the moral level, finally, Jesus is to be known in the Eucharist, not in memory or in imagination, in history or in allegory, but in action and in fact, once again in flesh but now veiled behind the *sacramentum* and hidden except to faith. At this stage the lover of Jesus takes him wholly into her body so that he becomes in all truth bone of her bone, flesh of her flesh.[63]

The movement from imagination to reality, the prismatic representation of a single moment of the soul, is frequently signaled by Aelred. Three times in *On Reclusion* he speaks of someone facing the judgment of Christ, the first and third times using much the same language: "Standing, sitting, and walking he so kept his face cast down and his eyes bent on the ground that he seemed to be standing in fear and trembling before God's judgment seat [*ut tremens et timens diuinis tribunalibus*]."[64] Again, "Imagine now that you are standing before Christ's judgment seat [*ante Christus tribunal*] between these two companies and have not yet been assigned to one or the other . . . .

[62] Aelred, *S. in Ypapanti Domini*, ed. Talbot, 51 {S 51.19; CCCM 2B:47; CF 80:59}.

[63] The two predominant eucharistic theologies of the Middle Ages, the Paschasian and what Macy calls the mystical, come together here for the Cistercians in this understanding. As Macy explains the Paschasian: "The image used here is biological. Just as the food we eat becomes part of ourselves, so we, in a sort of divine reversal, become part of Christ when we receive the Eucharist. Paschasius has made this perfectly clear, 'we become part of Christ because we eat him'" (Macy, *Theologies*, 70). And of the mystical, which Macy identifies as particularly Victorine and characteristic also of William, he says: "This more mystical approach to the Eucharist insisted that salvation came through a spiritual, mystical union with Christ rather than through a natural or substantial union, as the advocates of a Paschasian theology held . . . . [It] stressed the individual relationship of each believer to the risen Christ present in and through the sacrament" (Macy, *Theologies*, 103, 104).

[64] Aelred, Inst incl 22 (CCCM 1:655; CF 2:70).

Now stand in the middle, not knowing to which company the Judge's sentence will assign you. O what a dreadful waiting. Fear and trembling [*Timor et tremens*] have come upon me, and darkness has covered me. If he sends me to join those on the left I cannot complain of injustice; if he sets me among those on the right it is to be attributed to his grace, not to my merits."[65] The second such passage, though, is not hypothetical or imaginary, but fact: "I freely abandoned myself to all that is base, accumulating material for fire to burn me, for corruption to stifle me, for worms to gnaw me . . . . Your anger and your indignation, God, weighed down upon me, and I did not know it . . . . How generous was his grace in following me when I fled, in allaying my fears . . . . He rescued me from the world and welcomed me with kindness."[66]

In these three passages all the facts are the same, in memory and imagination are found present realities, and he who acts as though he is before the Judgment Seat or imagines that he is before the Judgment Seat must recall that he is in fact before the Judgment Seat, accumulating material for fire, corruption, and worms—were it not for God's grace. So too the various ways of loving Christ, historically—in memory—and allegorically—in imagination—come finally to the same thing, uniting in the moral stage of present act and actuality.[67]

The moral stage is the stage of unity with Christ, naturally and spiritually. At the historical level his lover kissed, embraced, carried, anointed, and drank from him but remained apart. At the allegorical she progressed to the nearest human approach to oneness, but as Wisdom explains, "They that eat

[65] Aelred, Inst incl 33 (CCCM 1:678–79; CF 2:99–100). Aelred's shift from second to first person in this passage is characteristic of this work, as I have discussed in Dutton Stuckey, "An Edition of Two Middle English Translations," 83–84.

[66] Aelred, Inst incl 32 (CCCM 1:674; CF 2:94–95).

[67] For William in fact the levels are sacramentally identical; meditation on the humanity of Christ is equivalent to reception of the Eucharist. See Ep frat 30.115–17 (SCh 223:237; CF 12:50–51), and 177 above.

me shall yet hunger, and they that drink me shall yet thirst."[68] But finally in the eating of his body and blood in the Eucharist he and she are indistinguishably one. All of the fathers insist on the union there of Christ and the transfigured soul. Bernard says, recalling both traditional images of God's self-revelation and the Eucharist,

> As a drop of water seems to disappear completely in a great quantity of wine, even assuming the wine's taste and color: as red, molten iron becomes so much like fire it seems to lose its primary state; as the air on a sunny day seems transformed into sunshine instead of being lit up: so . . . all human beings melt in a mysterious way and flow into the will of God.[69]

William also refers to this uniting of the soul and Christ in the Eucharist, using much the same language as Bernard:

> In wisdom, which is the cellar of wine, are fed love and affection. The riches of the storeroom are known; the riches of the cellar of wine are tasted. In the storerooms, one must labor diligently to understand; in the cellar of wine, one has but to rejoice in experiencing fruition . . . . The cellar of wine, indeed, is a certain secret of God's wisdom; it is the state of the soul that is more fully drawn to cleave to God . . . not under the cedar beams of faith and hope, but in the fullness of charity, which is the cellar of wine. For charity . . . is the cellar of wine, and the wine of this cellar is joy in the Holy Spirit. In the cellar of wine, therefore, nothing is found but wine. Whatever enters there, whatever is brought in, either is wine or becomes wine, because the fire of the love of God wholly claims and consumes it and, in the manner

[68] Sir 24:29; see John 4:13-14; see 52n17 above.

[69] Bernard, Dil 28 (SBOp 3:143; CF 13:119). The mixing of the water and wine in the chalice is often understood to represent the blending of the human and the divine in the Incarnate Christ and always to reiterate the water and blood that poured from Jesus' side.

> of the element of fire, converts it into its own substance, since to one who loves God all things work together unto good.[70]

Not only does Aelred use recognizably eucharistic language in urging the contemplative to receive Christ's body and blood and to enter into physical union with him on the cross; he is also propositionally explicit about the unitive goal of his teaching. Echoing the language of the Mass, he says,

> Let these things serve to increase your charity . . . . From all of them you must ascend to unity, for only one thing is necessary. That is the one thing, the unity which is found only in the One, by the One, with the One with whom there is no variation, no shadow of change. The one who unites himself with him becomes one spirit with him, passing into that unity which is always the same and whose years do not come to an end. This union is charity, as it were the edge and border of the spiritual vesture.[71]

This unity is for Aelred explicitly tied and indeed central to the three stages of the humanity of Christ. He places this eucharistic passage between an explanation of the significance of the anchoress's crucifix and a mention of her wedding garment,

[70] William, Cant 10.115–16 (SCh 82:150–253; CF 6:92–93). In this passage William also repeats the image of the two eyes for the sight of God, again emphasizing the distinction between reason and love, understanding and wisdom, and anticipating the banquet and the embrace.

[71] Aelred, Inst incl 26 (CCCM 1:659; CF 2:74). In the celebration of the Eucharist according to the Roman Rite, after the consecration of the elements the priest makes the sign of the cross with the Host three times over the chalice and twice between the chalice and himself, then raises the Host and chalice, saying meanwhile, "Per ipsum, et cum ipso, et in ipso, est tibi Deo Patri omnipotenti, in unitate Spiritus Sancti, omnis honor et gloria." Replacing the Host and chalice upon the altar, he says: "Per omnia saecula saeculorum" (*The Missal in Latin and English* [Westminster, 1959], 683). Aelred's words here are not identical to those—he says "in uno, apud unum, cum uno . . . in illud unum quod semper idem ist"—but inescapably recall the language of the Mass.

which introduces his consideration of charity, the portion of the treatise that contains the three meditations provided so that "the sweet love of Jesus [may grow] in your affections."[72]

Just as the *sacramentum* is only to humans' darkened eyes distinct from the *res*, so the body and blood on the altar is only to mortal eyes distinct from the swaddled babe in the manger whose crib Christ's lovers embrace or the crucified lord whose limbs they bear to the tomb. So too that infant, lover, and mother whose body they kiss and hold until their lips are red with his blood[73] is only to their darkened imagination distinct from the bread and wine they eat and drink until their lips are red. As the Cistercians love in memory, in imagination, and in substance, so they may see him whom they love now and forever, the same face shining sweetly in this world and the next.

So the route to the face of God is for the Cistercians the face of Jesus. They love in order that they may love; they see in order that they may see and that they may possess. The sight of Jesus in the Eucharist leads to the eternal vision of God, and feeding upon him there leads to the heavenly banquet, the wedding supper of the Lord.

William explains this life's need to know God present:

> When the Bride remembered the Bridegroom, or thought of him, seeking understanding, she supposed him to be absent as long as her understanding turned not into love. But goodwill is already the beginning of love. And a passionate will, directed as if to an absent person, is desire; drawn to someone present, it is love; then what the lover loves is present to his understanding. For love of God itself is knowledge of him; unless he is loved, he is not known, and unless he is known, he is not loved. He is known only insofar as he is loved, and he is loved only insofar as he is known.[74]

[72] Aelred, Inst incl 28 (CCCM 1:663; CF 2:79).

[73] Aelred, Inst incl 31 (CCCM 1:671; CF 2:91).

[74] William, Cant 7.76 (SCh 82:188; CF 6:64).

## The Fruit of Charity: Cistercian Spirituality

The newly integrated knowledge and love of Jesus culminate in the union of the two eyes in charity, as William promised. But it does not stop there. For while Aelred advises the anchoress at the feet of the risen Jesus, "Linger here as long as you can, virgin. Do not let these delights of yours be interrupted by sleep or disturbed by any tumult from without," he immediately adds, "However . . . in this wretched life nothing is stable, nothing eternal, and one never remains in the same state."[75] Indeed, a central difference between her and the God with whom she reaches union on the cross, at the tomb, and in the Eucharist, between this world and the next, is that expressed in the words "temporality" and "eternity." In losing itself in God the eye of love has not yet attained eternal peace; the sight of God, charity, has become like God in activity and maternal love for the hungry who wait and yearn. William explains the process of participative transformation that accomplishes this likeness:

> Every bodily sense, in order to be a sense and to perceive at all, must be in some sort changed, by means of a certain sensible impression, into the thing perceived . . . . The sense, then, is no sense, neither can it perceive at all unless, when it has informed the reason of the thing perceived, the soul of the perceiver is changed by a certain transformation of itself into the reality perceived, or into its state . . . . That is how the soul's sense functions. For the soul's sense is love; by love it perceives whatever it perceives . . . . When the soul reaches out in love to anything, a certain change takes place in it by which it is transmuted into the object loved.[76]

So charity, produced through participation in the active, intimate love of God, through union not metaphorical but actual,

[75] Aelred, Inst incl 31 (CCCM 1:673; CF 2:92).
[76] William, Med 3.7–8 (PL 180:213; CF 3:105–6).

becomes Godlike. It is the golden hem on the seamless garment of the soul, the nuptial robe of the bride, in which her bridegroom is surely well pleased to see her; it is the visible evidence of their oneness in flesh and spirit.

And their nuptial union at once bears fruit, offspring of an active love toward those who have not yet been fortunate enough to see, love, and possess such a lover. At the allegorical stage of the argument these are the handmaidens, the daughters of Jerusalem, who accompany the bride as she searches through the streets of the city for her spouse. Literally they are the monks, the new Carthusians at Mont Dieu, the perhaps unknown anchoress—all those to whom the Cistercians are drawn to give service, guidance, direction.

The fruit of charity is itself a product of and in the likeness of Jesus. It is born of the spousal union with Christ the bridegroom, signaled by the pouring of milk from the breasts of the bride or from Christ the mother:

> While the bride is conversing about the Bridegroom, he, as I have said, suddenly appears, yields to her desire by giving her a kiss . . . . The filling up of her breasts is a proof of this. For so great is the potency of that holy kiss, that no sooner has the bride received it than she conceives and her breasts grow rounded with the fruitfulness of conception, bearing witness, as it were, with this milky abundance. Men with an urge to frequent prayer will have experience of what I say. Often enough when we approach the altar to pray our hearts are dry and lukewarm. But if we persevere, there comes an unexpected infusion of grace, our breast expands as it were, and our interior is filled with overflowing love; and if somebody should press upon it then, this milk of sweet fecundity would gush forth in streaming richness.[77]

When the bride longs to linger in the kiss, the Bridegroom's companions chastise her:

[77] Bernard, SC 9.7 (SBOp 1:46; CF 4:58).

> The favor you demand is rather for your own delight, but the breasts with which you may feed the offspring of your womb are preferable to, that is, they are more essential than the wine of contemplation. What gladdens the heart of one man cannot be placed on equal terms with that which gladdens many. Rachel may be more beautiful, but Lia is more fruitful. So beware of lingering amid the kisses of contemplation; better the breasts that flow in the preaching of God's word.[78]

The love and service produced through charity include increased love for Jesus himself, expressed in service to those whom he had defined as being equivalent to him: the poor, the hungry, the naked, the thirsty.[79] In fact, the *Exordium Parvum* includes that understanding and that service as essential to the lives of the first Cistercians, those who left Molesme: "Thus having rejected the riches of this world, the new soldiers of Christ, poor with the poor Christ, began to consult with one another as to the question of the way of life by which, and with what work or occupation, they should provide in this life for themselves as well as for guests who would come, rich and poor alike, whom according to the *Rule* they should receive as Christ."[80]

Aelred is especially clear about this responsibility. He defines beneficence—"to do good to those to whom you are able"—as a subdivision of charity, while explaining that the way in which beneficence may be practiced differs according to the life one has chosen. So while Marthas, those who follow the active life in community, are to give alms, do works of physical mercy, the anchoress, as Mary, is to exercise her be-

[78] Bernard, SC 9.8 (SBOp 1:47; CF 4:59).

[79] Matt 25:31-46.

[80] *The Exordium Parvum*, trans. Bede K. Lackner, in Louis J. Lekai, *The Cistercians: Ideals and Reality* (Kent, OH: Kent State University Press, 1977), 459; {*Exordium Parvum* <XV>, in *Narrative and Legislative Texts from Early Cîteaux*, ed. and trans. Chrysogonus Waddell (Cîteaux–Commentarii Cistercienses, 1999), 254.

neficence in "good will": "Let this be your offering. What is more useful than prayer? Let this be your largesse. What is more humane than pity? Let this be your alms. So embrace the whole world with the arms of your love . . . . Open to all the breast of your love, shed your tears, pour out for them your prayers."[81] The language of this passage is sufficiently similar to that of the crucifixion to alert the attentive reader to the likeness between the contemplative soul and Christ in these acts of charity; she not only serves him but bears his likeness in so doing.

Aelred's youthful introduction to the linking of Jesus and the needy appears in a story from David of Scotland, at whose court he grew to manhood. David once told Aelred of an incident from his own childhood, much of which was spent at the court of Henry I of England, where his sister, Matilda, was queen. Late one night Matilda summoned her brother. Finding her washing and kissing the feet of lepers, he cried out in horror, "Surely if the king were to know of this, your lips, polluted by the feet of lepers, would never again be dignified by the kisses of his lips!" She answered, smiling, "Who does not know that the feet of the eternal king are to be preferred to a mortal king's lips? I indeed have called you here, dearest brother, so that you might learn from my example to perform such things."[82]

The love to the human brother or sister who is Christ is reciprocal. Not only does it proceed from and participate in God's love for humankind, responding to God's initiative of love, and not only is it produced by the love between Jesus and the soul, but it is immediately mirrored by love and service from Jesus to the soul. The recluse in *On Reclusion* is to wash and dry Jesus' feet, with "that most blessed sinner,"[83] but then to allow him to wash and dry hers: "Give him your own feet

[81] Aelred, Inst incl 28 (CCCM 1:661–62; CF 2:74).

[82] Aelred, *Genealogia regum Anglorum* III (PL 195:736; {CCCM 3:55; CF 57:119–20}).

[83] Aelred, Inst incl 31 (CCCM 1:666; CF 2:83).

to wash."[84] Aelred is even more explicit in discussing the roles of Mary and Martha:

> You see, if Mary had been alone in the house, no one would have fed the Lord; if Martha had been alone, no one would have tasted his presence and his words. Martha thus represents the action, the labor accomplished for Christ, Mary the repose that frees from bodily labor, in order to taste the sweetness of the Lord in reading, prayer, or contemplation. That is why, my brothers, so long as Christ is on earth, poor, subject to hunger, to thirst, to temptation, it is necessary that these two women inhabit the same house, that in one soul the two activities occur. While we are on earth—you, me, others—for it is true that we are his members, he also will be on the earth. As long as his members endure hunger, thirst, temptation, just so long Christ also will endure hunger, thirst, will be tempted . . . . Do not neglect Mary for Martha, nor Martha for Mary. If you neglect Martha, who will serve Jesus? And if you neglect Mary, what will be the use of the visit of Jesus, since you will not taste his sweetness? Know, my brothers, that in this life it is necessary never to separate these two women. When the time comes that Jesus is no longer poor, no longer has hunger or thirst, is no longer tempted, then only Mary, the spiritual action, will occupy the dwelling of your soul.[85]

Mary and Martha, traditional symbols of active and contemplative love of God, both belong to Cistercian spirituality as inseparable and essential elements of charity in this life.

But the preeminent fruit of the fathers' union with Christ, the milk that spills from their union with him, is their own works of spiritual direction, their sermons and treatises, their "milk of doctrine offered to babes."[86] And as that fruit, that

[84] Aelred, Inst incl 31 (CCCM 1:668; CF 2:86).

[85] Aelred, *S. in assumptione b. Mariae*, PL 195:306; trans. Anthony Storey, "The Castle of the Soul," in *The Tablet* 198 (1951): 93; {Aelred, S 19.18–22; CCCM 2A:151; CF 58:269–79. See also Iesu 30–31 (CCCM 1:276–78; CF 2:37–39)}.

[86] Aelred, *S. in natale*, in Talbot, ed., *Sermones inediti* 133; {S 71.32; CCCM 2B:229; CF 80:288}.

milk, is produced by the union with Christ through the Holy Spirit, it is identical to it. The physical, enduring manifestation of Cistercian love of Jesus, the textually transmitted spirituality of the fathers, is incarnational and eucharistic: willed, active, and intimate.

Cistercian spirituality is a product of will rather than emotion, insisting that action produces affection rather than the other way around, for it is produced through the grace of the Holy Spirit, always understood by the fathers as will. In his introduction to *The Nature and the Dignity of Love*, David N. Bell says, "by love we are conformed to God; by love we are conjoined to him; by love the whole Trinity dwells within us. The basis of love, however, is will."[87] Bernard says the revelation of the Holy Spirit "lights the fire of love."[88] William explains: "When grace anticipates and cooperates, [the will] begins to cleave by its good assent to the Holy Spirit who is the Love and the Will of the Father and the Son. It begins ardently to will what God wills, and what memory and reason suggest it should will. By ardent willing it becomes love. For love is nothing other than the will ardently [fixed] on something good."[89] As Bell says, in fact, will is that which links reason and love, which allows the movement between the two eyes: "Reason 'forms' the will, directs it, endows it with the knowledge of the good and the desire for it, and reason itself finally 'mounts on high to become love [*amor*].' "[90]

Aelred reduces the theological to the practical:

> The love that comes about through feeling is pleasant but dangerous . . . . Love induced by mere feeling may well be good,

[87] David N. Bell, Introduction to William of St. Thierry, *The Nature and Dignity of Love*, trans. Thomas X. Davis, CS 30 (Kalamazoo, MI: Cistercian Publications, 1978), 7.

[88] Bernard, SC 8.5 (SBOp 1:38; CF 4:48).

[89] William, Nat am 4 (PL 184:390; CF 30:56).

[90] David N. Bell, *The Image and Likeness: The Augustinian Spirituality of William of St. Thierry*, CS 78 (Kalamazoo, MI: Cistercian Publications, 1984), 154.

> but what we love in this way we love because it is pleasant and nothing more. But in the full and perfect love [that comes from the collaboration of reason, feeling, and will] we love not because it is pleasant to do so, but because it is the love of something worthy.[91]

Love based on feeling fades when the feeling fades, when one "falls out of love," but love based on feeling, reason, and will, *chosen* love, endures. That is the love of the Cistercians for Christ.

Cistercian love of the humanity of Christ is also active rather than passive. For the Cistercians it is an error to identify contemplation with passive receptiveness, with infusion, and to distinguish it from anything resulting from activity. While the fathers all speak of infused joy, of "the sound of the Holy Spirit's breathing"[92] or of being suddenly filled with the Holy Spirit, usually they speak of the experience as an outcome of action, seeking, longing, actively reading and praying, running and insisting. It seldom catches them off guard, rarely comes without some effort on their part. Bernard begins his sermons on the Song of Songs by acknowledging the soul's hunger for her bridegroom and her active request for his kiss:

> In his own person "let him kiss me with the kiss of his mouth"; let him whose presence is full of love, from whom exquisite doctrines flow in streams, let him become "a spring inside me, welling up to eternal life." . . . For his living, active word is to me a kiss, not indeed an adhering of the lips that can sometimes belie a union of hearts, but an unreserved infusion of joys, a revealing of mysteries, a marvelous and indistinguishable mingling of the divine light with the enlightened mind, which, joined in truth to God, is one spirit with him.[93]

[91] Aelred, Spec car 3.20.48 (PL 195:594); {CCCM 1:128; CF 17:254}.
[92] William, Ep frat 251 (SCh 233:344; CF 12:93).
[93] Bernard, SC 2.2 (SBOp 1:9; CF 4:9).

Later he acknowledges that the request is bold, importunate: "'I cannot rest,' she said, 'unless he kisses me with the kiss of his mouth' . . . . There is no question of ingratitude on my part, it is simply that I am in love. The favors I have received are far above what I deserve, but they are less than what I long for. It is desire that drives me on, not reason. Please do not accuse me of presumption if I yield to this impulse of love. My shame indeed rebukes me, but love is stronger than all."[94] The love explains and justifies the importunity of the lover.

The activity of Cistercian seeking does not diminish the role of God in the experience, nor his power to choose his time of coming. Indeed, William is especially insistent on this point, saying: "I hear the Lord say to me: 'The Spirit blows whither he will.' And knowing even in myself that he breathes not when I will, but when he himself wills, I find everything devoid of taste and dead. And then I know that it is to you alone, O Fount of life, that I must lift up my eyes, that I may see light only in your light."[95]

Nonetheless, his crying out for God is constant, unremitting: "Do all you can, my soul, not so much by the exercise of reason as by the activity of love."[96] With the same explanation as Bernard he excuses the importunity of his love through its ardor and indicates its occasional reward:

> Yearnings, strivings, longings, thoughts, and affections, and all that is within me, come and let us go up to the mountain or place where the Lord both sees and is seen! . . . But alas, O Lord, alas! To want to see God when one is unclean in heart is surely quite outrageous, rash, and presumptuous, and altogether out of order and against the rule of the word of truth and of your wisdom! . . . I know I am behaving outrageously, but it is the love of your love that makes me do so, as you indeed can see for yourself, though I cannot see you . . . . And sometimes, when I gaze with

[94] Bernard, SC 9.2 (SBOp 1:43; CF 4:54).

[95] William, Contemp 12 (SCh 61:116; CF 3:62).

[96] William, Contemp 12 (SCh 61:126; CF 3:73).

> longing, I do see the back of him who sees me; I see your son Christ passing by in the abasement of his incarnation.[97]

In fact, it may be the fathers' very understanding that they cannot compel the Spirit to come upon them that urges them onward in their yearning, their struggling, their crying out. For as their longing for God is grounded in hope, they will not stop seeking. Further, as they conceive the love between God and humankind to be as ardent, as intimate, as real as that between two humans, they understand that in such affairs both partners are equally eager, equally seeking the union and reunion that defines the Song of Songs and their sermons and treatises based upon it.

Aelred urges the anchoress always forward, saying, "If he still will not let you approach his feet, be insistent, beseech him, raise your eyes to him brimming with tears and extort from him with deep sighs and unutterable groanings what you seek. Strive with God as Jacob did, so that he may rejoice in being overcome."[98] In *On Jesus as a Boy of Twelve* Aelred reminds Ivo of the times when he has moaned, been on fire, sought, longed—"impatient in [his] love"—cajoled, accused, complained, professed, presumed, tried to conquer "by a certain spiritual wrangling." He explains the value of such behavior, saying:

> Jesus, to be sure, loving as he is, is glad to be overcome in such a contest. He is delighted by so great constancy in such a soul and says proudly to the angels who stand around, "The voice of the turtledove has been heard in our land." For it is in the land of the living that such words of a soul on fire are heard, and the sweet fragrance of such great desire charms the whole city of God.[99]

[97] William, Contemp 2–3 (SCh 61:58–64; CF 3:36–38).
[98] Aelred, Inst incl 31 (CCCM 1:666; CF 2:83–84).
[99] Aelred, Iesu 21 (CCCM 1:265; CF 2:29).

And so the lover receives the reward:

> The soul is inflamed with the fire of an unutterable longing and enters upon a certain spiritual contest with God, until the whisper of a gentle breeze makes itself felt in its inmost depths. It gently captivates the affections, imposing silence on all movements, all anxieties, all words, all thoughts; it raises the soul in contemplation up to the very gates of the heavenly Jerusalem. Then he who has been sought so long, so often implored, so ardently desired, comely beyond the sons of men, "looking out of the lattice work," invites to kisses, "Rise up, hasten, my friend, and come." . . . Then there are embraces, then there are kisses, then "I have found him whom my soul loves, I have held him fast and will not let him go," then she abounds in delights and enjoys good things in Jerusalem, celebrating a feast day with joy and exultation.[100]

Here Aelred presents the essential elements of Cistercian contemplative understanding: a spiritual contest rewarded by the gift of the Holy Spirit, imposing silence and bringing vision, embrace, the celestial banquet. Quiet succeeds upon struggle, but it is not a distinct state, one for which the contemplative is required merely to wait, but rather a silence after storm, a respite after rain. It is a peace, a repose that emerges from the spiritual contest itself, from the very activity of yearning, seeking, hungering.[101] In fact, only when fast in intimate relationship with Jesus is the contemplative told by Aelred to linger.

[100] Aelred, Iesu 22 (CCCM 1:270; CF 2:30); Song 2:9.

[101] The fathers frequently write of repose as a mark of beatitude, a reward from the journey. But it is very often a result of the Spirit's working rather than the necessary condition for it. While Aelred three times speaks of the importance of silence, "imposing silence that her spirit may speak," "listening to Christ and speaking with him" (Inst incl 5 [CCCM 1:641; CF 2:50–51]), silence no more assures the coming of the Spirit than does active pursuit. God's coming is not to be compelled; his freedom to stay away or to come may not be restricted by active seeking or by passive receptivity. For further discussion of this theme, see Jean Leclercq, *Otia Monastica: Études sur le vocabulaire de la contemplation au Moyen Age*, *Studia Anselmiana* 51–52 (Rome, 1963).

At the Last Supper, after she has been told to allow Jesus to wash her feet, Aelred says, "Why are you in such a hurry to go out now? Wait a little while." Again when she observes the women clasping the feet of the risen Jesus, he says "Linger here as long as you can, virgin."[102] While peace is that sought, in Cistercian spirituality the seeking itself is unremitting, urgent, active.

Finally, not only is Cistercian spirituality willed and active; it is centrally intimate, constantly using the language of intimate love: the kiss, the embrace, the running to meet. It is the language of the Eucharist as well, of partaking, participating in, becoming one with, not following behind.

It is a nearly universal misconception that medieval devotion to the humanity of Christ is preeminently imitative. Jaroslav Pelikan speaks in *The Growth of Medieval Theology* at length of "the Discipline of Jesus," insisting that "The summons to 'take up the cross of the Redeemer' was the core of the Christian life of self-mortification" and that "the exhortation to imitate 'the example of the Lord' pertained to all who were 'his followers.'"[103] However, for the Cistercians that is rarely so. Theirs is not primarily a spirituality of exemplarism or mortification.

There are, of course, numerous passages in which the Cistercian fathers urge imitation of Christ, most commonly in his humility, although even in imitation they tend to move rapidly to intimacy with the one they imitate. Bernard, looking at the infant Christ, says: "Let us make every effort to be like this little child. Because he is meek and humble in heart, let us learn from him, lest he who is great, even God, should have been made a little man for nothing, lest he should have died to no purpose, and have been crucified in vain. Let us learn his

[102] Aelred, Inst incl 31 (CCCM 1:673; CF 2:86, 92).

[103] Jaroslav Pelikan, *The Growth of Medieval Theology (600–1300)*, The Christian Tradition, 3 (Chicago and London: University of Chicago Press, 1978), 126.

humility, imitate his gentleness, embrace his love, share his sufferings, be washed in his blood."[104] William's Christ says: "I shall show myself to man as a man despised and the least of all men, a man of sorrows and knowing infirmity, that he may be zealous to imitate my humility, through which he will come to the glory toward which he is hastening to rush."[105]

Aelred, like Bernard, urges imitation of the boy Jesus, saying: "Now this is the beginning of conversion, a spiritual birth as it were, that we should model ourselves upon the Child, take upon ourselves the marks of poverty, and, becoming like animals before you, Lord, enjoy the delights of your presence."[106]

While imitation of Jesus' life, suffering, and death is a less frequent theme than intimacy among the twelfth-century fathers, it also appears here and there. In a sermon on the passion Bernard urges memory of Christ's suffering in order to take on his strength, his likeness, "that I may follow in his footsteps."[107] And in a sermon for the Ascension Aelred says, "And so it is to these things that we have been called: that we may follow in the footsteps of him who, when he was reviled, did not revile, and who, when he suffered, did not threaten. Taking therefore Christ in his suffering as his model, let him who says he abides in Christ also walk even as he walked."[108]

But even in passages urging mortification, imitation of Christ's passion, the Cistercians move quickly into sharing of his pain, joining him within it, participating in intimacy rather than separately taking his pain upon themselves. So Aelred tells his anchoress to "have a representation of our Savior hanging on the Cross; that will bring before your mind his

[104] Bernard, Miss 3.14 (SBOp 4:45; CF 18:44).

[105] William, Nat am 3.34 (PL 184:389; CF 30:96).

[106] Aelred, Iesu 4 (CCCM 1:252; CF 2:1).

[107] Bernard, "Sermo in feria iv hebdomadæ sanctæ" 11 {SBOp 5:64; CF 52:123}.

[108] Aelred, "S. in Ascensione Domini de raptu Helye," ed. Talbot, 103; trans. Chrysogonous Waddell, "On the Rapture of Elijah"; {S 65.16; CCCM 2B:174; CF 80:224}.

passion for you to imitate; his outspread arms will invite you to his embraces, his naked breasts will feed you with the milk of sweetness to console you."[109]

Imitation for the Cistercians rapidly becomes a matter of participating with Jesus, of being intimate with him in his life and through that intimacy sharing his suffering when called upon to do so. The biblical source for Cistercian devotion to Christ is not Jesus' warning that "he who does not take his cross and follow me is not worthy of me,"[110] but his promise to the sons of Zebedee: "The cup that I drink you will drink; and with the baptism with which I am baptized, you will be baptized."[111] The passage in which the anchoress's actions of beneficence are described in language recalling the crucified Christ illustrate this blending of the ideas; there she might easily be understood either as imitating him and his works of mercy and thereby becoming like him or as ministering to him in the needy and so participating with him in his own works of mercy.[112] Aelred gives no clue as to his intention, and at this point the distinction becomes insignificant.

A similarly ambiguous example appears when Aelred suggests that the recluse should share her bridegroom's poverty, exchange her state for participation in his:

> How can you dare to take pride in riches or noble birth when you seek to appear as the bride of him who became poor although he was rich and chose for himself a poor mother, a poor family, a poor little house also, and the squalor of a manger? Is it any matter for pride that you have preferred the Son of God to the sons of men, that you have despised the uncleanness of the flesh for the beauty of virginity, that you have exchanged things which will become mere dung for the eternal riches and delights of heaven?[113]

[109] Aelred, Inst incl 26 (CCCM 1:659; CF 2:73).

[110] Mark 10:39.

[111] Matt 10:38.

[112] {223 above.}

[113] Aelred, Inst incl 24 (CCCM 1:656–57; CF 2:71).

Imitation for the Cistercians then is more often a matter of becoming like Christ by dwelling with and in him than by walking in his footsteps. And that imitation is equivalent to Jesus' imitation of and intimate participation in the human condition—so the word *imitare* comes to mean for the Cistercians. For them even the idea of imitation of Christ is essentially eucharistic, a matter of acting, choosing, participating. As Christ is taken into the self, so he is known and loved, and so his lover becomes like him.

But the most important imitation for Cistercian spirituality is an imitation of those who were intimate with Christ in his human life—his mother, most of all, his disciples, his friends. Mary is the great object of Cistercian imitation, not Christ, for through her the worshiper may conceive the heavenly sweetness, embrace the infant and the crucified, and finally be crowned as bride and queen. Bernard says of her: "You are told that she is a virgin. You are told that she is humble. If you are not able to imitate the virginity of this humble maid, then imitate the humility of the virgin maid."[114] Aelred tells the recluse to have on her altar two figures, of Mary and of John, as signs of the excellence of virginity and "to increase your charity."[115]

More important than Bernard's explicit call for imitation of Mary, though, is his speaking of her as the bride in the Song of Songs. So in the language used elsewhere by the fathers for the church or the soul as the bride of Christ, Bernard says,

> While the King was on his couch, the Virgin's nard was sending forth its fragrance, and a sweet-smelling smoke was rising up in the sight of his glory, and in this way she found grace in the Lord's eyes . . . . he was moved by so great a desire that he sped ahead of his messenger and came to the Virgin whom he loved, whom he had chosen for his own, whose beauty he ardently desired.[116]

[114] Bernard, Miss 1.5 (SBOp 4:15; CF 18:9).

[115] Aelred, Inst incl 26 (CCCM 1:659; CF 2:73–74).

[116] Bernard, Miss 3.2 (SBOp 4:43; CF 18:34–35; see Aelred, Inst incl 14 [CCCM 1:650; CF 2:63]).

Again, he urges Mary toward God:

> Only say the word and receive the Word: give yours and conceive God's. Breathe one fleeting word and embrace the everlasting Word. Why do you delay? Why be afraid? Believe, give praise, and receive. Let humility take courage and shyness confidence. This is the moment for virginal simplicity to forget prudence. In this circumstance, alone, O prudent Virgin, do not fear presumptuousness, for if your reserve pleased by its silence, how much more must your goodness speak. Blessed Virgin, open your heart by faith, your lips to consent, and your womb to the Creator. Behold, the long-desired of all nations is standing at the door and knocking. Oh, what if he should pass by because of your delay and, sorrowing, you should again have to seek him whom your soul loves? Get up, run, open! Get up by faith, run by prayer, open by consent.[117]

Aelred echoes this language in his address to the recluse and says to her that the annunciation was "on your account, virgin, that you might diligently contemplate the Virgin whom you have resolved to imitate and the Virgin's Son to whom you are betrothed," so acknowledging at once her role as mother and bride of Jesus.[118]

Cistercian spirituality outlasted the fathers, influencing Latin and vernacular literatures across Europe through the centuries to come.[119] Its essence was its sacramentalism, its

[117] Bernard, Miss 4.8 (SBOp 4:54; CF 18:54); see Aelred, Inst incl 31 (CCCM 1:668; CF 2:86–87): "Let love overcome shyness, affection drive out fear." The Cistercian emphasis on imitation of Mary in her intimacy with Jesus as mother and bride may explain some of the burst of Marian devotion in the twelfth century and beyond, not initially to her, but with her.

[118] Aelred, Inst incl 29 (CCCM 1:663; CF 2:81).

[119] Martin Thornton, *English Spirituality* (London: SPCK, 1963), 46, 48, says of this influence in England: "The Benedictine line follows into the Cistercian reform, of which the influence on England is apparent to anyone who has looked at our monastic history. This is the affective side, but English spirituality follows the Cistercianism of the more thoughtful William of St Thierry and the less austere Aelred of Rievaulx, rather than that of St Bernard. In the

grounding in the humanity of Christ, and its willed, active intimacy with Jesus. Its story developed at three levels: historical, allegorical, and moral. At the historical level the plot was that of the gospels, from the annunciation to the ascension, with Pentecost added to provide the *sententia* and bring it to life. At the allegorical level, the plot was that of the love between God and the church, between Christ and the soul, the story in fact of the Song of Songs. As William summarizes it:

> Here we have the entire sequence of the plot of this holy love song from beginning to end, its entire matter and action. The scenes are already marked out and harmoniously arranged: hope hastens, desire becomes a crucifixion, wisdom sets all in order, love speeds forward, and grace is there to meet it; until finally, at the end of the Song, the grief of the soul's desire is turned into the joy of fruition, the weariness of delay being at last exchanged for mutual union.[120]

At the moral level there is no plot, no narrative: only action, union with God in the flesh, becoming one with him through the mutual, reciprocal action of God and humankind. The late twelfth-century Baldwin of Forde's *Tractate on the Most Holy Sacrament of the Altar* contains a passage striking in its faithfulness to the center of Cistercian spirituality. Here is the importunity, the audacious love, the active seeking out of God who hides to be found in the sacrament. Here there is no passive receptivity, no waiting to be overcome by love, no imitation.

---

story of English religion, William of St Thierry plays the part of a kind of Jack–in-the-box: always popping up in unexpected places . . . . In the middle ages [England] could almost have been called the land of the Cistercians . . . . Devotion following from the Incarnation, necessarily coupled with the Blessed Virgin, is also Cistercian." Thornton also speaks of Bonaventure as the primary ascetic Franciscan influence on England; as Bonaventure himself was significantly influenced by Aelred, the importance of Cistercian spirituality in England is then greater even than Thornton realizes. See "The Cistercian Source: Aelred, Bonaventure, and Ignatius," chap. 7 below, 237–67.

[120] William, Cant 146 (SCh 82:310; CF 6:117).

Rather, here the faithful approaches the Eucharist and finds Christ there; the lover enters the bed-chamber, knowing that waiting there is the God who formerly assumed the flesh of humankind.

The Cistercian school of spirituality that began in the twelfth-century Cistercians' rational inquiry into questions of eucharistic theology has its fruition then in charity, in works of spiritual direction, and finally in a new generation of eucharistic theology:

> Christ was hidden from the beginning in the bosom of the Father; afterwards, he was hidden in the form of a servant that he assumed; and now he is hidden in the sacrament that he instituted. Faith finds him hidden in the bosom of the Father; no less does faith find him hidden in man; and it is faith that finds him hidden in the sacrament. The great power of faith possesses the great grace of intimacy with God. Wherever it finds him, it can approach him, and with a certain familiar and audacious intimacy, it rushes into his sanctuary and his bed-chamber. It gives no thought to being hindered by the guardians of the entrance or the door-keepers or the chamberlains; it enters carefree and unites itself confidently but reverently to the mysteries of God's intentions.[121]

[121] Baldwin of Ford, Tractate 1 (PL 204:403–4); {*Baudouin de Ford, Traités*, ed. and trans. R. Thomas, Pain de Cîteaux 35–40 (Chimay, Belgium: Notre-Dame de la Paix, 1972–1975), 28–29; Baldwin of Forde, *Spiritual Tractates*, trans. David N. Bell, 2 vols., CF 39 (Kalamazoo, MI: Cistercian Publications, 1986), 1:44.

*Chapter 7*

# The Cistercian Source: Aelred, Bonaventure, and Ignatius[1]

The medieval growth of affective spirituality and its close association with the school of Cîteaux is by now almost a commonplace. Ewert Cousins describes its development in the introduction to his 1978 translation of Bonaventure:

> The most characteristic form of Christian spirituality in the West focuses on the mystery of Christ, who is seen as the Mediator between God and man and the Savior freeing man from the burden of sin and leading him to salvation. In the Middle Ages this spirituality took the form of devotion to the humanity and passion of Christ, with concentration on vivid details, an awakening of human emotions, especially compassion, and the imitation of Christ in his moral virtues. This devotion is rooted in the fundamental orientation of Western culture toward the concrete, the particular, the human and the moral. Grounded in classical Roman culture, this orientation developed in the spirituality of the Middle Ages and blossomed in the 13th century

[1] I presented this paper in May 1984 at the Cistercian Studies Conference as part of the International Medieval Studies Congress; it was first published in *Goad and Nail: Studies in Medieval Cistercian History, X*, ed. E. Rozanne Elder, CS 84 (Kalamazoo, MI: Cistercian Publications, 1985), 151–78. It appears here by permission from Cistercian Publications.

In the notes below LV = *Lignum Vitae*, the Latin text of St. Bonaventure's work as it appears in the Quaracchi edition (n. 9 below); TL = *The Tree of Life*, in Ewert Cousins' 1978 translation (n. 2 below).

into a complex form of religious sensibility, with Francis of Assisi as its chief expression.[2]

The flowering of that affectivity in Francis and in Franciscan spirituality in the Middle Ages is also generally acknowledged, but the significant role played in its development by the twelfth-century English Cistercian Aelred of Rievaulx, his new approach to meditation, and its popularity throughout Western Europe have gone almost entirely unrecognized. Aelred's influence on Franciscan and Ignatian spirituality has largely escaped the notice of scholars. Because of the great importance of the Franciscan tradition of affective spirituality and of the Ignatian imaginative approach to meditation, and because of the attention given to both by modern scholarship, their common origins in the contemplative writings of Aelred should be recognized. Both Bonaventure's *The Tree of Life* and Ignatius's *Spiritual Exercises* find their ultimate source in Aelred's single treatise on the contemplative life, *De institutione inclusarum* or *On Reclusion*.[3]

In about 1160 Aelred, abbot of Rievaulx, wrote *On Reclusion*, a work of spiritual direction for an anchoress. In it he provided guidance for her life, its quotidian details, virtue, and loving search for God. Although in around 1155 at the request of a young monk for contemplative direction he had used one story from the life of Jesus to set forth the journey toward God, in

[2] Bonaventure, *The Soul's Journey into God, The Tree of Life, The Life of Saint Francis*, trans. and intro. Ewert Cousins, preface Ignatius Brady (New York: Paulist Press, 1978), 34.

[3] The standard edition of this work is C. H. Talbot, "The 'De institutis inclusarum' of Aelred of Rievaulx," ASOC 7 (1951): 12–217, repr. CCCM 1:636–82. It appears in translation by M. P. Macpherson, "A Rule of Life for a Recluse," CF 2 (Spencer, MA: Cistercian Publications, 1971), 43–102. The notes below cite page numbers from the CCCM text and from the CF 2 translation, but in cases of compared passages I have provided my own translations. I am using a straightforward rendering of the Latin title of *De institutione inclusarum*, one that better defines the work. Biblical phrases within quoted passages appear within quotation marks.

*On Jesus as a Boy of Twelve*,[4] the later treatise, *On Reclusion*, was unique in its concern with the life devoted to contemplation. It alone of his works was written for a woman, it alone exalted the life of Mary over that of Martha. Further, it guided the contemplative toward union not, like *On Jesus*, through imitation of Jesus, but through intimacy with him. This approach to contemplative union depended on the imaginative involvement of the contemplative in the human life of Jesus.

*On Reclusion* begins with attention to the anchoress's daily life, then turns to the three virtues that define her life: chastity, humility, and charity. As the contemplative life has to do centrally with the love of God, Aelred devotes the larger part of the entire work to three meditations, on the past, present, and future.[5] He intends these to nourish the contemplative's affections, to enable "the sweet love of Jesus to grow in" them.[6]

The first of the three contains an extended narrative of Jesus' life. In it Aelred directs the contemplative to participate in the events of that life, to love Jesus with those who loved him then, to minister to him with those who ministered to him, and finally to know him and to become one with him in his crucifixion. This meditation ends with the post-resurrection appearance of Jesus to Mary Magdalene in the garden and with her finally being allowed to "come close and clasp his feet."[7] In the third meditation, that on the future, Jesus appears again, but this meditation concentrates less on Jesus than on the Judgment and the beatitude prepared for the blessed. It is the first portion, with its presentation of the life of Jesus and the contemplative's participation in that life, that was so new in Christian spiritual writing; it is this approach to contemplation and the search for union with God as seen in the meditation on the past that influenced those who followed Aelred.

[4] Ed. Anselm Hoste, CCCM 1:247–78; trans. Theodore Berkeley, *On Jesus at the Age of Twelve*, CF 2:1–39.

[5] {Aelred actually refers to them as a single "threefold meditation."}

[6] Aelred Inst incl 29 (CCCM 1:662; CF 2:79).

[7] Aelred, Inst incl 31 (CCCM 1:673; CF 2:92).

Aelred's first meditation is one extended narrative, interrupted by occasional spontaneous prayers. The narrative itself is largely imperative or third-person subjunctive, "let the contemplative." It includes little theological explanation or exposition, gives no attention to imitation of Christ, and concentrates primarily on the contemplative's imaginative going forward to love and to minister to Jesus. Aelred's constant gentle exhortation and admonition, an approach to meditation imitated by Bonaventure in *The Tree of Life*, functions within *On Reclusion* as guidance toward contemplative union; it is the keystone in Aelred's approach to meditation and contemplation.

Aelred's *On Reclusion* probably became known to Bonaventure in Paris between 1257 and 1267. By that time he had completed his studies at the University of Paris and been elected Minister General of the Franciscan Order. He is thought during this period to have written his spiritual works; Ewert Cousins says in the introduction to his translation of three of these that this time in Bonaventure's life "flowers in a host of spiritual writings which have a distinctive Franciscan flavor."[8]

The three most important of Bonaventure's "mystical opuscula" are *The Triple Way*, *The Soul's Journey into God*, and *The Tree of Life* (*Lignum Vitae*), which Cousins describes as "his classic meditation on the life of Christ."[9] In the first of these Bonaventure most systematically sets forth his understanding of the three stages of the spiritual life; the second is abstract, highly speculative, and heavily influenced by Richard of St. Victor's discussion of the ascent to the vision of God in *The Mystical Arc.*

[8] Cousins, *The Soul's Journey*, 10. Three manuscripts of *On Reclusion* are still to be found in Paris, though all postdate Bonaventure. In view of Aelred's popularity and the number of Cistercian houses in France, manuscripts of *On Reclusion* must have been widespread in France for many centuries.

[9] Cousins, *The Soul's Journey*, 10. The standard edition of Bonaventure is the Quaracchi critical edition, *Doctoris seraphici S. Bonaventurae Opera Omnia*, ed. studio et cura pp. collegii a S. Bonaventura, 10 vols. (Quaracchi: Collegium S. Bonaventurae, 1882–1902). *The Tree of Life, Lignum Vitae*, is in vol. 8, *Opuscula varia ad theologiam mysticam*, 68–87.

*The Tree of Life* is a very different kind of work. It is a much simpler work of affective spirituality, devoted to the life and passion of Jesus and to his glorification. This is Bonaventure's primary work of affective spirituality; it must be central in any consideration of Franciscan influence in that tradition.[10] Its indebtedness to Aelred's *On Reclusion*, almost exclusively to the first of the three meditations, is overwhelming.

The influence of *On Reclusion* on Ignatius and his *Spiritual Exercises* has been more widely recognized and therefore demands less attention here than that given to Bonaventure. The link between Aelred and Ignatius is Ludolph of Saxony, a Carthusian monk who in about 1330, probably while at Mainz, wrote a work sometimes referred to as the most influential work of popular spirituality of the Middle Ages. Ludolph's *Vita Jesu Christi*, a lengthy compilation of patristic writings, contains among other things the entire first meditation of *On Reclusion*—credited to Anselm, to whom Aelred's three meditations were long attributed from the fourteenth century on—some of the third meditation, and large pieces of {Aelred's} *On Jesus as a Boy of Twelve*, credited to Bernard.[11] In 1502–1503

[10] John V. Fleming says, "What are usually called his 'mystical opuscula' . . . are among the most beautiful and most influential of all the hundreds of spiritual books in the Middle Ages. The *Lignum Vitae* . . . demonstrates the pleasing harmony of the visual and verbal imaginations of Bonaventure's pastoral writings" (*An Introduction to the Franciscan Literature of the Middle Ages* [Chicago: Franciscan Herald Press, 1977], 203–4).

[11] *Vita Jesu Christi*, ed. L. M. Rigollot, 4 vols. {Paris: Palmé, 1865, 1870, 1878}. *Vita Christi*'s translation history has been examined in two studies: Mary Immaculate Bodenstedt, *The Vita Christi of Ludolphus the Carthusian*, The Catholic University of America Studies in Medieval and Renaissance Latin Language and Literature, vol. 16 (Washington, DC: The Catholic University of America Press, 1944); and Elizabeth Salter, "Ludolphus of Saxony and his English Translators," *Medium Aevum* 33 (1964): 26–35. Salter points out that since its printing in 1472 it has been edited sixty times and that during the fifteenth and sixteenth centuries it was translated into almost every European language. {The work now exists in a full English translation: Ludolph of Saxony, *The Life of Jesus Christ*, trans. and intro. Milton T. Walsh, 4 vols., CS 267, 282, 283, 284 (Collegeville, MN: Cistercian Publications, 2018, 2019, 2021, 2022). For a discussion of the history of the *Vita*, see Walsh, Introduction to *The Life of Jesus Christ*, vol. 1, xxiii–xxv.}

Ferdinand and Isabella of Spain commissioned a translation of the *Vita Jesu Christi* by Ambrose Montesino, a Franciscan; he translated about two-thirds of the work into Castilian.[12]

After receiving a leg wound in the siege of Pamplona in 1521, Ignatius asked his sister-in-law for chivalric romances to read while recuperating. When she could find none in the family castle at Loyola, she substituted two popular—and hence easily available—books of piety, a *Flos Sanctorum* (probably Voragine's *Golden Legend*) and Ludolph's *Vita Christi.* Ignatius was so delighted with these books that he copied extracts from them into a quarto volume of three hundred leaves: "The words of Christ he wrote in red ink and those of Our Lady in blue, on polished and lined paper in a good hand, for he was an excellent penman."[13] All discussions of Ignatius and of the *Spiritual Exercises* insist on the role played by the *Vita Christi* in their composition.[14]

Not only did the *Vita Christi* effect Ignatius's conversion, but it—and so its sources—directly influenced his later writings, most recognizably the *Spiritual Exercises*. In the *Dictionnaire de Spiritualité* article on "Application des sens," regarding the characteristic meditative approach of the *Spiritual Exercises*, Jean Maréchal traces this method so associated with Ignatius from Bernard through Aelred, Richard of St. Victor, Henry Suso, and Ludolph to Ignatius. Of Aelred Maréchal cites *On Jesus as a Boy of Twelve* and *On Reclusion*, saying that in them Aelred "gives counsel and example of a concrete contemplation of the Gospel events, one that here and there becomes an application of the senses, whether imaginative or spiritual."[15]

[12] Bodenstedt, *Vita Christi*, 22.

[13] Ignatius Loyola, *Saint Ignatius' Own Story as Told to Luis González de Cámera*, trans. William J. Young (Chicago: Henry Regnery, 1956), 7–11. See also "Ignace de Loyola," *Dictionnaire de Spiritualité* 7 (1971): 1267.

[14] Besides Bodenstedt and Salter, e.g., Emmerich Raitz von Frentz, "Ludolph, le Chartreux, et Les Exercises de S. Ignace de Loyola," *Revue d'ascètique et de mystique* 25 (1949): 375–88; and Henry Watrigant, *La genèse des exercises de saint Ignace de Loyola* (Amiens: Yvert & Tellier, 1897).

[15] "Application des Sens," *Dictionnaire de Spiritualité* 1 (1937): 823–24. Regarding Bernard's role in the development of this approach, Maréchal cites

As Maréchal's words indicate, Aelred's influence on Ignatius and even on Bonaventure has not gone unnoticed by scholars. In 1944 Sr. Mary Immaculate Bodenstedt published her Catholic University dissertation, *The Vita Christi of Ludolphus the Carthusian*. In it she noted that Ludolph occasionally attributed passages incorporated into his work to Anselm when they had in fact originated with Aelred, but as she had no text of *On Reclusion* available, she was unable to be specific about either the extent of Ludolph's borrowing from Aelred or his treatment of the borrowed passages.

In 1958 Anselm Hoste mentioned that at least four exact citations from *On Reclusion* appeared in Ludolph's *Vita Christi*. He repeated the observation in the introduction to his 1958 parallel-text edition of *On Jesus as a Boy of Twelve* and again in his 1962 *Bibliotheca Aelrediana*.[16]

Following Hoste, Charles Dumont discussed Aelred's influence on Ludolph and through him Ignatius at length in the introduction to his 1961 French-Latin parallel-text edition of Aelred's treatise, *La Vie de Recluse*, saying "Ludolph the Carthusian, while writing his *Vita Christi*, had the text of Aelred's meditation constantly under his eyes. He believed it to be by Anselm, but that matters little . . . . To conclude his work, he quotes the last lines of Aelred's treatise."[17] Regarding the meditative technique of Aelred, that seen later in both *The Tree of Life* and *Spiritual Exercises*, Dumont says,

> Saint Bernard was doubtless the originator of this new method, but he was too intellectual, too speculative to do all with it that one might do. It was up to Aelred, imaginative and sensitive, to

---

the Third Sermon on the Nativity, saying, "Nothing very remarkable from our point of view, except the affective and imagistic genre of devotion to the incarnate Word, a new genre in patristic literature."

[16] Anselm Hoste, "Marginalia bij Aelred's De Institutione Inclusarum," *Cîteaux in de Nederlanden* 9 (1958): 133; *Quand Jesus eut douze ans*, trans. Joseph Dubois (Paris: Les Éditions du Cerf, 1958), 32; *Bibliotheca Aelrediana* (Steenbrugge: In Abbati sancti Petri, 1962), 1945.

[17] Charles Dumont, *La Vie de Recluse*, SCh 76 (Paris: Les Éditions du Cerf, 1961), 35–36.

> accomplish this little masterpiece and in it to apply the method, following its creator but with an ease and freedom that gave it the richness of his own experience.[18]

Not surprisingly, in light of Ludolph's care to acknowledge his sources and Bonaventure's failure to do so, scholarly recognition of Aelred's influence on *The Tree of Life* has been much slighter. In 1923 André Wilmart, in his introduction to D. A. Castel's French translation of Anselm's meditations and prayers, commented, "I believe that [Bonaventure] had direct recourse to Aelred's *De institutis inclusarum*, perhaps already attributed to St. Augustine (viz. *Lignum vitae*, par. 9)." In 1958 Anselm Hoste, in the same article as that mentioned above, said that five citations from *On Reclusion* appeared in *The Tree of Life.*

The long-time attribution of Aelred's meditations to both Augustine and Anselm is part of the problem for both Bonaventuran and Ludolphan studies. J.-P. Migne printed most of *On Reclusion* among the works of Augustine in the Patrologia Latina, though he noted there that it was in fact Aelred's, as Lucas Holstenius had recognized in his 1661 *Codex Regulam.* In the same note Migne pointed out that roughly a third of the work {the threefold meditation, in fact,} appeared in the Patrologia among the meditations of Anselm as number 15, 16, and 17. But in that volume he made no mention of Aelred, saying merely in a footnote to meditation 15, "S. Anselm wrote this to his sister."[19]

[18] André Wilmart, "Le recueil des prières de S. Anselme," in *Méditations et prières de S. Anselme*," trans. D. A. Castel, Pax XI (Paris: Abbaye de Maredsous, 1923), xvi. I have also noted Aelred's influence on Bonaventure and Ludolph in my 1981 dissertation and a 1983 article: Marsha Dutton Stuckey, "An Edition of Two Middle English Translations of Aelred's *De Institutione inclusarum*," PhD dissertation, University of Michigan, 1981, 28; "A Prodigal Writes Home: Aelred of Rievaulx's *De institutione inclusarum*," in *Heaven on Earth: Studies in Medieval Cistercian History IX*, ed. E. Rozanne Elder, CS 68 (Kalamazoo, MI: Cistercian Publications, 1983), 35.

[19] PL 32:1451–74 (Augustine); 158:785a–98b (Anselm).

In 1924 Wilmart discussed the history of printing and attribution of *On Reclusion*, and in 1927 he again identified the three meditations as Aelred's. Because of his work there should no longer be any confusion about the authorship of the various "Anselmian" meditations.[20]

As a further complication, not only are Aelred's meditations often attributed to Augustine and Anselm, but passages attributed by modern scholars to Anselm may in fact have been written not only by Anselm or Aelred, but also by a number of others. Wilmart lists thirteen authors, six named and seven unnamed, for the twenty-one meditations printed in the Patrologia as Anselm's. Of the nine passages that the Quaracchi edition of *The Tree of Life* attributes to Anselm and three others noted as resembling his (eight of which are attributed in Cousins' translation to Pseudo-Anselm), only one is by Aelred;[21] the other eleven come from the meditation printed by Migne as meditation nine, "On the humanity of Christ." The author of that meditation was actually the twelfth-century Ecbert of Schönau in the diocese of Trier.[22]

[20] André Wilmart, "La tradition des prières de S. Anselme," *Revue Bénédictine* 36 (1924): 52–71; "Les Méditations VII et VIII attribuées à Saint Anselme: La Série des 21 Meditations," *Revue d'ascétique et de mystique* 8 (1927): 249–82. Wilmart's attention to the corpus of devotional works traditionally attributed to Anselm has identified as his three of the twenty-one meditations in PL 158; these three have been printed in a critical edition by Franciscus Schmitt, *S. Anselmi Cantuariensis Archiepiscopi: Opera Omnia*, vol. 3 (Edinburgh: Thomas Nelson and Sons, 1946). See also André Wilmart, *Auteurs spirituels et textes devots du moyen* âge *latin*, Études d'histoire littéraire (Paris: Bloud et Gay, 1932), 162–201.

[21] That one passage, identified by the Quaracchi editors and by Cousins as coming from Anselm's meditation fifteen, is in paragraph nine of *The Tree of Life*, the passage on the nativity. One additional passage not indicated by the Quaracchi editors as Anselmian is identified by Cousins as coming from one of the three authentic Anselmian meditations, Meditation two in PL, "About the terror of judgment, to excite fear," PL 158:724–25 = Schmitt, Med. 1, "Meditatio ad concitandum timorem," 76–79.

[22] Wilmart, "Méditations," 273.

Despite the occasional recognition of Aelred's influence on Bonaventure and Ludolph and the now-general awareness that some of what has long been considered Anselmian meditation originated with Aelred, Franciscan scholars have remained unaware of Aelred's role.[23] In the preface to Cousins' 1978 translation, Ignatius Brady says about *The Tree of Life*, "The opuscule is, quite evidently, a highly original work. Apart from frequent anonymous use of the meditations once ascribed to Saint Anselm, it reveals no dependence on other writers. . . ."[24]

Brady's statement of course depends on Cousins' analysis of the work's sources. Unfortunately, although Wilmart in 1924, 1927, and 1932 showed Anselm to have written only three of the meditations long attributed to him, Cousins in 1978 apparently merely accepted the 1882–1902 Quaracchi edition's attribution of eight passages to Anselm.[25] Nor does he appear to have sought out non-biblical sources other than those familiar from the Quaracchi edition. His neglect of the question

[23] Dunstan Dobbins, *Franciscan Mysticism*, Franciscan Studies, no. 6 (New York: J. F. Wagner, 1927), 82, states that Bonaventure's "principal sources . . . are the Gospels, the writings of St Anselm and St Bernard, and the characteristically Franciscan traditions begun by the 'Poverello' . . . . it is to these that he is indebted for his conception and presentation of the mystical value of this practical devotion to Christ. . . . Both in the dogmatic and in the scriptural treatises already mentioned, and in the *Opuscula*, he constantly appeals to the earlier writers for confirmation."

[24] Cousins, *The Soul's Journey*, xvi. Brady's phrase "frequent anonymous use" appears to contradict his conclusion of "no dependence." In fact, besides the "Anselmian" passages noted by him and Cousins and the multiple Aelredian usages that Cousins does not recognize, Cousins footnotes two passages in the work from Bede and one from Boethius. Further, there is some evidence that Bonaventure may have known and been influenced by Robert Grosseteste's *Moralia super Evangelia*, probably delivered to the Franciscans of Oxford in about 1230 (see S. Harrison Thomson, *The Writings of Robert Grosseteste: Bishop of Lincoln 1235–1253* [Cambridge, UK: Cambridge University Press, 1940], 134); this work may have been the immediate source for Bonaventure's use of the authentic Anselmian meditation.

[25] Cousins does not follow the Quaracchi editors in attributing to "Anselm's" meditation some nine lines in *The Soul's Journey*, 29, titled "Jesus, sol morte pallidus."

of sources for Bonaventure's treatise and of the implications of the Pseudo-Anselmian passages within it has caused him and Brady to regard *The Tree of Life* as essentially original and to leave that impression with their readers.

Cousins has recognized the similarities of method between *The Tree of Life* and Ignatius's *Spiritual Exercises*, but he attributes their origin to Bonaventure, saying in the introduction to his translation,

> Bonaventure can be seen in relation to the *Spiritual Exercises* of Ignatius of Loyola. Bonaventure's *The Tree of Life* is in many respects a forerunner of Ignatian meditation, in both its subject matter and its techniques. . . . From one point of view, the Ignatian *Exercises* can be seen as an initiation into the contemplative vision that Bonaventure proposes in *The Soul's Journey*; and from another point of view, one could follow Bonaventure's suggestions as how to open the meditation on the humanity of Christ in the *Exercises* to a more mystical contemplation of Christ.[26]

In a Franciscan Studies session at the 18th annual Congress of Medieval Studies at Kalamazoo, Michigan, on May 7, 1983, Cousins combined these two comments in a paper titled "St Bonaventure's *Lignum Vitae*: Mysticism of Historical Events." In his paper he argued that in *The Tree of Life* Bonaventure invented a new kind of affective approach to God, an approach that he termed "mysticism of historical events," and suggested again that this meditative approach directly influenced Ignatius in his writing of the *Spiritual Exercises*.[27]

[26] Cousins, *The Soul's Journey*, 37. See also below, n. 48.

[27] As Cousins notes Bonaventure's use of one passage from the authentic Anselm and eight from the Pseudo-Anselm, as well as the two from Boethius and one from Bede, it is hard to explain his suggestion that Bonaventure invented the method. Of the nine passages attributed by him to Anselm or Pseudo-Anselm, six urged the soul to participate imaginatively in the historical events of Jesus' life. Despite his ignorance of Aelred's influence, Cousins clearly knew that Bonaventure followed at least two previous authors, Anselm and Ecbert (his pseudo-Anselm), in his use of this approach

Cousins is quite right in recognizing the influence of this form of spirituality in the *Spiritual Exercises*; his error lies in considering Bonaventure its originator and in failing to recognize him as, like Ignatius, a beneficiary of Cistercian affective spirituality and, specifically, of Aelred's unique contribution to that tradition. In fact, Bonaventure's *The Tree of Life* is largely derivative, truly original only apparently in its external structure and not at all in content or meditative approach and style.

Bonaventure's *The Tree of Life*, written about a hundred years after Aelred's *On Reclusion*, declares two purposes. First, it is intended to create in the Christian an ability to declare with Paul in Galatians, "With Christ I am nailed to the cross,"[28] that is, to guide the Christian to imitate Christ. In a characteristically Bonaventuran understanding, Christ appears from the beginning of the treatise as the exemplum of the Christian life.

After beginning his work with this general statement of purpose, Bonaventure continues with greater specificity to define the purpose and subject matter of his treatise. Where in the first paragraph he refers to Christ crucified as the "bundle of myrrh" whom the contemplative will "carry about continuously, both in his soul and in his flesh," in the second the bundle of myrrh becomes the work itself, now understood as the life of Christ, to be used as a stimulus to devotion and faith.

He is no less specific about his source: "the forest of the holy Gospel." Unfortunately for later scholars, Bonaventure does not follow either of the two familiar medieval patterns of source acknowledgement, either alluding to all the fathers as the inspiration and source or neglecting to mention any source at all. Had he either modestly and conventionally acknowl-

---

to meditation through the historical events of Jesus' life. The immediate impact of Cousins' paper and its coining of a new term of reference for the meditative approach that Bonaventure found in Aelred may be seen in a paper presented at the 19th Congress of Medieval Studies in Kalamazoo, May 1984. The program booklet of the conference for 11 May 1984 includes a paper by William Hood, "Franciscan Pilgrimage Sanctuaries of the Renaissance: A Case of Cousin's [*sic*] Mysticism of the Historical Event."

[28] Gal 2:19; Bonaventure, LV Prol. 1, p. 68; TL p. 119.

edged widespread assistance in his literary and spiritual task or admitted to none, readers and scholars in all subsequent periods would have searched intently for the literary origins of *The Tree of Life*. Rather, he acknowledges a source, the obvious, necessary, and, one would think, sufficient one. While the ubiquity of medieval plagiarism is a byword of medieval scholarship, this work is unusual in disguising its heavy reliance on an important source through apparent forthrightness of acknowledgement. In this Bonaventure is, I would argue, disingenuous, intentionally misleading.

Finally Bonaventure details the full complexity of the large image that shapes his treatment of the life of Christ, a tree of life with twelve branches and twelve fruits:[29]

> To enkindle in us this affection, to shape this understanding and to imprint this memory, I have endeavored to gather this bundle of myrrh from the forest of the holy Gospel, which treats at length the life, passion, and glorification of Jesus Christ. I have bound it together with a few ordered and parallel words to aid the memory. I have used simple, familiar, and unsophisticated terms to avoid idle curiosity, to cultivate devotion, and to foster the piety of faith. Since imagination aids understanding, I have arranged in the form of an imaginary tree the few items I have collected from among many, and have ordered and disposed them in such a way that in the first or lower branches the Savior's origin and life are described; in the middle, his passion; and in the top, his glorification.[30]

The work is divided into a prologue and three main divisions, devoted to the origins, passion, and glorification of Christ. Within each of these divisions appear four sections, "fruits," each of which contains four separate meditations. At the end

[29] {This image is not Aelredian, but based on the tree of life of Revelation 22:2, which bears twelve fruits. Bonaventure's tree of life also has twelve fruits, but growing on twelve branches. In the original version of this chapter I referred to this image as non-biblical, having failed to recognize Revelation as Bonaventure's source here.}

[30] Bonaventure, LV Prol. 2, p. 68; TL 119–20.

of the whole comes a prayer to obtain the seven gifts of the Holy Spirit.

Of the forty-eight meditations, forty begin with short narrative passages, sometimes only a sentence or two, followed by a lyrical prayer, exhortation, or exclamation. Most are exhortations to the soul, though the intended audience is most clearly defined in the prologue to the work: "The true worshipper of God and disciple of Christ, who desires to conform perfectly to the Savior of all men crucified for him."[31] Almost all of the borrowings from Aelred come in these lyrical exhortations.

Throughout *The Tree of Life* Bonaventure moves rhythmically from third-person indicative narration of Jesus' life to second-person conditional—"if you could"—or imperative and back again. The pattern is not quite regular, however, for sometimes he addresses God in these passages or speaks cohortatively. The rhetorical function of these passages in *The Tree of Life* is not altogether clear, but they reflect the pervasive influence of *On Reclusion* upon *The Tree of Life* and indicate Bonaventure's desire in this work to imitate Aelred's meditative approach while not fully understanding its purpose.

In his discussion of *The Tree of Life* Cousins describes the meditative approach of the work and addresses the question of its purpose:

> In *The Tree of Life*, however, Bonaventure provides a meditation that touches the very heart of Franciscan devotion to the humanity and passion of Christ . . . . In each specific meditation, Bonaventure summarizes the narrative details of an event in Christ's life, with references to the foreshadowing in Old Testament texts. There is a vivid application of the senses, an imaginative recreation of the Gospel scene, a drawing of the reader into the drama of the event as a witness and a participator. Most of the meditations contain a prayer or direct address to the reader, evoking strong emotions through graphic, dramatic imagery. . . . In this type of meditation, one applies the senses

[31] Bonaventure, LV Prol. 1, p. 68; TL 119.

> to a vividly imagined scene and evokes human emotions ranging from tender love to anguish.[32]

In *The Tree of Life* all Aelredian passages come from *On Reclusion*, all but three from the first of the three meditations. These three are not in fact certainly borrowings—they are similar in language and function, but that similarity could be coincidence or simply reflect the Gospel accounts that underlie both works. Two of these come from the third meditation, that on the Judgment, and one from the section on humility just before Aelred's three meditations.

The passages in *The Tree of Life* revealing influence from Aelred fall into four rough categories: (1) near-identity with slight variation in phrasing, (2) extensive verbal parallels with embellishment or rearrangement, (3) some verbal similarity and likeness in technique and purpose but with considerable independence in phrasing, and (4) stylistic imitation of Aelred with little overlap of content or phrasing. These classifications are highly inexact and fluid; they indicate a continuum between passages unmistakably taken from *On Reclusion* and minimally adapted in *The Tree of Life* and passages merely reminiscent of Aelred's meditative approach as seen in *On Reclusion*.

However, Aelred's influence is markedly greater than this description would indicate, because it seems clear that Bonaventure's purpose in writing this work and his internal structure, the movement from a third-person indicative narrative of Christ's life to second- and third-person exhortation, comes directly from Aelred. Bonaventure surely intended in *The Tree of Life* to follow Aelred's lead in writing a work of affective spirituality based on the life of Christ, using Aelred's style and often words, but in so doing to transform what was for Aelred only one portion of a work written for the specific needs of very specific audience, an anchoress, into a single, unified work of spiritual direction drawn from the life of Christ, expanded and adapted for a much more general audience.

[32] Cousins, Introduction to *The Soul's Journey*, 35–36.

There are nine instances of category one. These include Aelred's direction to the contemplative to accompany Mary to visit Elizabeth, to embrace the manger at the nativity, to "let love overcome bashfulness, affection dispel fear,"[33] to accompany the holy family to Egypt, and so on. These appear with minor variants—a word inserted, an embellished phrase, a verb replaced by another of the same root—all changes that might but probably do not reflect minor manuscript variants. Frequently Bonaventure inserts a sentimental word or two or a brief theological statement into Aelred's direction. Usually, though not always, the borrowed passages appear in the same position in *The Tree of Life* as in *On Reclusion*. For example, most of the words in which Aelred speaks of the nativity are directly transferred to Bonaventure's meditation on the nativity, but one phrase of direction, that mentioned above, is transferred from Aelred's nativity passage to Bonaventure's presentation in the temple {which is not present in *On Reclusion*}.

An instance of this category appears in the visitation passage:

> But now with your most sweet lady go up into the mountains and gaze at the sweet embrace of the barren one and the virgin and at their greeting, in which the little servant recognized and greeted with unspeakable joy the lord, the herald the judge, the voice the word, the one confined in the old woman's womb, the other enclosed in the womb of the virgin.

Bonaventure's version says:

> If you might hear with joy the virgin singing, if you might go up with your lady into the mountains, if you might gaze at the sweet embrace of the barren one and the virgin and at their greeting, in which the little servant recognized the lord, the herald the judge, the voice the word, I believe that then with the most

[33] A[elred]: *uincat uerecundiam amor, timorem depellat affectus* (Inst incl 29 [CCCM 1:663; CF 2:81]). B[onaventure]: *vincat verecundiam amor, depellat timorem affectus* (LV 7, p. 72; TL p. 131).

> blessed virgin you would sing in sweet measure that sacred song, "My soul magnifies the Lord." And you, at one with the little prophet, will adore the marvelous virginal conception, rejoicing and exulting.[34]

Here Bonaventure changes Aelred's imperative mood to a conditional followed not by direction but by a result clause: Aelred urges the imaginative participation of the contemplative; Bonaventure, the consideration of what it would be like for the contemplative if only.

In this passage Bonaventure adds to the Aelredian passage the suggestion that the soul sing with Mary, in the words of the *Magnificat*. In *On Reclusion* Aelred four times asks the contemplative to sing with those hymning Jesus' coming: once at the annunciation, twice at the nativity, and once at the entry into Jerusalem on Palm Sunday. But in Aelred's work the contemplative who so joins her voice always associates herself with worshipers of Jesus divine and human, never with Mary or Jesus himself. Bonaventure, in imitation and adaptation of this meditative technique, advises the soul to sing—or says that the soul will sing—with thirteen others in seven passages: with Mary at the visitation, with angels at the nativity, with the spouse from the Song of Songs, and with Simeon at the presentation, with six recipients of miracles, with Peter at the transfiguration, and with the Psalmist (from Psalm 41) at the Last Supper. Aelred's instruction to the contemplative has her singing as one among worshipers, while Bonaventure's various

[34] A: *Iam nunc cum dulcissima domina tua in montana conscende, et sterilis et uirginis suauem intuere complexum, et salutationis officium, in quo seruulus dominum, praeco iudicem, uox uerbum, inter anilia uiscera conclusus, in Virginis utero clausum agnouit, et indicibili gaudio salutauit* (Inst incl 29 [CCCM 1:663; CF 2:81]).

B: *Si Virginem canentem cum iubilo posses audire, si cum Domina tua in montana conscendere, si sterilis et Virginis suavem intueri complexum et salutationis officium, in quo servulus Dominum, praeco Iudicem, vox Verbum agnovit: puto, quod canticum illud sacrum: "Magnificat anima mea Dominum" etc., cum beatissima Virgine suavi tunc modulatione concineres mirumque conceptum virginem una cum Propheta Parvulo exsultans et iubilans adorares!* (LV 3, p. 71; TL 127–28).

such passages are disparate, incorporating the idea of the contemplative's imaginative involvement but without such clear sense of purpose or definition of the contemplative's role in the biblical scene.

In the visitation passage, then, Bonaventure not only directly incorporates Aelred's visitation scene but also imitates an Aelredian feature that Aelred himself omits, exemplifying category four as well as category one. This combination of direct verbal borrowing and imitation of technique indicates the ubiquity of Aelred's influence on Bonaventure in *The Tree of Life*.

Another nine passages fall into category two, those containing marked verbal similarities or parallels to Aelred's but with a rearrangement of phrases and a conflation of what are in *On Reclusion* separate passages, discrete narrative events. In these the inspiration and the words both clearly come from Aelred's parallel passages. For example, Aelred's nativity concentrates on the birth, then considers Mary's joy at the birth and the assistance of the contemplative at that birth, next the contemplative's embracing the crib and kissing the infant's feet, and finally the angels' visit and the coming of the magi. After the angels' song—with which the contemplative is asked to sing along—Aelred directs her attention in one sentence to the magi and the flight to Egypt. He says nothing about the gifts or worship of the magi; the movement is straightforward and unbroken; it occupies three and a half sentences and seven imperative verbs.

In his parallel treatment of these scenes Bonaventure gives only narrative space to the fact of the birth, placed within a theological statement, perhaps an imitation of Aelred's passage on humility well before the meditation on the past.[35] He de-

[35] A: *Qua enim fronte de diuitiis uel natalibus gloriaris quae illius uis sponsa uideri, qui pauper factus cum esset diues, pauperem matrem, pauperem familiam, domum etiam pauperculam, et praesepii uilitatem elegit?* (Inst incl 24 [CCCM 1:656–57; CF 2:71]).

B: *qui, cum magnus esset et dives, pro nobis effectus parvus et pauper, extra domum in diversorio nasci elegit, panniculis involvi, lacte virgineo pasci et inter bovem et asinum in praesepio reclinari* (LV 4, pp. 71–72; TL 128).

votes one sentence in the passage to the soul's embracing the manger and kissing the infant's feet, then moves rapidly to the shepherds' watch and the angels' song. The magi's coming is distinct from the nativity passage (the fourth meditation of the first fruit; the magi the second meditation of the second fruit). In *The Tree of Life,* Jesus' circumcision, a {non-biblical} incident not included by Aelred, intervenes. Still later, as the fourth meditation of the second fruit, Bonaventure conflates the flight to Egypt with the story of the twelve-year-old Jesus in Jerusalem.

Another example of category two comes from Peter's denying Jesus. Aelred directs the contemplative's attention in this scene primarily to Jesus and his response to Peter's denial, then acknowledges his own guilt and asks Jesus' compassion on him. He identifies himself with the sinner as one in need of grace, and the contemplative washes Jesus' face out of love and compassion for him rather than a desire to atone. Her compassion precedes and is separate from the guilt and repentance of Peter and the author.

Bonaventure reports Peter's denial in a lengthy narrative paragraph on the guilt and personal atonement of the listening contemplative; for him the emphasis is not on compassion for Jesus' suffering, Jesus' mercy toward the sinner, or his own guilt; rather, he concentrates on his audience's guilt and ability to make satisfaction.

Aelred says to the contemplative:

> Follow him rather "to the courtyard of the prince of priests," and with your tears wash his most beautiful face, which they are smearing with spittle. Regard how compassionate his eyes, how mercifully, how effectually he looked back at Peter denying him

---

This passage may not have resulted from Bonaventure's familiarity with Aelred; it is a natural kind of exposition of the details of the nativity, and by the thirteenth century it was commonplace in all devotional literature. But in view of Bonaventure's constant use of Aelred, it may occur here through his influence. It suggests familiarity with more of *On Reclusion* than just the three meditations.

for the third time when Peter, turned about and returned into himself, "wept bitterly." Good Jesus, would that your sweet eyes might look upon me who so often at the voice of the shameless serving girl, that is, my flesh, have denied you by evil deeds and affections.

Bonaventure says here:

> "Yet Peter," more faithful, "followed at a distance even to the courtyard of the prince of priests," where at the voice of a serving girl, he with an oath denied that he knew Christ and repeated it a third time. Then, the cock crowing, the gentle master looked back at the beloved disciple with a look of compassion and grace, by which Peter, reminded, "going outside, wept bitterly." O, whoever you are, who at the voice of an insistent serving girl, that is, your flesh, have shamelessly denied Christ, either by will or by act, Christ who for you suffered, remember the passion of your beloved master and go out with Peter to weep most bitterly over yourself. When the one who looked upon the weeping Peter looks upon you, you will be inebriated with "the wormwood" of a twofold bitterness: remorse for yourself and compassion for Christ, so that having atoned with Peter for the guilt of your crime, you will be filled with the spirit of holiness.[36]

[36] A: *Sequere potius eum ad atrium principis sacerdotum, et speciosissimam eius faciem, quam illi sputis illiniunt, tu lacrymas laua. Intuere quam piis oculis, quam misericorditer, quam efficaciter tertio negantem respexit Petrum, quando ille conuersus, et in se reuersus, fleuit amare. Vtinam, bone Iesu, tuus me dulcis respiciat oculus, qui te totiens ad uocem ancillae procacis, carnis scilicet meae, pessimis operibus affectibusque negaui* (Inst incl 31 [CCCM 1:669; CF 2:88]).

B: *"Petrus, tamen," tanquam fidelior, "secutus est a longe usque in atrium principis sacerdotum," ubi ad vocem ancillae, se Christum nosse cum iuramento negavit tertioque repetit, donec, gallo cantante, respexit benignus Magister praedilectum discipulum respexit miserationis et gratiae; quo commonitus Petrus et "foras egressus flevit amare," O quisquis es, qui ad vocem impetentis ancillae, carnis videlicet tuae, Christum pro te passum negasti procaciter vel voluntate vel actu; rememorans passionem dilectissimi Magistri, foras cum Petro egredere, ut te ipsum amarissime defleas, si quando te respeciat qui Petrum lacrymantem respexit, geminae quoque amarictionis "compunctionis" scilicet pro te et "compassionis" ad Christum, inebrieris absinthio, ut, expiatus cum Petro a reatu sceleris, replearis cum Petro spiritu sanctitatis* (LV 21, p. 76; TL 144–45).

Ten passages fall into category three. They contain similarities with parallel passages in *On Reclusion* and are clearly influenced by Aelred's meditative style, but they might not be recognized as by him did they not appear in this heavy Aelredian context. For example, Aelred says to the contemplative in the passion narrative,

> And what of you? It is not surprising if when the sun mourns you mourn with it, if when the earth trembles you tremble with it, if when rocks are rent your heart is rent, if with the women weeping at the cross you weep as well.

Bonaventure says:

> And you also, redeemed man, consider . . . at whose passing over heaven and earth mourn and hard rocks rend as if from natural compassion. Oh human heart, you are harder than any hardness of rocks if at the recollection of such great sacrifice you are not struck with terror or moved with compassion or rent with compunction or softened with devotion.[37]

Category four, containing roughly seven to twelve passages, shows Bonaventure's imitation of Aelred's meditative approach. An example comes after his sentence-long summary of miracles done by Jesus (a topic intentionally avoided by Aelred):

---

Aelred is always aware that the sinner cannot make recompense, that one is dependent on God's unmerited mercy. Note also that for Aelred *inebriate* is an essentially contemplative word; one who receives God's grace, one who knows union with God, experiences inebriation. Cf. Acts 2:13; Inst incl 31 (CCCM 1:668; CF 2:87).

[37] A: *Quid tu? Non mirum si sole contristante, tu contristaris, si terra tremiscente, tu contremiscis, si scissis saxis, tuum cor scinditur, si flentibus iuxta crucem mulieribus, tu collacrymaris* (Inst incl 31 [CCCM 1:670; CF 2:89–90]).

B: *Considera et tu, homo redempte, . . . cuius que transitum et caelum luget et terra, et lapides duri quasi naturali compassione scinduntur. O cor humanum omni lapidum duritia durius, si ad tanti rememorationem piaculi nec terrore concuteris nec compassione afficeris nec compunctione scinderis nec pietate molieris?* (LV 29, p. 79; TL 154).

> To him our sinning conscience calls out like the faithful leper, "Lord, if you wish, you can make me clean." Now like the centurion: "Lord, my servant boy is lying at home paralyzed and is suffering intensely." Now like the woman of Canaan: "have mercy on me, son of David." Now like the woman with the issue of blood: "If I touch the hem of his garment, I will be cured." Now with Mary and Martha: "See, Lord, the one you love is ill."[38]

This passage attempts in pedestrian fashion to provide an Aelredian meditation where none is available.

Aelred's influence on *The Tree of Life* is not limited to instances of parallel usage; Bonaventure's repeated borrowing reveals an enormous stylistic debt to Aelred. The work as a whole—its style and approach of imaginative involvement in Jesus' human experience, intimacy with him, and growing nearness to God—continuously resonates of Aelred's first meditation. Knowledge of the regularity with which Bonaventure relies on Aelred for language and style allows the reader to recognize Bonaventure's dependence on him in the individual instance. For example, at the beginning of *The Tree of Life* Bonaventure defines his audience as

> one who, not unmindful of the Lord's passion nor ungrateful, contemplates the labor, suffering, and love of Jesus crucified, with such vividness of memory, such sharpness of intellect, and such charity of will that he can truly say with the bride: "A bundle of myrrh is my beloved to me; he will linger between my breasts."[39]

Immediately after this sentence, Bonaventure defines his purpose in *The Tree of Life*: "To enkindle in us this affection, to shape this understanding, and to imprint this memory, I have endeavored to gather this bundle of myrrh from the forest of the holy Gospel."[40] In both cases Bonaventure uses Song of

[38] Bonaventure, LV 11, p. 73; TL 135.
[39] Bonaventure, LV Prol.1, p. 68; TL 119.
[40] Bonaventure, LV Prol.2, p. 68; TL 119.

Songs 1:12 in reference to Jesus crucified, as he does in *The Life of Saint Francis* [*Legenda Maior*] when he says, "Jesus Christ crucified always *rested like a bundle of myrrh in the bosom* of Francis's soul."[41]

Bernard of Clairvaux had also used this verse to refer to Christ in sermons forty-three and forty-five on the Song of Songs, in the former case defining Christ as the lover of the bride and speaking of his humility, the suffering of the present time, and the anticipation of glory to come. In sermon forty-five Bernard explicitly identifies the myrrh as Christ crucified: "And yet when reproved [the bride] repented and said, 'My beloved is to me a little bundle of myrrh that lies between my breasts.' As much as to say, 'it is enough for me: I desire to know nothing any longer except Jesus and him crucified.'"[42]

Bonaventure might well have taken his understanding of this verse from Bernard, but awareness of his intimate acquaintance with and constant reliance on *On Reclusion* leads the reader to examine Aelred's work for the immediate source—and apparently to find it. At the moment in *On Reclusion* when Joseph of Arimathea takes Christ down from the cross, Aelred says to the contemplative, "then could that holy man say, 'My beloved is a bundle of myrrh for me, he shall rest upon my breast.'"[43] It is surely Aelred's use of this verse that influences both of Bonaventure's identifications of the crucified Christ as a bundle of myrrh upon the believer's breast.

Some thirty-five to forty instances of the four categories of borrowing appear in *The Tree of Life*. Aelred's life of Christ in the first meditation of *On Reclusion* is clearly Bonaventure's primary source: it and Ecbert's meditation on the humanity of Christ ("Anselm's" meditation nine) shape the content and

[41] Bonaventure, *Legenda Sancti Francisci*, in *Opuscula varia ad theologiam mysticam*, 8.9.2; Cousins, *The Soul's Journey*, 263.

[42] Bernard, *On the Song of Songs II*, trans. Kilian Walsh, CF 7 (Kalamazoo, MI: Cistercian Publications, 1976), 223, 234.

[43] Aelred, Inst incl 31 (CCCM 1:671; CF 2:91).

style of the work. {Besides the probable origin of the work's structural image, Revelation's tree of life, Bonaventure's} only other important source is probably the Gospels themselves.[44]

At the same time *The Tree of Life* is very different from Aelred's life of Christ in overall structure and purpose. Although Bonaventure apparently wrote his life of Christ out of admiration for Aelred's first meditation and used it as the core of his own work, he was not satisfied merely to duplicate it; he chose to add to it on both ends—largely extra-canonically—and in the middle, with attention to Gospel events that showed forth Jesus' ministry and divinity. Bonaventure's life of Christ begins with a theological statement about the begetting of Jesus and ends with fourteen meditations after the resurrection, including the ascension, and providing a number of theological summaries of Jesus' identity in glory, such as Jesus' Extraordinary Beauty and Jesus Given Dominion over the Earth. He includes the transfiguration, as Aelred does not, and concentrates on the Last Supper not, like Aelred, as a human event whose immediate interest lies in the relationships of those present, in its provision of a eucharistic model for contemporary union, or in it as an incident in Jesus' human life, but as a theological and sacramental event.

Aelred's life of Christ begins with the annunciation, ends with the resurrection, and omits the transfiguration, miracles, and most of Jesus' ministry. He includes some events that Bonaventure omits: Jesus' washing the disciples' feet; the paralytic man let down through the roof; dinner with Mary, Martha, and Lazarus; and Mary's anointing of Jesus. He treats separately some stories conflated by Bonaventure, such as the woman taken in adultery and her later anointing Jesus, but treats the details of the passion as part of a whole, a narrative that picks up speed and coherence as it develops, rather than as a series of individual events, as does Bonaventure.

[44] See n. 29.

Further, Bonaventure's contemplative theology as enunciated in *The Tree of Life* is radically different from Aelred's. Bonaventure insists on coming to God by imitation of Jesus rather than by intimacy with him. Where Aelred regularly directs the soul to minister to, to anoint, to love Jesus, Bonaventure's emphasis is always on following Jesus' lead, on reaching toward identification with him, likeness to him, through meditation on his life and its meaning for humankind rather than on coming to union with him, even in passages in which the soul must naturally identify herself with those who love Jesus rather than with Jesus himself. While in the meditation on the magi he urges veneration of Jesus with gifts of gold, myrrh, and frankincense, he concludes, "you will return to your country in the footsteps of the humble Christ."[45] When Jesus is nailed to the cross he asks, "Who will grant me that my request should come about and that God will give me what I long for, that having been totally transpierced in both mind and flesh, I may be fixed with my beloved to the yoke of the cross?"[46]

In the parallel passages Aelred says nothing about the magi except to note their coming, but he urges the contemplative to weep at the passion, to stand with Mary and John, and finally to drink the blood and water from Jesus' side, to enter into his wound, and finally to bear up his limbs and save the falling drops of blood. Aelred guides the contemplative towards spiritual union with Christ through love of him, not toward perfection through imitation of him, suggesting that such perfection, such imitation, is neither possible nor necessary.

Bonaventure's treatise is finally less concerned with the humanity of Jesus and with the events of his human life than with a theological understanding of that humanity, placed within the context of his divinity. Thus he leads his reader to Jesus through two statements about his origins, statements not taken from the Gospel accounts, titled "Jesus Begotten of God"

[45] Bonaventure, LV 6, p. 72; TL 130–31.

[46] Bonaventure, LV 26, p. 78; TL 149.

and "Jesus Prefigured." Neither of these passages allows any human involvement with Jesus, and neither has the usual lyrical passage. The top four branches on Bonaventure's tree again contain meditations from outside the human life of Jesus, with scenes from his glorification. Even within the events of Jesus' life Bonaventure is concerned to provide theological definition and explication.

Bonaventure's concern, then, is more speculative and didactic than affective or contemplative. He is essentially concerned with leading his reader to understand and perhaps to effect a change in behavior as a result of that understanding. His treatise appears more truly concerned with a moral reading of the Gospel than a contemplative one; its center is cognitive, not contemplative; its concerns doctrinal and moral. Because of a radically different purpose in the work, Bonaventure uses Aelred's direction to the contemplative, his constant urging her forward, not as a way of bringing her to closeness with Jesus in his humanity and thus to God, but rather as a stylistic variant, a different way of explaining Christ's dual nature and of leading his audience to imitate it so as to come to God. His treatise on the life of Christ emerges from a radically different understanding from Aelred's of the road to mystical knowledge of God. At the same time *The Tree of Life* is consciously emotive, urging the reader, the soul, to ever greater levels of emotional intensity in hearing and responding to the Gospel events. It accomplishes Bonaventure's moral and theological goals through emotional appeal, a familiar and valuable heuristic approach. The reader is led to feel as well as to think, to become involved in order to understand.

Cousins misunderstands the work, though, when he tries to present it as a contemplative work, one leading toward mystical knowledge of or union with God. He comments in his introduction that "Bonaventure meditates on Christ as the beginning, the middle and the end of the journey; but in each case he focuses not on the historical Jesus in the concrete details of his earthly life as an example of moral virtue, but on the mystical Christ who opens the deeper dimensions of the soul and leads to union with God."[47] That statement is hard to support on the basis of the work itself, and in fact Cousins' own suggestion that *The Tree of Life* cannot stand alone as a contemplative treatise, that it requires combination with either *The Soul's Journey into God* or *Spiritual Exercises* to allow such a passage to union, bears more conviction.[48]

Like Bonaventure, Ludolph the Carthusian directs the reader of his *Vita Christi* to imitation of Christ; it is his work and his emphasis on this meditative approach that is generally understood as underlying the *imitatio* school of spirituality, notably in the works of Thomas à Kempis and Francis de Sales.

Each of the eighty-nine chapters of Ludolph's *Vita Christi* is given to a different aspect of the life of Jesus (some actually to Mary), and each ends with a brief appended prayer, essentially the only parts of the whole thought actually to have originated with Ludolph. That pattern of narrative followed by semi-spontaneous prayer, seen also in *The Tree of Life*, may itself have been influenced by the similar brief prayers interjected by

[47] Cousins, *The Soul's Journey*, 35.

[48] Cousins in fact recognizes the heavy moral emphasis of *The Tree of Life* despite his attempt here to deny it as central, saying on the next page: "In this type of meditation, one applies the senses to a vividly imagined scene and evokes human emotions ranging from tender love to anguish. In the history of Christian piety, this form of meditation has been problematic, especially in its focus on the passion of Christ. Since it evokes human emotions, it can fall into a superficial sentimentalism. If it avoids this, it might remain exclusively on the moral level, proposing Christ's virtues for imitation in everyday life. It can, however, be a gateway into deeper mystical states of consciousness. Bonaventure indicates how this can be done when in the soul's journey he speaks of Christ as the doorway into the Franciscan contemplative vision, then later as the bridegroom of the soul, and finally as the passage to mystical ecstasy. If one were, for example, to link Bonaventure's meditations on the life of Christ in *The Tree of Life* to these three points, he could integrate these two forms of meditation in an organic fashion" (Cousins, *The Soul's Journey*, 37). Aelred's *On Reclusion* does in fact integrate the two forms of meditation, not sequentially but organically, leading the contemplative to mystical union through intimacy rather than imitation.

Aelred into his life of Christ in *On Reclusion*, but it is of course a pattern not restricted to any one author. Anselm Le Bail has suggested it as a characteristic of Cistercian spirituality:

> These men . . . find it necessary to interrupt their exposition with prayers, with flights upward to God, with chants of praise . . . . Here perhaps we see the quintessence of the style of the Cistercian spirituality of the twelfth and thirteenth centuries. It is a search for God, and the moment the insight is attained the heart bursts forth in chants of praise.[49]

While such movement from third-person objective narration to first-person prayer is perhaps characteristic of Cistercian spirituality, it is clearly a natural one and not restricted to any one school. It need not depend on any non-biblical source, but if one were sought it might as well be Augustine as Aelred.

Ludolph, unlike Bonaventure, makes no pretense of having drawn his lengthy life of Christ from the Gospels alone. He appears to have used every author and every manuscript available to him, and he cites every borrowed passage both before and after its use.[50] Passages quoted from *On Reclusion* begin *Hic dicit Anselmus* and end *Haec Anselmus*. A few times, at the appropriate place in his narrative, he quotes from *On Jesus as a Boy of Twelve*, known to him as written by Bernard, and before and after those passages he writes *Hic dicit Bernardus* and *Haec Bernardus*. His treatise is finally more a carefully annotated florilegium than an independent work.

Like Bonaventure, Ludolph breaks Aelred's uninterrupted narrative into brief topical blocks, on the annunciation, the visitation, the nativity, and so on. Like Bonaventure, he begins at the beginning of time and ends with the Judgment, so not

[49] Anselm Le Bail, "La Spiritualité cistercienne," *Les Cahiers du Cercle Thomiste Fémine* 7 (1927): 491; cited in Aelred of Rievaulx, "On Jesus as a Boy of Twelve," trans. Theodore Berkeley, in *Treatises; Pastoral Prayer*, CF 2 (Kalamazoo, MI: Cistercian Publications, 1971), 80 n. 8.

[50] {For Ludolph's sources, see Ludolph, *The Life of Jesus Christ*, 1:xlvi–xlvii.}

all of Aelred fits into his scheme. Further, he puts much more emphasis on the public ministry of Jesus than does Aelred, and so has no material from Aelred for those portions of his treatise. It is clear, however, that he wrote with a manuscript of Aelred at hand, for the entire first meditation, almost word for word, appears in blocks at the appropriate places in his work. He omits only words in which Aelred indicates a transition from one scene to another—"Now, sister," "linger no longer here"—or too great specificity of audience: "O, virgin."

Ludolph's access to Aelred is unquestionably independent of Bonaventure. Not only does he include all of the first meditation, as Bonaventure does not, but he does not ever adapt, rearrange, embellish, or conflate Aelred's narrative as Bonaventure always does. It is also clear that Ludolph has more than one "Anselmian" manuscript available to him. In his account of the annunciation, he begins *De hac Verbi Incarnatione, sic dicit anselmus*, and he follows that with a Prayer for the Son not taken from *On Reclusion*. After the prayer he adds *Idem ad sororem suam* and continues with Aelred's urging the contemplative to await with Mary the coming of the angel.[51]

Both Bonaventure and Ludolph used the first meditation of Aelred's *On Reclusion* extensively in the composition of their own lives of Christ. The evidence of their use argues that perhaps they wrote in direct response to that meditation, out of deep admiration for it and desire to replicate it in a work devoted to that one purpose. That desire is more clear in the case of Bonaventure than that of Ludolph, given the great number of authors represented in Ludolph's work. Both later writers were perhaps frustrated with what they saw as Aelred's truncated treatment of the Gospel account, beginning only with the annunciation and ending with the meeting in the garden after the resurrection, and both wanted more theological definition.

[51] Ludolph, *Vita Iesu Christi* 1.5.27, vol. 1:44.

Not only had Aelred both begun too late and ended too early in his portrayal of Christ, he had not even dealt with all of Christ's human experiences, especially those that showed forth divinity—miracles, teaching, and so on. Aelred was much more interested in *On Reclusion* as in all his works in Jesus' human relationships during his life and the model they suggested for men and women of all times to come into relationship with Jesus. Bonaventure and Ludolph then added not only to the beginning and end of Aelred's account of Jesus' life but to the middle as well.

Both also failed to understand Aelred's concern for the contemplative's life and purpose, the yearning effort to come into union with God. Because Aelred writes his work not as a theological treatise or as an allegorized representation of the Gospel, but rather as a simple work of guidance in the life of contemplation toward the goal of that life, his meditation on the life of Christ exemplifies that purpose.

And Aelred's understanding of the way to communion with God was like his understanding of human union: it comes through love, through intimacy. His meditation exemplifies that understanding of contemplative union throughout, and his meditative method of imaginative involvement in the human life of Jesus—the only life in which a contemplative can involve oneself (that being the point of the incarnation, after all)—grows out of that understanding.

Bonaventure and Ludolph were able to use Aelred's words and, in the case of Bonaventure, to imitate his method, but in the absence of Aelred's particular purpose and understanding—and with their own understanding of Christ as exemplar and of contemplative union as emerging from imitation of Christ—they were never really able to understand what Aelred had in mind. It did not matter so much in Ludolph's *Vita Christi*, because he merely quoted Aelred, but in Bonaventure the passages borrowed from Aelred sometimes fit awkwardly, as in the passage on the magi. Aelred's *On Reclusion* is, finally, contemplative, theirs devotional and theological, given over to meditation and exposition.

Ludolph's effect on Ignatius was also devotional and theological, finally leading toward exemplarism; the *Spiritual Exercises* reflect his stylistic and didactic influence. The resemblance of Bonaventure and Ignatius has clearly been misleading; it is far too easy to trace Ignatius to Bonaventure and to his *Application des sens* in *The Tree of Life*, even though Ignatius, like Ludolph and unlike Bonaventure, acknowledged the origin of his spiritual insight. Oddly, then, Franciscan and Ignatian spirituality resemble one another more than they do Aelred and Cistercian spirituality. Nonetheless, both schools trace their heritage to the Cistercian Aelred.

Aelred said in the second meditation of *On Reclusion* (the one never borrowed or imitated so far as I know, and omitted almost entirely from many manuscripts),

> In men's opinion the graciousness of the giver and the good fortune of the recipient are so connected that they praise not only him to whom praise alone is due, the giver, but also him who has received the gift. What does a man possess that he has not received? And if he has received freely, why is he praised as if he had deserved the gift?[52]

Well might he ask. Aelred's gift of the meditation on the humanity of Christ has been the good fortune of Bonaventure, Ludolph, Ignatius—and all of Western Christian spirituality.

[52] Inst incl 32 (CCCM 1:675; CF 2:95).

*Appendix*

# Aelred's Works

## Bibliographies

Burton, Pierre-André. "Bibliotheca Aelrediana Secunda: Supplementa." In *A Companion to Aelred of Rievaulx (1110–1167)*, edited by Marsha L. Dutton. Brill Companions to the Christian Tradition 76. Leiden/Boston: Brill, 2017. 295–324.

Burton, Pierre-André. *Bibliotheca Aelrediana Secunda: Une Bibliographie Cumulative (1962–1996)*. Textes et Études du Moyen Âge 7. Louvain-la-Neuve, Belgium: Fédération Internationale des Instituts d'Études Médiévales, 1997.

Dutton, Marsha L. "Aelred of Rievaulx." In *Oxford Bibliographies in Medieval Studies*, edited by Paul E. Szarmach. Rev. ed. New York: Oxford University Press, 2025. https://www.oxfordbibliographies.com/.

Hoste, Anselm. *Bibliotheca Aelrediana: A Survey of the Manuscripts, Old Catalogues, Editions and Studies Concerning St. Aelred of Rievaulx*. Instrumenta Patristica 2. The Hague: Nijhoff, 1962.

## Grouped Editions of Aelred's Treatises

Aelred of Rievaulx. *Writings on Body and Soul*. Edited by Bruce Venarde. Dumbarton Oaks Medieval Library. Cambridge, MA, and London: Harvard University Press, 2021.

Aelredi Rievallensis. *Opera Omnia 1. Opera Ascetica*. Edited by Anselm Hoste and C. H. Talbot. CCCM 1. Turnholt: Brepols, 1971.

Aelredi Rievallensis. *Opera Omnia 6. Opera Historica et Hagiographica*. Edited by Domenico Pezzini. CCCM 3. Turnhout: Brepols, 2017.

Aelredi Rievallensis. *Opera Omnia 7. Opera Historica et Hagiographica.* Edited by Francesco Marzella. CCCM 3A. Turnhout: Brepols, 2017.

Ailredi Abbatis Rievallensis. "Historia bello standardii tempore Stephani Regis," "Genealogia regum Anglorum [including part of *Eulogium Davidis*]," "Vita et miraculis Edwardi Regis et Confessoris," "De quodam miraculo mirabili." In *Historiae Anglicanae Scriptores Decem*, edited by Roger Twysden. London: Cornelius Bee, 1652. 333–422.

Beati Aelredi Rievallis Abbatis. *Operum Pars Prima—Ascetica; Operum Pars Secunda—Historica*. Edited by J.-P. Migne. Paris, 1855. PL 195:500–796.

## Editions and English Translations of Aelred's Treatises in Accepted Order of Appearance[1]

*Speculum Caritatis* (ca. 1142) Spec car

*Speculum caritatis.* Edited by C. H. Talbot. 1971. CCCM 1:1–161.

*Speculum charitatis.* Edited by J.-P. Migne. 1855. PL 195:501–620.

*The Mirror of Charity.* Translated by Elizabeth Connor. Introduction by Charles Dumont. CF 17. Kalamazoo, MI: Cistercian Publications, 1990.

*Relatio de Standardo* (1153–1154) Stand

*Relatio de Standardo*. Edited by Domenico Pezzini. 2017. CCCM 3:57–73.

*De Bello Standardii tempore Stephani regis.* Edited by J.-P. Migne. 1855. PL 195:701–12.

"The Battle of the Standard." Translated by Jane Patricia Freeland. In Aelred of Rievaulx, *The Historical Works*, edited by Marsha L. Dutton. CF 56. Kalamazoo, MI: Cistercian Publications, 2005. 245–69.

"Relatio Venerabilis Aelredi, Abbatis Rievallensis, de Standardo." In *Chronicles of the Reigns of Stephen, Henry II., and Richard I.*

[1] Editions precede translations; each category is listed in reverse chronological order.

Edited by Richard Howlett. 4 vols. Rolls series. London: Longman, 1884–1886. 3:179–99.

"Æthelredi Descriptio de Bello inter Regem Scotiæ et Barones Anglie apud Standardum." In Johannis de Fordun, *Chronica Gentis Scotorum*, edited by William F. Skene. Appendix 4. Edinburgh: Edmonston and Douglas, 1871. 438–48.

*Vita Davidis* (1153) Vita D

"Liber de vita religiosi David regis Scotie." In *Genealogia de Regum Anglorum*, edited by Domenico Pezzini. Turnhout: Brepols, 2017. CCCM 3:5–21.

"Eulogium Davidis regis Scotorum." In *Pinkerton's Lives of the Scottish Saints*, edited by W. M. Metcalfe. 2 vols. Paisley, UK: Alexander Gardner, 1889. 2:267–85.

"De sancto rege Scotorum David." In *Genealogia de Regum Anglorum*. 1855. Edited by J.-P. Migne. PL 195:713–16.

"Eulogium Davidis regis Scotorum ex Ailredi Revalensis." In *Vitæ antiquæ sanctorum qui habitaverunt in ea parte Britanniæ nunc vocata Scotia vel in ejus insulis*, edited by Johannes Pinkerton. London: Johannis Nichols, 1789. 439–56.

"Lament for David, King of the Scots." Translated by Jane Patricia Freeland. In Aelred of Rievaulx, *The Historical Works*, edited by Marsha L. Dutton. CF 56. Kalamazoo, MI: Cistercian Publications, 2005. 45–70.

*Genealogia de Regum Anglorum* (1153–1154) Gen Angl

*Genealogia de regum Anglorum*. Edited by Domenico Pezzini. Turnhout: Brepols, 2017. CCCM 3:1–56.

*Genealogia de regum Anglorum*. Edited by J.-P. Migne. Paris, 1855. PL 195:711–38.

"The Genealogy of the Kings of the English." Translated by Jane Patricia Freeland. In Aelred of Rievaulx, *The Historical Works*, edited by Marsha L. Dutton. CF 56. Kalamazoo, MI: Cistercian Publications, 2005. 71–122.

*De Sanctis Ecclesie Haugustaldensis et Eorum Miraculis.* (1155) SS Haug

*De Sanctis Ecclesie Haugustaldensis et Eorum Miraculis*. Edited by Domenico Pezzini. Turnhout: Brepols, 2017. CCCM 3:75–110.

"De sanctis ecclesiae Haugustaldensis et eorum miraculis libellus." In *The Priory of Hexham, its Chroniclers, Endowments, and Annals*, edited by James Raine. 2 vols. Surtees Society 44. Durham, UK: Andrews and Co, 1864. 1:173–203.

"The Saints of the Church of Hexham and their Miracles." Translated by Jane Patricia Freeland. In Aelred of Rievaulx, *Lives of the Northern Saints*, edited by Marsha L. Dutton. CF 71. Kalamazoo, MI: Cistercian Publications, 2006. 65–107.

*Vita Sancti Niniani* (1155) Vita N

*Vita Sancti Niniani.* Edited by Domenico Pezzini. Turnhout: Brepols, 2017. CCCM 3:111–34.

"Vita Niniani." In *Pinkerton's Lives of the Scottish Saints*, edited by W. M. Metcalfe. 2 vols. Paisley, UK: Johannis Nichols, 1889. 1:9–47.

"Vita Sancti Niniani." In *Lives of S. Ninian and S. Kentigern*, edited by Alexander Penrose Forbes. Edinburgh: Edmonston and Douglas, 1874. 137–57.

"Vita Niniani ab Ailredo." In *Vitæ antiquæ sanctorum qui habitaverunt in ea parte Britanniæ nunc vocata Scotia vel in ejus insulis.* Edited by Johannes Pinkerton. London: Johannis Nichols, 1789. 1–23.

"The Life of Saint Ninian, Apostle of the Southern Saints." Translated by Jane Patricia Freeland. In Aelred of Rievaulx, *Lives of the Northern Saints*, edited by Marsha L. Dutton. CF 71. Kalamazoo, MI: Cistercian Publications, 2006. 33–63.

"The Life of Ninian." Translated by Winifred MacQueen. In John MacQueen, *St. Nynia with a Translation of the Miracula Nynie Episcopi and the Vita Niniani.* Edinburgh: Polygon, 1990. 102–33.

*De Iesu Puero Duodenni* (?1160) Iesu

*De Iesu Puero Duodenni.* Edited by Anselm Hoste. Turnhout: Brepols, 1971. CCCM 1:245–78.

*Tractatus de Jesu Puero Duodenni.* Edited by J.-P. Migne. Paris, 1862. PL 184:849–70.

*On Jesus as a Boy of Twelve.* Translated by Theodore Berkeley. In Aelred of Rievaulx, *Treatises; The Pastoral Prayer.* CF 2. Kalamazoo, MI, and Spencer, MA: Cistercian Publications, 1971. 1–39.

*De institutione inclusarum* (?1160) Inst incl

"Teachings for Recluses." In Aelred of Rievaulx, *Writings on Body and Soul*, edited and translated by Bruce Venarde. Dumbarton Oaks Medieval Library. Cambridge, MA, and London: Harvard University Press, 2021.

*De institutione inclusarum.* Edited by C. H. Talbot. Turnhout: Brepols, 1971. CCCM 1:635–82.

*De vita eremitica ad sororem.* In *Augustini Hipponensis Episcopi Opera Omnia.*[2] Edited by J.-P. Migne. Paris, 1844. PL 32:1451–74, 158:784–98.

"A Rule of Life for a Recluse." Translated by Mary Paul Macpherson. In *Aelred of Rievaulx: Treatises; The Pastoral Prayer.* CF 2. Kalamazoo, MI, and Spencer, MA: Cistercian Publications, 1971. 41–102.

"Informacio Alredi, abbatis monasterii de Rieualle, ad sororem suam inclusam," and "A tretys that is a rule and a forme of lyuing perteynyng to a Recluse," in *Aelred of Rievaulx's De Institutione Inclusarum: Two English Versions*, edited by John Ayto and Alexandra Talbot Barratt. Early English Text Society 87. [14th–15th centuries.] Oxford: Oxford University Press, 1984.

*Vita Sancti Edwardi, Regis et Confessoris* (1161–1163) V Ed[3]

*Vita Sancti Edwardi, regis et confessoris.* Edited by Francesco Marzella. Turnhout: Brepols, 2017. CCCM 3A:9–181.

*Vita S. Edwardi regis et confessoris auctore Beato Aelredo.* Edited by J.-P. Migne. Paris, 1855. PL 195:737–90.

"The Life of Saint Edward, King and Confessor." Translated by Jane Patricia Freeland. In Aelred of Rievaulx, *The Historical Works*, edited by Marsha L. Dutton. CF 56. Kalamazoo, MI: Cistercian Publications, 2005. 123–243.

[2] While including this in the works of Augustine, Migne credits it to Aelred in the introductory note on PL 32:1451 and again in PL 195:701–2.

[3] For a history of translations of Aelred's *De Vita Edwardi*, see Domenico Pezzini, "Aelred of Rievaulx's *Vita Sancti Edwardi Regis et Confessoris*: Its Genesis and Radiation," *Cîteaux* 69 (2009): 27–77.

*The Life of St. Edward the Confessor by St. Aelred of Rievaulx*. Translated by Jerome Bertram. Guildford, UK: St. Edward's Press, 1990.

"The Lyf of Saint Edward." In *The Golden Legend*, edited by Jacobus Voragine. Modernized by Frederick Startridge Ellis. 6 vols. Hammersmith: Kelmscott Press, 1892. 6:1–45.

*The Middle English Verse Life of Edward the Confessor*. Edited by Grace Edna Moore. 1438; Philadelphia: University of Pennsylvania Press, 1942.

*The Vita Sancti Ædwardi Versifice.* Edited by Francesco Marzella. 1163–1173. Turnhout: Brepols, 2017. CCCM 3A:183–318.

*De Quodam Miraculo Mirabili* (1162?) Mira

"A Certain Wonderful Miracle." In Aelred of Rievaulx, *Writings on Body and Soul*, edited and translated by Bruce Venarde. Dumbarton Oaks Medieval Library. Cambridge, MA, and London: Harvard University Press, 2021.

*De quodam miraculo mirabili.* Edited by Domenico Pezzini. 2017. CCCM 3:135–46.

*De Sanctimoniali de Wattun.* Edited by J.-P. Migne. Paris, 1855. PL 195:789–96.

"A Certain Wonderful Miracle." Translated by Jane Patricia Freeland. In Aelred of Rievaulx, *Lives of the Northern Saints*, edited by Marsha L. Dutton. CF 71. Kalamazoo, MI: Cistercian Publications, 2006. 109–22.

"The Nun of Watton." Translated by Oliver Gutman. In *Women and Writing in Medieval Europe: A Sourcebook*, edited by Carolynne Larrington. Abingdon, UK: Routledge, 1995. 128–33.

"The Nun of Watton." Translated by John Boswell. In John Boswell, *The Kindness of Strangers*. New York: Pantheon Books, 1988. 452–58.

*De Spiritali Amicitia* (1164–1167) Spir am

"Spiritual Friendship." In Aelred of Rievaulx, *Writings on Body and Soul*, edited and translated by Bruce Venarde. Dumbarton Oaks Medieval Library. Cambridge, MA, and London: Harvard University Press, 2021.

*De spiritali amicitia.* Edited by Anselm Hoste. 1971. CCCM 1:279–350.

*De spirituali amicitia liber.* Edited by J.-P. Migne. Paris, 1855. PL 195:659–702.

*Spiritual Friendship.* Translated by Lawrence C. Braceland. Edited by Marsha L. Dutton. CF 5. Collegeville, MN: Cistercian Publications, 2010.

*Aelred of Rievaulx's* Spiritual Friendship. Translated by Mark F. Williams. Scranton, PA: Scranton University Press, 1994, 2002.

*Spiritual Friendship.* Translated by Mary Eugenia Laker. CF 5. Kalamazoo, MI: Cistercian Publications, 1977.

*Christian Friendship by S. Aelred of Rievaulx.* Translated by Hugh Talbot. London: Catholic Book Club, 1942.

*De Anima* (1164–1167) Anima

*Dialogus de anima.* Edited by C. H. Talbot. Turnhout: Brepols, 1971. CCCM 1:683–754.

*Dialogue on the Soul.* Translated by C. H. Talbot. CF 22. Kalamazoo, MI: Cistercian Publications, 1981.

*Oratio Pastoralis* (1165–1167) Orat

"A Pastoral Prayer," in Aelred of Rievaulx, *Writings on Body and Soul,* edited and translated by Bruce Venarde. Dumbarton Oaks Medieval Library. Cambridge, MA, and London: Harvard University Press, 2021.

*For Your Own People.* Edited by Marsha L. Dutton. Translated by Mark DelCogliano. CF 73. Kalamazoo, MI: Cistercian Publications, 2008.

*Oratio Pastoralis.* Edited by André Wilmart. Turnhout: Brepols, 1971. CCCM 1:755–63.

*The Pastoral Prayer.* Translated by R. Penelope Lawson. In Aelred of Rievaulx, *Treatises; The Pastoral Prayer.* CF 2. Kalamazoo, MI, and Spencer, MA: Cistercian Publications, 1971. 103–18.

## Editions and Translations of Aelred's Sermons[4]

Aelredi Rievallensis. *Opera Omnia. Sermones I–XLVI* (*Collectio Claraevallensis Prima et Secunda*). Edited by Gaetano Raciti. CCCM 2A. Turnholt: Brepols, 1989.

Aelredi Rievallensis. *Opera Omnia. Sermones XLVII–LXXXIV* (*Collectio Dunelmensis. Sermones Lincolnienses*). Edited by Gaetano Raciti. CCCM 2B. Turnhout: Brepols, 2001.

Aelredi Rievallensis. *Opera Omnia. Sermones LXXXV–CLXXXII* (*Collectio Radingensis*). Edited by Gaetano Raciti. CCCM 2C. Turnhout: Brepols, 2012.

Aelredi Rievallensis. *Opera Omnia 5. Homiliae de oneribus propheticis Isaiae*. Edited by Gaetano Raciti. CCCM 2D. Turnholt: Brepols, 2005.

Beati Aelredi Rievallis Abbatis. *Operum Pars Prima—Ascetica*. Edited by J.-P. Migne. Paris, 1855. PL 195:209–501.

*Sermones Inediti B. Aelredi Abbatis Rievallensis.* Edited by C. H. Talbot. Series Scriptorum S. Ordinis Cisterciensis, vol. 1. Rome: Curia Gen, O.Cist., 1952.

*Homilies on the Prophetic Burdens of Isaiah*. Translated by Lewis White. Introduction by Marsha L. Dutton. CF 83. Collegeville, MN: Cistercian Publications, 2018.

"*In translacione sancti Edwardi confessoris*: The Lost Sermon by Aelred of Rievaulx Found?" Edited by Peter Jackson. CSQ 40 (2005): 45–83.

*The Liturgical Sermons: The First Clairvaux Collection. Advent through All Saints. Sermons 1–28.* Translated by Theodore Berkeley and Basil Pennington. CF 58. Kalamazoo, MI: Cistercian Publications, 2001.

*The Liturgical Sermons: The Durham and Lincoln Collections. Sermons 47–84.* Translated by Katherine Krug, Lewis White, and the *Catena Scholarium*. Introduction by Ann Astell. CF 80. Collegeville, MN: Cistercian Publications, 2018.

*The Liturgical Sermons. The Reading-Cluny Collection, 1 of 2. Sermons 85–133.* Translated by Daniel Griggs. Introduction by Marjory Lange and Marsha L. Dutton. CF 81. Collegeville, MN: Cistercian Publications, 2021.

[4] Editions precede translations, each group listed in alphabetical order.

*The Liturgical Sermons. The Reading-Cluny Collection, 2 of 2. Sermons 134–182.* Translated by Daniel Griggs. Introduction by Marjory Lange. CF 87. Collegeville, MN: Cistercian Publications, 2022.

*The Liturgical Sermons: The Second Clairvaux Collection. Sermons 29–46. Christmas through All Saints.* Translated by Marie Anne Mayeski. Introduction by Domenico Pezzini. CF 77. Collegeville, MN: Cistercian Publications, 2016.

"A Sermon upon the Translation of Saint Edward, Confessor." Translated by Tom License. CSQ 40 (2005): 45–83. Repr. CF 87:379–88.

# Works Cited

## Primary Sources

Aelred of Rievaulx. "The 'De institutis inclusarum' of Aelred of Rievaulx." Edited by C. H. Talbot. ASOC 7 (1951): 12–217. Repr. CCCM 1:636–82.

Aelred of Rievaulx. *Dialogue on the Soul.* Translated by C. H. Talbot. CF 22. Kalamazoo, MI: Cistercian Publications, 1981.

Aelred of Rievaulx. *La Vie de Recluse.* Translated by Charles Dumont. SCh 76. Paris: Les Éditions du Cerf, 1961.

Aelred of Rievaulx. *The Mirror of Charity.* Translated by Elizabeth Connor. Introduction by Charles Dumont. CF 17. Kalamazoo, MI: Cistercian Publications, 1990.

Aelred of Rievaulx. "On Jesus as a Boy of Twelve." Translated by Theodore Berkeley. In Aelred of Rievaulx, *Treatises; The Pastoral Prayer.* CF 2. Spencer, MA: Cistercian Publications, 1971. 1–39.

Aelred of Rievaulx. *Quand Jesus eut douze ans.* Translated by Joseph Dubois. Paris: Les Éditions du Cerf, 1958.

Aelred of Rievaulx. "A Rule of Life for a Recluse." Translated by M. P. Macpherson. In Aelred of Rievaulx, *Treatises; The Pastoral Prayer.* CF 2. Spencer, MA: Cistercian Publications, 1971. 43–102.

Aelred of Rievaulx. "S. in Ascensione Domini de raptu Helye." In *Sermones inediti B. Aelredi abbatis Rievallensis*, edited by C. H. Talbot. Series Scriptorum S. Ordinis Cisterciensis. Rome: Curia gen., O.Cist., 1952. {Aelred. "In Ascensione Domini," S 65. Edited by Gaetano Raciti. CCCM 2B:170–76; CF 80:224.}

Aelred of Rievaulx. ["S. in Ascensione Domini de raptu Helye."] "An Ascension Day Sermon by Saint Aelred: On the Rapture of Elijah, Presentation and Translation." Translated and introduced by Chrysogonus Waddell. *Liturgy* 14, no. 1 (1980): 47–76. {Aelred. S 65, "In Ascensione Domini." CCCM 2B:170–76; CF 80:219–26.}

Aelred of Rievaulx. "S. in Assumptione b. Mariae." PL 195:303.

Aelred of Rievaulx. "S. in Assumptione b. Mariae." In "The Castle of the Soul," translated by Anthony Storey. *The Tablet* 198 (11 August 1951): 91–94. {Aelred. "In Assumptione Sanctae Mariae," S 19. Edited by Gaetano Raciti. CCCM 2A:147–54; CF 58:263–74.}

Aelred of Rievaulx. "S. in Epiphania de tribus generibus nuptiarum." In *Sermones inediti B. Aelredi abbatis Rievallensis*, edited by C. H. Talbot. Series Scriptorum S. Ordinis Cisterciensis. Rome: Curia gen., O.Cist., 1952. {Aelred. "In Epiphania Domini," S 50. Edited by Gaetano Raciti. CCCM 2B:26–39; CF 80:26–39.}

Aelred of Rievaulx. "S. in natale apostolorum Petri et Pauli." In *Sermones inediti beati Aelredi abbatis Rievallensis*, edited by C. H. Talbot. Series S. Ordinis Cisterciensis. Rome: Curia gen., O.Cist., 1952. {Aelred. "In Festivitate Apostolorum Petri et Pauli," S 71. Edited by Gaetano Raciti. CCCM 2B:220–31; CF 80:277–90.}

Aelred of Rievaulx. "S. in Nativitate Domini." In *Sermones inediti beati Aelredi abbatis Rievallensis*, edited by C. H. Talbot. Series S. Ordinis Cisterciensis. Rome: Curia gen., O.Cist., 1952. {Aelred. "In Nativitate Domini," S 49. Edited by Gaetano Raciti. CCCM 2B:22–25; CF 80:28–31.}

Aelred of Rievaulx. *S. in Ypapanti Domini*. In *Sermones inediti B. Aelredi abbatis Rievallensis*, edited by C. H. Talbot. Series Scriptorum S. Ordinis Cisterciensis. Rome: Curia gen., O.Cist., 1952. {Aelred. "In Ypapanti Domini," S 51. Edited by Gaetano Raciti. CCCM 2B:40–47; CF 80:50–60.}

Aelred of Rievaulx. *Spiritual Friendship*. Translated by Mary Eugenia Laker. CF 5. Kalamazoo, MI: Cistercian Publications, 1977.

Aelred of Rievaulx. *Spiritual Friendship*. Translated by Lawrence C. Braceland. Edited by Marsha L. Dutton. CF 5. Collegeville, MN: Cistercian Publications, 2010.

Ambrose. *De officiis*. Edited and translated by Ivor J. Davidson. 2 vols. Oxford: Oxford University Press, 2001.

Ambrose. *De officiis ministrorum*. Edited by Antonio Cavasin. Corona Patrum Salesiana. Turin: Società Editrice Internazionale, 1938.

Ambrose. *De sacramentis*. Edited by J.-P. Migne. Paris, 1845. PL 16:417–62.

Ambrose. *De spiritu sancto.* Edited by J.-P. Migne. Paris, 1845. PL 16:703–816.

Ambrose. *De spiritu sancto.* Edited by Gerhard Crone. Münster: Aschendorff, 1978.

Ambrose. *De virginibus.* Edited by Otto Faller. Bonnae: Hanstein, 1933.

Ambrose. *On Virgins.* In *Ambrose*, translated by Boniface Ramsey. The Early Church Fathers. London: Routledge, 1997. 11–116.

Ambrose. *Sancti Ambrosii Mediolanensis*, Part 5. *De Officiis.* Edited by Maurice Testard. CCSL 15. Turnhout: Brepols, 2000.

Ambrose. *Theological and Dogmatic Works.* Translated by Roy J. Deferrari. Washington, DC: The Catholic University of America Press, 1963.

Anselm. *S. Anselmi Cantuariensis Archiepiscopi: Opera Omnia.* 6 vols. Edited by Franciscus Schmitt. Vol. 3. Edinburgh: Thomas Nelson and Sons, 1946.

*The Apostolic Tradition of Hippolytus.* Translated by Burton Scott Easton. Cambridge, UK: Cambridge University Press, 1934; repr. ed. 1962.

Aristotle. *Nichomachean Ethics.* Translated by Harris Rackham. Loeb 23. Cambridge, MA: Harvard University Press, 1926.

Augustine. *Confessions.* Translated by R. S. Pine-Coffin. London: Penguin, 1961.

Augustine. *Confessionum Libri XIII.* Edited by Lucas Verheijen. In Sancti Augustini Opera. CCSL 27. Turnholt: Brepols, 1990.

Augustine. *De bono conjugali.* Edited by J.-P. Migne. Paris, 1865. PL 40:373–96.

Augustine. *De bono coniugali, De sancta virginitate.* Translated by P. G. Walsh. Oxford: Clarendon Press, 2001.

Augustine. *De civitate Dei.* Edited by J.-P. Migne. Paris, 1864. PL 41:13–804.

Augustine. *De doctrina Christiana.* Translated by D. W. Robertson, Jr. Indianapolis: Liberal Arts Press, 1958.

Augustine. "De Genesi ad litteram libri dvodecim." In *Sancti Avreli Avgvstini*, edited by Joseph Zycha. CSEL 28. Vienna: Tempsky, 1894.

Augustine. *De sancta virginitate*. Edited by J.-P. Migne. Paris, 1865. PL 40:354–430.

Augustine. *De Trinitate*. Edited by J.-P. Migne. Paris, 1865. PL 42:819–1098.

Augustine. *Holy Virginity*. Translated by John McQuade. In Saint Augustine, *Treatises on Marriage and Other Subjects*. The Fathers of the Church: A New Translation 27. Washington, DC: The Catholic University of America Press, 1955.

Augustine. *Select Letters*. Loeb. Cambridge, MA: Harvard University Press, 1980.

Augustine. *St. Augustine's Confessions*. Edited by P. Knöll. 2 vols. Loeb. Cambridge, MA: Harvard University Press, 1989.

Augustine. *St Augustine's Confessions*. Translated by William Watts. 2 vols. Loeb. Cambridge, MA: Harvard University Press, 1912.

Augustine. *The Trinity*. Translated by Edmund Hill. Brooklyn: New City Press, 1990.

Baldwin of Forde. *De sacramento altaris*. Edited by J.-P. Migne. Paris, 1855. PL 204:641–774.

Baldwin of Forde. *De sacramento altaris*. Edited by John Morson. In *Baudouin de Ford: Le sacrement de l'autel*, translated by E. de Solms. SCh 93–94. Paris: Cerf, 1963.

Baldwin of Forde. *Spiritual Tractates*. Translated by David N. Bell. 2 vols. CF 39. Kalamazoo, MI: Cistercian Publications, 1986.

Baldwin of Forde. *Tractatus de sanctissimus sacramento eucharistiae*. Edited by J.-P. Migne. Paris, 1855. PL 204:403–14.

Baldwin of Forde. *Tractatus de sanctissimus sacramento eucharistiae*. In *Baodouin de Ford, Traités*, edited and translated by Robert Thomas. Pain de Cîteaux 35–40. Chimay, Belgium: OEIL, 1973–1975.

Benedict. *The Rule of St. Benedict in Latin and English with Notes*. Edited by Timothy Fry. Collegeville, MN: Liturgical Press, 1981.

Bernard of Clairvaux. *De diligendo Deo*. Edited by Jean Leclercq and H. M. Rochais. Rome: Editiones Cistercienses, 1957–1999. SBOp 3:138–44.

Bernard of Clairvaux. "Epistola ad Aelredum abbatem." Edited by Jean Leclercq and H. M. Rochais. Rome: Editiones Cistercienses, 1957–1999. SBOp 8:486–89.

Bernard of Clairvaux. "Epistola Beati Bernardi Abbatis Clarevallis ad Aelredum Abbatem." In *Speculum Caritatis*, edited by C. H. Talbot. Turnhout: Brepols, 1971. CCCM 1:3–4.

Bernard of Clairvaux. *On the Song of Songs II*. Translated by Kilian Walsh. CF 7. Kalamazoo, MI: Cistercian Publications, 1976.

Bernard of Clairvaux. "S. de Passione Domini." Edited by Jean Leclercq and H. M. Rochais. Rome: Editiones Cistercienses, 1957–1999. SBOp 5:56–67.

Bernard of Clairvaux. *Sermones super Cantica Canticorum*. Edited by Jean Leclercq and H. M. Rochais. Rome: Editiones Cistercienses, 1957–1999. SBOp 1–2.

Bonaventure. *Legenda Sancti Francisci*. In *Opuscula varia ad theologiam mysticam*. 10 vols. *Doctoris seraphici S. Bonaventurae Opera Omnia*. Quaracchi: Collegium S. Bonaventurae, 1882–1902. 8:504–64.

Bonaventure. *Lignum Vitae*. In *Opuscula varia ad theologiam mysticam*. 10 vols. *Doctoris seraphici S. Bonaventurae Opera Omnia*. Quaracchi: Collegium S. Bonaventurae, 1882–1902. 8:68–87.

Bonaventure. *The Soul's Journey into God, The Tree of Life, The Life of Saint Francis*. Translation and introduction by Ewert Cousins. New York: Paulist Press, 1978.

"Carta Caritatis Prior V." In *Narrative and Legislative Texts from Early Cîteaux*, edited by Chrysogonus Waddell. Studia et Documenta, vol. 9. *Cîteaux*, 1999. 261–82.

Cicero. *De Amicitia*. Translated by William Armistead Falconer. Loeb. Cambridge, MA: Harvard University Press, 1953.

Cicero. *De Amicitia*. Translated by William Armistead Falconer. In *Cicero: De senectute, De amicitia, De divinatione*. Loeb. London: Heinemann, 1923.

Dutton Stuckey, Marsha, ed. "An Edition of Two Middle English Translations of Aelred's *De institutione inclusarum*." PhD dissertation, University of Michigan, 1981.

"The Exordium Parvum." Translated by Bede K. Lackner. In Louis J. Lekai, *The Cistercians: Ideals and Reality*. Kent, OH: Kent State University Press, 1977. 451–61.

"The Exordium Parvum." In *Narrative and Legislative Texts from Early Cîteaux*, edited by Chrysogonus Waddell. Studia et Documenta, vol. 9. *Cîteaux*, 1999. 197–259.

Gregory I. *The Life of Saint Benedict by Gregory the Great: Translation and Commentary*. Translated by Terrence Kardong. Collegeville, MN: Liturgical Press, 2009.

Gregory I. *Moralia in Iob*. Edited by J.-P. Migne. Paris, 1862. PL 75–76.

Gregory I. *Moralia in Iob.* Edited by Marcus Adriaen. 2 vols. CCSL 143, 143A, 143B. Turnhout: Brepols, 2005.

Gregory the Great. *Moral Reflections on the Book of Job.* Translated by Brian Kerns. Introduction by Mark DelCogliano. 6 vols. CS 249, CS 257–261. Collegeville, MN: Cistercian Publications, 2014, 2015, 2016, 2017, 2019, 2022.

Gregory of Nyssa. *Dogmatic Treatises*. Translated by William Moore and Henry Astin Wilson. Nicene and Post-Nicene Fathers. 2nd series, 5. New York: Wipf and Stock, 1893.

Ignatius Loyola. *Saint Ignatius' Own Story as Told to Luis González de Cámera*. Translated by William J. Young. Chicago: Henry Regnery, 1956.

Isaac de l'Étoile. *Sermons.* Vol. 3. Edited by Anselm Hoste with Gaetano Raciti. SCh 339. Paris: Les Éditions du Cerf, 1987.

Isaac of Stella. *Epistola ad Joannem Episcopum Pictaviensem de officio missae*. Edited by J.-P. Migne. Paris, 1855. PL 194:1889–96.

Isaac of Stella. *Sermons on the Christian Year.* Vol. 2. Translated by Lewis White. CF 66. Collegeville, MN: Cistercian Publications, 2019.

Ludolph of Saxony. *The Life of Christ.* Translated and introduced by Milton T. Walsh. 4 vols. CS 267, 282, 283, 284. Collegeville, MN: Cistercian Publications, 2018, 2019, 2021, 2022.

Ludolph of Saxony. *Vita Jesu Christi*. Edited by L. M. Rigollot. 4 vols. Paris and Brussels: Palmé, 1865, 1879, 1878.

Paschasius Radbert. *De corpore et sanguine domini. Epistola ad Fredugarum*. Edited by Bede Paulus. CCCM 16.

Tertullian. *De corona militis* 3. Edited by J.-P. Migne. Paris, 1844. PL 2:73–102.

Walter Daniel. *The Life of Aelred of Rievaulx and the Letter to Maurice.* Translated by Maurice Powicke. CF 57. Kalamazoo, MI: Cistercian Publications, 1994.

Walter Daniel. *Vita Ailredi Abbatis Rievall'*. Edited, translated, and introduced by Maurice Powicke. 1950; Oxford: Clarendon, 1978.

William of Saint-Thierry. *De sacramento altaris*. Edited by J.-P. Migne. Paris, 1855. PL 180:341–66.

## Secondary Sources

Starred items are reprinted in this volume.

"Application des Sens." *Dictionnaire de Spiritualité* 1 (1937): 823–24.

Ayto, John, and Alexandra Talbot Barratt, eds. *Aelred of Rievaulx's De Institutione Inclusarum: Two English Versions*. Early English Text Society 87. Oxford: Oxford University Press, 1984.

Bell, David N. *Handmaid of the Lord: Mary, the Cistercians, and Armand-Jean de Rancé*. CS 293. Collegeville, MN: Cistercian Publications, 2021.

Bell, David N. *The Image and Likeness: The Augustinian Spirituality of William of Saint Thierry*. CS 78. Kalamazoo, MI: Cistercian Publications, 1984.

Bell, David N. *An Index of Authors and Works in Cistercian Libraries in Great Britain*. CS 130. Kalamazoo, MI: Cistercian Publications, 1992.

Bell, David N. Introduction to William of St. Thierry, *The Nature and Dignity of Love*. Translated by Thomas X. Davis. CS 30. Kalamazoo, MI: Cistercian Publications, 1978. 5–43.

Bell, David N. "Lists and Records of Books in English Cistercian Libraries." *Analecta Cisterciensia* 43 (1987): 181–222.

Bodenstedt, Mary Immaculate. *The Vita Christi of Ludolphus the Carthusian*. The Catholic University of America Studies in Medieval and Renaissance Latin Language and Literature, vol. 16. Washington, DC: The Catholic University of America Press, 1944.

Book of Common Prayer. New York: Church Hymnal Corporation, 1979.

Boquet, Damien. "Affectivity in the Spiritual Writings of Aelred of Rievaulx." In *A Companion to Aelred of Rievaulx (1110–1167)*, edited by Marsha L. Dutton. Brill's Companions to the Christian Tradition 76. Leiden/Boston: Brill Academic, 2017. 167–96.

Braceland, Lawrence C. "Bernard and Aelred on Humility and Obedience." In *Erudition at God's Service: Studies in Medieval Cistercian History, XI*, edited by John R. Sommerfeldt. CS 98. Kalamazoo, MI: Cistercian Publications, 1987. 149–59.

Brady, Ignatius. Preface to Bonaventure, *The Soul's Journey into God, The Tree of Life, The Life of Saint Francis*. Translation and introduction by Ewert Cousins. New York: Paulist Press, 1978. xiii–xviii.

Brown, Peter. *Augustine of Hippo: A Biography*. Berkeley: University of California Press, 1967.

Brown, Peter. *The Body and Society: Men, Women, and Sexual Renunciation in Early Christianity*. Lectures on the History of Religions, n.s. 13. New York: Columbia University Press, 1988.

Burt, Donald X. *Friendship and Society: An Introduction to Augustine's Practical Philosophy.* Grand Rapids, MI: Eerdmans, 1999.

Burt, Donald X. "Friendship and Subordination in Earthly Societies." *Augustinian Studies* 22 (1991): 83–123.

Burton, Pierre-André. *Aelred of Rievaulx (1110–1167): An Existential and Spiritual Biography*. Translated by Christopher Coski. CS 276. Collegeville, MN: Cistercian Publications, 2021.

Butler, Cuthbert. *Western Mysticism*. London: Constable, 1922.

Bynum, Caroline Walker. *Jesus as Mother: Studies in the Spirituality of the High Middle Ages.* Berkeley: University of California Press, 1982.

Caldwell, Ellen C. "The *loquaces muti* and the *Verbum infans*: Paradox and Language in the *Confessiones* of St. Augustine." In *Collectanea Augustiniana*, edited by Joseph C. Schnaubelt and Frederick Van Fleteren. New York: Peter Lang, 1990. 101–11.

Carruthers, Mary. *The Book of Memory: A Study of Memory in Medieval Culture*. 2nd ed. Cambridge Studies in Medieval Literature 10. Cambridge, UK: Cambridge University Press, 2008.

Carruthers, Mary. *The Craft of Thought: Meditation, Rhetoric, and the Making of Images, 400–1200*. Cambridge Studies in Medieval Literature 34. Cambridge, UK: Cambridge University Press, 2000.

Chadwick, Henry. *Augustine*. Oxford: Oxford University Press, 1986.

Chenu, M.-D. "Theology and the New Awareness of History." In *Nature, Man, and Society in the Twelfth Century*, translated by Jerome Taylor and Lester K. Little. Chicago: University of Chicago Press, 1968. 162–201.

Clark, Elizabeth. "'Adam's Only Companion': Augustine and the Early Christian Debate on Marriage." *Recherches Augustiniennes* 21 (1986): 139–62.

Coleman, Janet. *Ancient and Medieval Memories: Studies in the Reconstruction of the Past.* Cambridge, UK: Cambridge University Press, 1992.

Connor, Elizabeth. "Saint Bernard's Three Steps of Truth and Saint Aelred of Rievaulx's Three Loves." In *Bernardus Magister*, edited by John R. Sommerfeldt. CS 135. Kalamazoo, MI: Cistercian Publications, 1991; *Cîteaux* 42, nos. 1–4 (1991): 225–38.

Courcelle, Pierre. "Ailred de Rievaulx à l'école des *Confessions*." *Revue des Études Augustiniennes* 3 (1957): 163–74.

Courcelle, Pierre. *Les Confessions de saint Augustin dans la tradition littéraire. Antécédents et postérité.* Paris: Études Augustiniennes, 1963.

Cousins, Ewert. Introduction to Bonaventure, *The Soul's Journey into God, The Tree of Life, The Life of Saint Francis.* Translated by Ewert Cousins. New York: Paulist Press, 1978. 1–48.

Coyle, Alcuin F. "Cicero's De Officiis and De Officiis Ministrorum of St. Ambrose." *Franciscan Studies* 15 (1955): 244–56.

Davidson, Ivor. Introduction to Ambrose, *De officiis*, edited and translated by Ivor J. Davidson. 2 vols. Oxford: Oxford University Press, 2001. 1:1–112.

Dobbins, Dunstan. *Franciscan Mysticism: A Critical Examination of the Mystical Theology of the Seraphic Doctor, with Special Reference to the Sources of His Doctrines.* Franciscan Studies, no. 6. New York: J. F. Wagner, 1927.

Donaldson, E. Talbot. "Chaucer the Pilgrim." PMLA 69 (1954): 928–36.

Doyle, Teresa Ann. "Aelred of Rievaulx's Rule for a Recluse." *The Benedictine Review* 6, no. 2 (1951): 33–37.

Dumont, Charles. "Aelred de Rievaulx: introduction à sa vie et à ses écrits." In *Une éducation du coeur.* Pain de Cîteaux 3,10. Oka, Canada: Abbaye Cistercienne Notre-Dame-du-Lac, 1996. 193–236.

Dumont, Charles. "Aelred of Rievaulx: His Life and Works." In Aelred of Rievaulx, *Mirror of Charity*, translated by Elizabeth Connor. CF 17. Kalamazoo, MI: Cistercian Publications, 1990. 11–67.

Dumont, Charles. "Chercher Dieu dans la communauté selon Aelred de Rievaulx." In *Une éducation du coeur*. Pain de Cîteaux 3,10. Oka, Canada: Abbaye Cistercienne Notre-Dame-du-Lac, 1996. 275–308.

Dumont, Charles. "*L'amitié spirituelle* d'Ælred de Rievaulx." In *Une éducation du coeur.* Pain de Cîteaux 3,10. Oka, Canada: Abbaye Cistercienne Notre-Dame-du-Lac, 1996. 349–58.

Dumont, Charles. "L'amour fraternel dans la doctrine monastique d'Ælred de Rievaulx." In *Une éducation du coeur.* Pain de Cîteaux 3,10. Oka, Canada: Abbaye Cistercienne Notre-Dame-du-Lac, 1996. 335–47.

Dumont, Charles. *Saint Aelred de Rievaulx*. Namur, Belgium: Soleil Levant, 1960.

Dumont, Charles. *Une éducation du coeur: La spiritualité de saint Bernard et de saint Ælred*. Pain de Cîteaux 3,10. Oka, Canada: Abbaye Cistercienne Notre-Dame-du-Lac, 1996.

Dutton, Marsha L. "Aelred of Rievaulx on Friendship, Chastity, and Sex: The Sources." CSQ 29 (1994): 121–96.

Dutton, Marsha L. "Aelred's Historical Works: A Mirror for Twelfth-Century England." Introduction to Aelred of Rievaulx, *The Historical Works*, translated by Jane Patricia Freeland, edited by Marsha L. Dutton. CF 56. Kalamazoo, MI: Cistercian Publications, 2005. 1–37.

Dutton, Marsha L. "Antiphonal Learning: Listening and Speaking in the Works of Aelred of Rievaulx." CSQ 54, no. 3 (2019): 267–85.

*Dutton, Marsha L. "Christ Our Mother: Aelred's Iconography for Contemplative Union." In *Goad and Nail: Studies in Medieval Cistercian History, X*, edited by E. Rozanne Elder. CS 84. Kalamazoo, MI: Cistercian Publications, 1985. 21–45.

*Dutton, Marsha L. "The Cistercian Source: Aelred, Bonaventure, and Ignatius." In *Goad and Nail: Studies in Medieval Cistercian History, X*, edited by E. Rozanne Elder. CS 84. Kalamazoo, MI: Cistercian Publications, 1985. 151–78.

*Dutton, Marsha L. "Eat, Drink, and Be Merry: The Eucharistic Spirituality of the Cistercian Fathers." In *Erudition at God's Service: Studies in Medieval Cistercian History*, XI, edited by John R. Sommerfeldt. CS 98. Kalamazoo: Cistercian Publications, 1987. 1–31.

Dutton, Marsha L. "The Feet and the Face of God: The Humanity of Christ in Bernard of Clairvaux and Aelred of Rievaulx." In *Bernardus Magister*, edited by John R. Sommerfeldt. CS 135. Kalamazoo, MI: Cistercian Publications, 1992. 203–23.

*Dutton, Marsha L. "Friendship and the Love of God: Augustine's Teaching in the *Confessions* and Aelred of Rievaulx's Response in *Spiritual Friendship*." ABR 56 (2005): 3–40.

Dutton, Marsha L. "A Historian's Historian: The Place of Bede in Aelred's Contributions to the New History of his Age." In *Truth as Gift: Studies in Cistercian History in Honor of John R. Sommerfeldt*, edited by Marsha L. Dutton, Daniel M. La Corte, and Paul Lockey. CS 204. Kalamazoo, MI: Cistercian Publications, 2004. 407–48.

*Dutton, Marsha L. "Intimacy and Imitation: The Humanity of Christ in Cistercian Spirituality." In *Erudition at God's Service: Studies in Medieval Cistercian History*, XI, edited by John R. Sommerfeldt. CS 98. Kalamazoo, MI: Cistercian Publications, 1987. 33–70.

Dutton, Marsha L. Introduction to Aelred, *Spiritual Friendship*. CF 5. Kalamazoo, MI: Cistercian Publications, 2010. 13–50.

*Dutton, Marsha L. "A Model for Friendship: Ambrose's Contribution to Aelred of Rievaulx's *Spiritual Friendship*." ABR 64, no. 1 (2013): 39–66.

Dutton, Marsha L. "A Prodigal Writes Home: Aelred of Rievaulx's *De institutione inclusarum*." In *Heaven on Earth: Studies in Medieval Cistercian History*, edited by E. Rozanne Elder. CS 68. Kalamazoo, MI: Cistercian Publications, 1983. 35–42.

Dutton, Marsha L. "The Sacramentality of Community in Aelred." In *A Companion to Aelred of Rievaulx (1110–1167)*, edited by Marsha L. Dutton. Brill's Companions to the Christian Tradition. Leiden/Boston: Brill, 2017. 246–67.

Dutton, Marsha L. "The Vocation and Conversion of Aelred of Rievaulx: A Historical Hypothesis." In *England in the Twelfth Century*, edited by Daniel Williams. London: Boydell, 1990. 31–49.

Dutton, Marsha L. "'When I Was a Child': Spiritual Infancy and God's Maternity in Augustine's *Confessions*." In *Collectanea Augustiniana*, edited by Joseph Schnaubelt and Frederick Van Fleteren. New York: Lang, 1987. 113–40.

Dutton-Stuckey, Marsha. "Getting Things the Wrong Way Round: Composition and Transposition in Aelred of Rievaulx's *De institutione inclusarum*." In *Heaven on Earth: Studies in Medieval Cistercian History*, edited by E. Rozanne Elder. CS 68. Kalamazoo, MI: Cistercian Publications, 1983. 90–101.

Fiske, Adele M. "The Survival and Development of the Ancient Concept of Friendship in the Early Middle Ages." 2 vols. Dissertation, Fordham University, 1955.

Fleming, John V. *An Introduction to the Franciscan Literature of the Middle Ages*. Chicago: Franciscan Herald Press, 1977.

Fleming, John V. *Reason and the Lover*. Princeton, NJ: Princeton University Press, 1984.

Freeman, Elizabeth. *Narratives of a New Order: Cistercian Historical Writing in England, 1150–1220*. Medieval Church Studies 2. Turnholt: Brepols, 2002.

Friedman, Lionel J. "Jean de Meun and Ethelred of Rievaulx." *L'Esprit Createur* 2 (1962): 135–41.

Geary, Patrick J. *Phantoms of Remembrance: Memory and Oblivion at the End of the First Millennium*. Princeton, NJ: Princeton University Press, 1994.

Ghislain, Gabriel. "À la recherche de la réponse juste: un novice interroge son père maître." In *Intentio cordis*. Coll 73, no. 1 (2011): 78–109.

Gilson, Étienne. *The Mystical Theology of St Bernard*. Translated by A. H. C. Downes. CS 120. 1940; Kalamazoo, MI: Cistercian Publications, 1990.

Gusdorf, Georges. "Conditions and Limits of Autobiography." Translated by James Olney. In *Autobiography: Essays Theoretical and Critical*, edited by James Olney. Princeton, NJ: Princeton University Press, 1980. 28–48.

Hallier, Amédée. *The Monastic Theology of Aelred of Rievaulx: An Experiential Theology*. Translated by Columban Heaney. CS 2. Kalamazoo, MI: Cistercian Publications, 1999.

Hallier, Amédée. *Un Éducateur Monastique: Aelred de Rievaulx*. Dublin: Irish University Press, 1969.

Heffernan, Thomas J. *Sacred Biography: Saints and Their Biographers in the Middle Ages*. New York: Oxford University Press, 1988.

Hood, William. "Franciscan Pilgrimage Sanctuaries of the Renaissance: A Case of Cousin's [*sic*] Mysticism of the Historical Event." Presentation at the May 1984 International Medieval Studies Congress, Kalamazoo, MI.

Hoste, Anselm. "Aelred of Rievaulx and the Monastic *Planctus*." *Cîteaux* 18 (1967): 385–98.

Hoste, Anselm. *Bibliotheca Aelrediana*. Steenbruge: Martinus Nijhoff, 1962.

Hoste, Anselm. "Marginalia bij Aelred's *De Institutione Inclusarum*." *Cîteaux in de Nederlanden* 9 (1958): 132–36.

Hyatte, Reginald. *The Arts of Friendship: The Idealization of Friendship in Medieval and Early Renaissance Literature*. Leiden: Brill, 1994.

"Ignace de Loyola." *Dictionnaire de Spiritualité* 7 (1971): 1267.

Inge, W. R. *Christian Mysticism*. London: Charles Scribner's Sons, 1899.

Knowles, David. "Ailred of Rievaulx." In *Saints and Scholars: Twenty-Five Medieval Portraits*. Cambridge, UK: Cambridge University Press, 1962. 34–50.

Lange, Marjorie. "The Performance of Doctrine in Aelred's Narrative Writings." Presentation at the 2019 Cistercian Studies Conference. Kalamazoo, MI.

Le Bail, Anselm. "La Spiritualité cistercienne." *Les Cahiers du Cercle Thomiste Fémine* 7 (1927): 388–413, 463–91.

Leclercq, Jean. "Friendship and Friends in the Monastic Life." CSQ 24 (1989): 293–300.

Leclercq, Jean. *Otia Monastica: Études sur le vocabulaire de la contemplation au Moyen Age. Studia Anselmiana* 51–52. Rome, 1963.

Leclercq, Jean. "Solitude and Solidarity: Medieval Women Recluses." In *Peace Weavers*, edited by John A. Nichols and Lillian Thomas Shank. Medieval Religious Women, vol. 2. CS 72. Kalamazoo, MI: Cistercian Publications, 1987. 67–83.

Lewis, C. S. *The Four Loves*. 1960; repr. San Diego: Harcourt, 1988.

Lienhard, Joseph T. "Friends, Friendship." In *Augustine through the Ages: An Encyclopedia*, gen. ed. Allan D. Fitzgerald. Grand Rapids, MI: Eerdmans, 1999. 372–73.

Long, Kevin M. "Echoes of Friendship: *Amicitia* and *Affectus* in the Writings of Aelred of Rievaulx with Special Reference to His Minor Works and the Monastic Foundations of His Theory." Dissertation, University of Western Australia, 1993.

Macy, Gary. *The Theologies of the Eucharist in the Early Scholastic Period.* Oxford: Oxford University Press, 1984.

Madigan, Mary Felicitas. *The Passio Domini Theme in the Works of Richard Rolle.* Salzburg: Institut für englische Sprache und Literatur, The University of Salzburg, 1978.

Mandel, Barrett J. "Full of Life Now." In *Autobiography: Essays Theoretical and Critical*, edited by James Olney. Princeton, NJ: Princeton University Press, 1980. 49–72.

McDonie, R. Jacob. *Friendship and Rhetoric in the Middle Ages: Language and Intimacy from Cicero to Aelred.* Philadelphia: Routledge, 2019.

McEvoy, James. "*Anima una et cor unum*: Friendship and Spiritual Unity in Augustine." *Recherches de théologie ancienne et médiévale* 53 (1986): 40–92.

McEvoy, James. "Notes on the Prologue of St Aelred of Rievaulx's 'De Spirituali Amicitia,' with a Translation." *Traditio* 37 (1981): 396–411.

McEvoy, James. "*Philia* and *Amicitia*: The Philosophy of Friendship from Plato to Aquinas." *Sewanee Medieval Colloquium,* Occasional Papers 2 (1984): 1–23.

McGuire, Brian Patrick. *Friendship and Community: The Monastic Experience, 350–1250.* CS 95. Kalamazoo, MI: Cistercian Publications, 1988.

McGuire, Brian Patrick. "Sexual Awareness and Identity in Aelred of Rievaulx (1110–67)." ABR 45 (1994): 184–226.

McNamara, Marie Aquinas. *Friendship in Saint Augustine.* Studia Friburgensia, n.s. 20. Fribourg: University Press, 1958.

Monagle, John F. "Friendship in St. Augustine's Biography." *Augustinian Studies* 2 (1971): 81–92.

Morrison, Karl. "The End of Christian Art." 5 May 2000. Plenary address at the 35th International Medieval Studies Congress, Kalamazoo, Michigan.

Nolte, Venantius. *Augustins Freundschaftsideal in seinen Briefen.* Wurzburg: Rita-Verlag u.-Druckerei, 1939.

Nouzille, Philippe. *Expérience de Dieu et Théologie Monastique au XII[e] Siècle.* Paris: Cerf, 1999.

Nouzille, Philippe. "Temps et Liturgie: Présence et Representation." In *Intentio Cordis: Temps, histoire, mémoire chez Aelred de Rievaulx.* Coll 73, no. 1 (2011): 174–86.

Pelikan, Jaroslav. *The Growth of Medieval Theology (600–1300).* The Christian Tradition, 3. Chicago and London: University of Chicago Press, 1978.

Pezzini, Domenico. "Aelred of Rievaulx's *Vita Sancti Edwardi Regis et Confessoris*: Its Genesis and Radiation." *Cîteaux* 69 (2009): 27–77.

Pezzini, Domenico. "Aelred's Doctrine of Charity and Friendship." In *A Companion to Aelred of Rievaulx (1110–1167)*, edited by Marsha L. Dutton. Brill's Companions to the Christian Tradition. Leiden/Boston: Brill, 2017. 221–45.

Pezzini, Domenico. Introduction to Aelredo di Rievaulx, *Gesù Dodicenne; Preghiera Pastorale*, translated and introduced by Domenico Pezzini. Letture Cristiane del Secondo Millennio 29. Milan: Paoline Editoriale Libri, 2001. 17–65.

Pizzolato, Luigi. *L'Amicizia nel mondo giudaico e cristiano antico.* Turin: Giulio Einandi, 1993.

Posset, Franz. "*Christi Dulcedo*: 'The Sweetness of Christ' in Western Christian Spirituality." CSQ 30 (1995): 245–65.

Posset, Franz. "The Sweetness of God." ABR 44 (1993): 143–78.

Pourrat, Pierre. *Christian Spirituality*, vol. 2, *The Middle Ages*. Translated by S. P. Jacques. 4 vols. Westminster, MD: Newman Press, 1953.

Pourrat, Pierre. *La spiritualité chrétienne.* 4 vols. Paris: Gabalda, 1921, 1924, 1927, 1928.

Raitz von Frentz, Emmerich. "Ludolph, le Chartreux, et Les Exercises de S. Ignace de Loyola." *Revue d'ascètique et de mystique* 25 (1949): 375–88.

Ramsey, Boniface. *Ambrose.* London: Routledge, 1997.

Russell, J. Stephen. "Cicero, Dialogue, and the Structure of Aelred's *Spiritual Friendship.*" Presentation at the 2011 Cistercian Studies Conference, Kalamazoo, MI.

Russell, J. Stephen. "The Dialogic of Aelred's *Spiritual Friendship.*" CSQ 47, no. 1 (2012): 47–69.

Salter, Elizabeth. "Ludolphus of Saxony and his English Translators." *Medium Aevum* 33 (1964): 26–35.

Schnaubelt, Joseph, and Frederick van Fleteren, eds. *Collectanea Augustiniana*. New York: Lang, 1987.

Scholl, Edith. "Sensing God." ABR 47 (1996): 341–57.

Scholl, Edith. "The Sweetness of the Lord: *Dulcis* and *Suavis*." CSQ 27 (1992): 359–66.

Sellner, Edward C. "Like a Kindling Fire: Meanings of Friendship in the Life and Writings of Augustine." *Spirituality Today* 43 (1991): 240–57.

Sommerfeldt, John R. *Aelred of Rievaulx: On Love and Order in the World and the Church*. New York and Mahwah, NJ: Newman Press, 2006.

Sommerfeldt, John R. "The Vocabulary of Contemplation in Aelred of Rievaulx' *On Jesus at the Age of Twelve, A Rule of Life for a Recluse*, and *On Spiritual Friendship*." In *Heaven on Earth: Studies in Medieval Cistercian History*, edited by E. Rozanne Elder. CS 68. Kalamazoo, MI: Cistercian Publications, 1983. 72–89.

Squire, Aelred. *Aelred of Rievaulx: A Study*. CS 50. 1950; Kalamazoo, MI: Cistercian Publications, 2020.

Stone, Darwell. *A History of the Doctrine of the Holy Eucharist*. 2 vols. New York and London: Longmans, Green, 1909.

Talbot, C. H. Introduction to Aelred of Rievaulx, *On the Soul*. Translated by C. H. Talbot. CF 22. Kalamazoo, MI: Cistercian Publications, 1981. 5–34.

TePas, Katherine M. "Spiritual Friendship in Aelred of Rievaulx and Mutual Sanctification in Marriage." CSQ 27 (1992): 63–76.

*Thesaurus Augustinianus*, curante CETEDOC. Corpus Christianorum, Thesaurus patrum Latinorum. Turnholt: Brepols, 1989.

Thomson, S. Harrison. *The Writings of Robert Grossteste: Bishop of Lincoln 1235–1253*. Cambridge, UK: Cambridge University Press, 1940.

Thornton, Martin. *English Spirituality*. London: SPCK, 1963.

Truax, Jean. *Aelred the Peacemaker: The Public Life of a Cistercian Abbot*. CS 251. Collegeville, MN: Cistercian Publications, 2017.

Verheijen, Luc. "The *Confessiones* of Saint Augustine: Two Grids of Composition and Reading." In *Collectanea Augustiniana*, edited by Joseph Schnaubelt and Frederick van Fleteren. New York: Lange, 1990. 175–201.

Walsh, Milton T. Introduction to *The Life of Jesus Christ*. 4 vols. CS 267, 282, 283, 284. Collegeville, MN: Cistercian Publications, 2018–2022. 1:xxiii–xlvii.

Watrigant, Henry. *La genèse des exercises de saint Ignace de Loyola*. Amiens: Yvert & Tellier, 1897.

White, Carolinne. *Christian Friendship in the Fourth Century*. Cambridge, UK: Cambridge University Press, 1992.

Wilmart, André. *Auteurs spirituels et textes devots du moyen âge latin*. Études d'histoire littéraire. Paris: Bloud et Gay, 1932.

Wilmart, André, "Jean l'Homme de Dieu, auteur d'un traité attribué à saint Bernard." In *Auteurs spirituels et textes dévots du moyen âge Latin*. Paris: Études Augustiniennes, 1971. 64–100.

Wilmart, André. "La tradition des prières de S. Anselme." *Revue Bénédictine* 36 (1924): 52–71.

Wilmart, André. "Le recueil des prières de S. Anselme." In *Méditations et prières de S. Anselme*, translated by D. A. Castel. Pax XI. Paris: Abbaye de Maredsous, 1923. i–xlii.

Wilmart, André. "Les Méditations VII et VIII attribuées à Saint Anselme: La Série des 21 Méditations." *Revue d'Ascètique et de Mystique* 8 (1927): 249–82.

Ziolkowski, J. M. "Translation and Commentary on Aelred of Rievaulx: *De spiritali amicitia* 2.27–29." In *Corpus Christianorum 1953–2003: Xenium Natalicum: Fifty Years of Scholarly Editing*, edited by John Leemans. Turnhout: Brepols, 2003. 314–18.

# Index of Names

Names are identified by the page number; n following the page number indicates a name that appears only in a footnote.

# General Index

References are by page number. Page numbers followed by n indicate items present only in a footnote on that page. Abbreviations: adj. (adjective), ger. (gerund), n. (noun), vb. (verb).